CHRISTOPAGANISM

About the Authors

Joyce and River Higginbotham have taught Paganism classes throughout the past decade. They have planned and organized local and national Pagan gatherings, written articles for Pagan publications, appeared on radio and television broadcasts, spoken at Christian and Unitarian Universalist churches, and attended interfaith councils. They also helped found the Council for Alternative Spiritual Traditions, which hosted public Pagan and alternative events in the Midwest.

CHRISTOPAGANISM

JOYCE & RIVER HIGGINBOTHAM

An Inclusive Path

Llewellyn Publications
Woodbury, Minnesota

First Edition
First Printing, 2009

Cover design by Lisa Novak
Cover image © Brand X/Superstock
Illustrations on pages 62, 63, 65, and 69 from *Monumental Christianity* by J. P. Lundy (New York: J.W. Bouton, 1876).
All other illustrations by Llewellyn Art department
Interior book design by Joanna Willis

Permission to reprint credits:
414 words, adapted, from *The Lost Gospel: The Book of Q and Christian Origins* by Burton L. Mack.
Copyright © 1992 by Burton L. Mack.
Reprinted by permission of HarperCollins Publishers.

224 words, adapted, from *Stages of Faith: The Psychology of Human Development and the Quest for Meaning* by James W. Fowler.
Copyright © 1981 by James W. Fowler.
Reprinted by permission of HarperCollins Publishers.

299 words, adapted, from *In Search of 'Ancient Israel'* by Philip R. Davies.
Reprinted by kind permission of Continuum International Publishing, Ltd.

Material from the following sources has also been incorporated:
Integral Spirituality, by Ken Wilber, © 2006 by Ken Wilber.
Sex, Ecology, Spirituality, by Ken Wilber, © 1995, 2000 by Ken Wilber.
A Theory of Everything, by Ken Wilber, © 2000 by Ken Wilber.
Reprinted by arrangement with Shambala Publications Inc., Boston, MA. www.shambala.com.

A paraphrased summary of the colors of the Spiral has been adapted from *Spiral Dynamics: Mastering Values, Leadership, and Change* by Don Edward Beck and Christopher C. Cowan, © 1996. Used by permission of Blackwell Publishing, a division of John Wiley & Sons, Inc.

Llewellyn is a registered trademark of Llewellyn Worldwide, Ltd.

LIBRARY OF CONGRESS CATALOGING-IN-PUBLICATION DATA
Higginbotham, Joyce, 1961–
  ChristoPaganism : an inclusive path / Joyce & River Higginbotham.—1st ed.
    p. cm.
  Includes bibliographical references (p.   ) and index.
  ISBN 978-0-7387-1467-7
  1. Spiritual life—Neopaganism. 2.
Neopaganism—Relations—Christianity. 3. Christianity and other religions—Neopaganism. I. Higginbotham, River,
1959– II. Title.
  BP605.N46H54 2009
  299´.94—dc22
                        2008045986

Llewellyn Worldwide does not participate in, endorse, or have any authority or responsibility concerning private business transactions between our authors and the public.
    All mail addressed to the author is forwarded but the publisher cannot, unless specifically instructed by the author, give out an address or phone number.
    Any Internet references contained in this work are current at publication time, but the publisher cannot guarantee that a specific location will continue to be maintained. Please refer to the publisher's website for links to authors' websites and other sources.

Llewellyn Publications
A Division of Llewellyn Worldwide, Ltd.
2143 Wooddale Drive, Dept. 978-0-7387-1467-7
Woodbury, MN 55125-2989, U.S.A.
www.llewellyn.com

Printed in the United States of America

Definition

ChristoPaganism *n.*

[Christo: OE *Crist*, Lat. *Christus*, Gk. *Khristos*, anoint or anointed one.
Paganism: Lat. *paganus*, country dweller, civilian, from *pagus*, country,
rural district.]

1. A spirituality that combines beliefs and practices of Christianity with beliefs and practices of Paganism, or that observes them in parallel.

2. A blended eclectic spiritual tradition involving magickal or earth-centered religions and orthodox or non-orthodox Christianity.

3. An example of an interspiritual or multifaith religious tradition.

Also by Joyce and River Higginbotham

Paganism:
An Introduction to Earth-Centered Religions

Pagan Spirituality:
A Guide to Personal Transformation

CONTENTS

FIGURES

Acknowledgments

Many thanks to our volunteers in the final section of the book, who gave so generously of their time to this project.

We wish to thank translator Marie Taris for her translation from the French of the St. Anselm scarab passage in chapter 3.

We are grateful to Kathleen Hill for her input and her brainstorming on several topics, including suggesting the title for the book.

Thanks to those on the CUUPS Café e-list who offered their assistance in locating Unitarian-Universalist Pagan population data, and to Diane at the UUA headquarters for her assistance in finding and supplying copies of surveys and reports.

We are especially grateful to the tireless librarians at our county branch and the interlibrary loan staff, who helped us locate hundreds of books for our research, some of them quite difficult to find.

INTRODUCTION

In our years as Pagan teachers, community leaders, organizers, and speakers, we have encountered a growing number of people who combine aspects of Christianity and Paganism within their spirituality. Many of the people we have met identify themselves as Pagan but include some Christian practices in their spirituality, such as observing both the Christian and Pagan liturgical years, praying the rosary, chanting the psalms, observing a form of communion, attending charismatic prayer services or Mass, or being devoted to the Virgin Mary. These people frequently call themselves ChristoPagans, or if their Pagan background is in Wicca, then perhaps Christian Wiccans.[1] Others we have met identify themselves as Christian, but incorporate Pagan or other earth-centered practices into their spirituality. We've met a number of Christian churchgoers, ministers, priests, and nuns who observe solstices, use tarot cards, worship in circles, honor the divine as experienced in other faiths, smudge, go on vision quests, drum, recognize a Divine Feminine, practice yoga and other forms of meditation, and experience the divine in nature. These people may or may not apply the word *Pagan* to any of their combined practices. In this book, our focus is on the first group rather than the second, although many of our observations about blended paths are applicable to both.

In our experience, those who blend practices or beliefs of various traditions do not do so carelessly or flippantly. They often feel deeply moved to adopt certain practices or beliefs with a sense of profound respect for the cultures from which they are drawn. We have yet to meet anyone combining Christian and Pagan practices whose intention is to mock or dishonor one faith or the other. If anything, ChristoPagans often feel that their awareness and conscious adoption of other practices is a way to bring a sense of honoring, perhaps even of healing, to the traditions involved. To such a person, the blending is itself a spiritual act.

The blending of traditions, from within Paganism at least, is not going to go away. We believe it is a sign of a shift in the culture to a worldview that some call "postindustrial" or "aperspectival,"[2] which means the ability to hold multiple perspectives at once in an honoring way that does not need to choose one over the other, or to resolve seeming contradictions between them. Ken Wilber, philosopher, calls this perspective "vision-logic."[3] Beck and Cowan, the Spiral Dynamics social scientists, call it "Green" or "HumanBond."[4] James Fowler, sociologist on matters of Christian faith, calls it "conjunctive."[5] The blending of traditions, then, is not happening in a vacuum but as part of the well-understood pattern of human development. This postindustrial developmental space is an emerging one, so it has not yet come into its full strength. Beck and Cowan, in fact, place only 10% of the world's population in this space at present.[6] Spiritual writers are also noticing and commenting on this approach. Catholic lay brother Wayne Teasdale, for example, calls it "interspirituality," and we explore more of his reflections in the first chapter. As more people move into the postindustrial worldview and become comfortable with a variety of perspectives, the combining of spiritualities may become even more common.

We believe that modern Paganism is essentially a postindustrial religious movement shaped by the postindustrial worldview, and that Neo-Paganism generally anchors many of its belief structures in the honoring of different perspectives and pathways to the divine. The experience of blended practices or interspiritual paths such as ChristoPaganism is a common one to many Pagans, both on a personal level and in their interactions within the greater Pagan community. Even if the form of the blending is not with Christianity per se, many Pagans are already quite familiar with combinations of some sort and frequently experience blending at large festivals or public rituals involving many Pagan groups and traditions. An entire tradition within Paganism, called the Eclectic path, is comprised of those who routinely blend interspiritual practices and beliefs. Understanding the basis for such spiritualities in general, and ChristoPaganism in particular, will be a benefit to everyone as such practices become more common.

We offer this book as one perspective on interspiritual paths generally and on ChristoPaganism in particular, as it is currently being experienced within Paganism. We do not claim to speak for every Pagan or ChristoPagan or represent every point of view within the greater movement, but we hope our effort here will encourage further discussion among those interested in these issues. We also hope that other writers will be moved to share their experiences in blended spiritualities, whether from the Pagan perspective or otherwise. For those who had no idea such practices were becoming common, we hope this book is enlightening and informative. For those of you who are attracted to or practicing a form of blended spirituality, we hope this material helps you realize that you are not alone.

As with our previous books, we use the word *Pagan* throughout to refer to the modern Neo-Pagan religious movement, not to ancient or historical Paganism. If we intend to discuss historical Paganism, or ancient people or cultures, as we do specifically in chapters 4 and 5, we will refer to them explicitly.

We do not assume that the reader of this book is Pagan, so we approach this material from the beginning, laying out a working understanding of both Paganism and Christianity, and issues of faith development within both. Our purpose is to examine interspiritual or blended traditions from three perspectives. The first is by looking at "what's out there" in the outer landscape of belief—the structure of the Pagan and Christian religions, and their beliefs and practices. These are the forms and structures you think of when you say "Christianity" or when you say "Paganism." You may believe that it is impossible for these two traditions to mix well with each other. From this perspective, you are looking "out there" because you are definitely not looking inside yourself. Yet two ingredients go into interspirituality—one is the spiritualities themselves, and the other is you and what is within you that allows one belief or practice to co-exist peacefully with another. So in the second perspective, we look at "what's in here" in the inner landscape of belief, and what is within you as a person that makes interspirituality attractive, repulsive, or a necessity. In the third perspective, we turn our attention to the lived experience of ChristoPaganism and discover what it is like through the shared stories and conversations of practicing ChristoPagans.

This book is divided into three parts, one for each of these perspectives. Part I examines "what's out there," the outer landscape of belief that contains ChristoPaganism. It begins with an overview of blended paths and interspirituality in general, and then gives a brief overview of Paganism. This is followed by a brief overview of Christianity, where we also offer some thought-provoking perspectives concerning the development of Christian belief and dogma. However, all of these perspectives are essentially mainstream, and all of them assume that Jesus existed as a historical person. In the chapter that follows the overview, we then present the research of non-mainstream scholars who do not believe in the historicity of Jesus. We discuss the impact such a result might have on Christianity and on interspiritual practice. Part I ends with a discussion of the development of monotheism and the compilation of the Old Testament, and contains the findings of both mainstream and non-mainstream scholars.

Part II examines "what's in here" in the inner landscape through an exploration of human and faith development, and the various capacities that social scientists believe people can grow into and in what sequence. We develop the idea of the holon, which we will explain, to include ideas, and we show how ideas also increase their capacity to hold more and bigger perspectives. We discuss how and why religions must teach and encourage their members to grow to the most expansive faith capacity they are capable of, and how the structures of the religious group can help, hinder or support continued development. Part III examines lived experience by approaching real ChristoPagans and asking them how and why they came to their faith, how they combine or incorporate the two spiritualities, how they live their path, what reactions they get from others, and where they see ChristoPaganism going in the future.

Since we are first and foremost teachers of spirituality, we see the discussion of any spiritual topic as an opportunity to explore one's self, beliefs, goals, and values. Those of you familiar with our writing know that our first books are designed as workbooks. We move away from that format here, but we can't entirely help ourselves! We see so many avenues for honest questioning, self-examination, re-evaluation of judgments and assumptions, and perhaps even an opportunity for personal growth within this topic. So we offer journaling questions periodically, which you may work on privately if you choose, or which can be adapted for classroom discussion or assignments. We encourage you to get a notepad or some paper on which to answer these questions, even if you are only reading this book because the topic seems strange to you or you are merely curious. We encourage you to give the questions a shot regardless of whether you are a Christian, a Pagan, or something else altogether. The questions are not designed to convince you to become a Pagan, a ChristoPagan, or anything else for that matter. They are designed to help you become aware of your current beliefs, their meaning to you, and how they shape and inform your spiritual practice, whatever it may be.

PART I
THE OUTER LANDSCAPE

Chapter 1

INTERSPIRITUALITY
AND BLENDED PATHS

The landscape of religious belief and practice is changing. Ideas are coming together in unique ways, and these combinations are generating new and unconventional spiritual experiences. The fact that a word like *Christo-Pagan* exists and a book can be written about it illustrates this point. But this may not be news to you. No doubt you have observed the rise of interfaith dialogue and interfaith councils in the past several decades. Maybe you've been a part of multifaith efforts to host special events, take social action, operate food pantries, or provide relief to disaster areas. It is likely that you have friends who have studied or experienced other religions and spiritual practices. Perhaps you have done the same. Maybe you and your friends have wrestled over the question of whether God is a woman or has a feminine aspect; whether every culture's concept of God ultimately points toward the same thing or not; whether beliefs and dogmas created by political necessity and power are or were ever valid, and to what extent religion should enter into political decisions today. Perhaps you have wondered whether or not religious belief is helping to build a better world and a sustainable future that can peacefully accommodate the world's cultures and religions, and how your own religious belief and practice fits into such a future.

The shift in the landscape of religious belief and practice is nothing less than a shift in worldview. People are changing the way they think about religion and religious practice, who is "us" and who is "them," and whether such distinctions make sense in a global, interdependent environment. Wayne Teasdale, Catholic lay brother and interfaith advocate, calls this new view "interspirituality." It encompasses interfaith dialogue, a sharing of traditions, and the blending of traditions and their practices. Teasdale notes that interspirituality is not about eliminating diverse religious expression, but making available to everyone the various forms that spiritual journeys can take.[1]

Is there any validity to interspirituality? Does it have any basis in the truth of lived experience or is it all wishful thinking? Or might it be even worse and spring from an inability to make a commitment to one form of spirituality or another? Teasdale answers that he believes interspirituality expresses a fundamental truth, that of the spiritual interdependence of all religions. He says this interdependence exists because the cosmos is one interrelated system, and "the religions themselves share in this one system of reality, life, and being."[2]

It is true that humanity has basic things in common, which governments, cultures, and religions cannot change. For example, all humans experience the cycles of day and night; the changing of the seasons; universal laws such as gravity, the speed of light, motion, and thermodynamics; and the experience of a body, with its birth, death, and physical and emotional needs. Humanity is already connected by these shared experiences. Since religions generally address the human condition, its purpose, meaning, and final end, they are also interconnected through the experience of a shared reality. This has always been true. But human beings have not always been at a point in their personal and cultural development where they can see this truth. Sometimes a person has to grow into the capacity to see something before he or she can see it. Interspirituality, then, is not a recent invention, just a recent recognition. It requires people who have developed the capacity to be able to see and appreciate the interconnectedness of human experience. It also requires people who are strongly grounded spiritually, who place a high value on spiritual sharing and who are willing to work to make such sharing real. Teasdale notes that interspirituality can be a world-changing force when it is pursued by people "who have a viable spiritual life, coupled with their determination, capacity, and commitment to the inner search across traditions."[3]

Beyond a recognition of humanity's common experience and connectedness, interspirituality promotes values that can help humanity create a joyful and sustainable future. It encourages dialogue among people and groups and may help lead to global understanding and the lowering of global tensions. The lowering of global tensions can lead in turn to better decision-making, better allocation of resources, preservation of the environment, and reduction of war. In general, interspirituality promotes values that have the potential to bring human beings to a greater appreciation of each other and more cooperative interaction. Teasdale sums up these values when he says that interspirituality honors more than just our own tradition, it "honors the totality of human spiritual insight, whether or not it is God-centered. To leave out any spiritual experience is to impoverish humanity."[4]

Paganism's blended traditions, of which ChristoPaganism is one, arise from this growing interspiritual awareness. ChristoPaganism does not desire to do away with the diversity of religious expression, but adds itself as one more diverse expression. ChristoPagans know that the spiritual journey takes many forms, and they are willing to share within and across traditions. Many ChristoPagans believe that everything in the cosmos is part of a related system and that physical and nonphysical reality are interconnected. This interconnected reality includes spirituality. Blended traditions reflect the diversity and interconnectedness inherent in the universe. They also support the many differences among individuals by permitting persons to find their unique point of intersection with the universe and to describe their experience with the divine in terms unique to themselves. Paganism in general and its interspiritual traditions in particular allow this wide range of experience without being threatened by it, or requiring it to be codified into dogma.

In Paganism, responsibility for matters of belief rests directly on the individual. Some fear that such a responsibility is too great and cannot be exercised with good results, that people should not be left to make such choices on their own. But the problem with this position is that responsibility for your beliefs is not one that can be avoided. If you do nothing and hope the issue goes away, then by your choice not to act you have exercised your responsibility, and your beliefs will reflect the value you put on nonaction. If you decide to join a particular religion and adopt its beliefs, then by that action you have exercised your responsibility, since joining a particular group or religion is a choice to adopt their beliefs and practices. This responsibility to choose is a power you hold. You can ignore it, give it away to others, use it purposefully, or unconsciously, but it is not a responsibility that can be avoided. When it comes to your spirituality, you are stuck with being responsible for what you choose to believe and, based on your beliefs, how you choose to act in the world.

The Nature of Belief

A discussion of Christianity and Paganism is nothing if not a discussion of beliefs. To be drawn to the work of interspirituality is to be willing to grapple with issues of belief and still find a way forward. The blending of traditions is a deliberate mixing and balancing of belief and practice that reflects an individual's personal history and experience of the divine. Since belief is central to this topic, it will be helpful to understand what we mean by it and what we think its characteristics are.

We define a belief as an idea that you hold to be true. Because a belief contains a piece of "how the world really is" to you, it acts as a filter for your reality. The filters of your beliefs are so strong that they typically allow in only information that matches the filters and will screen out contradictory input. A concept or idea that does not match your filters will generally be ignored or rejected.

The ideas you consciously choose as your beliefs, and also the ideas you unconsciously hold, will literally create your world. If you believe you cannot do certain things, then you won't. If you believe you can experience God in only one way, place, or time, then you will probably not experience God in any other way, place, or time. If you believe that the world must be a certain way, then you will not try to build a different one. At the individual level, beliefs are interior, subjective events that are not readily seen or measurable until an action or behavior occurs that demonstrates the underlying belief. At the level of culture, beliefs show themselves in a shared worldview, fashions, assumptions, prejudices, social conventions, and religious values. The individual and the cultural realms come together to create the buildings, institutions, laws, governments, armies, charities, and economies that give physical shape to shared beliefs. Not only do beliefs shape your reality, but with them you shape society and the world.

One feature of beliefs is that they tend to group together, reinforcing each other to form a belief system or structure. Within a belief structure, ideas are generally consistent, with one concept building on another, and another, each acting to support the ones that follow. As an example, take a look at the structure formed by the political philosophy of the United States, which is based on a constitutional form of government, bill of rights, and institutions built from them (fig. 1.1). This illustration is also found in our book *Paganism: An Introduction to Earth-Centered Religions* (2002), where belief systems are discussed in greater detail.

A building provides a good visual example of how beliefs take physical form and build a structure, whether this structure is visible or invisible. Buildings also illustrate

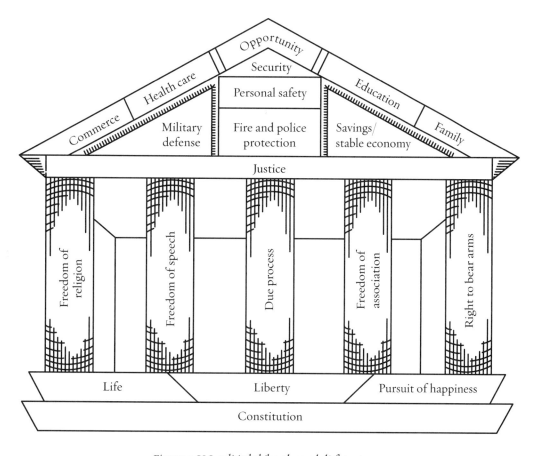

Figure 1.1. U.S. political philosophy as a belief structure

the constructed nature of beliefs. Remember that beliefs consist of ideas and concepts that people hold to be true. These concepts may have come from observing nature, or from scientific experiments, human relationships, political decisions, or survival needs. Or they may have been inspired by a spiritual experience, vision, shamanic journey, or revelation. Whatever the source of the idea, it is still articulated by people, put into a cultural context, and used to construct a pattern of values, which is the belief system. It is people who design concepts and group them together; assign meaning and value to them; rank them in importance; empower them politically, religiously, and socially; and choose to act or not act upon them.

Even entertaining the thought that beliefs and belief systems are human constructions has sometimes been difficult for our students. Many of them come from backgrounds in which the nature and source of belief is never overtly considered, and certain beliefs are never questioned. For them belief itself is sacred and cannot be approached objectively, and to do so brings on great anxiety. As you will see in Fowler's explanation of faith development in Part II, this is a normal aspect of spiritual growth. It is a perspective that shaped and informed many of the world's mainstream religions and is still very common today. Many people are raised to believe that certain beliefs are absolutes. They believe they have no power to examine their beliefs and the ideas that comprise them. They cannot question their beliefs, challenge them, or insist they be useful, healthy, or productive for themselves and their society. If the beliefs are not particularly helpful, many people believe that they are simply stuck with them. Many believe that they cannot change, abandon, or reconstruct such beliefs. So, in effect, they relinquish their responsibility and power for holding these beliefs to the system out of which they arise.

Paganism asserts that you have the right to examine any idea or belief you wish. You may pick up any concept you choose and look at it from every angle, question it, examine it, and put it to the test. You are not obligated to accept any idea as true until you experience it to be true yourself, personally and directly. This is a right or freedom of choice that Paganism values very highly. You have this right, or power, because in Paganism you are responsible for the beliefs you choose to adopt. With the right comes the responsibility, and conversely, with the responsibility comes the freedom or right. You cannot blame others for your values or your choices.

When a person is able to see beliefs as human constructions, then entire structures—such as religions, governments, cultural taboos, economic philosophies, and so on—can be viewed with greater objectivity. When you are not emotionally bound to a belief, you can more readily explore it and its consequences. You are then more free to choose beliefs that work best for you and the world you want to create from them. You will also feel more free to examine your beliefs whenever you wish and, if they are not meeting your expectations, explore why that is so and what you want to do about it.

You interact with a variety of belief systems every day, whether or not you realize it. You are immersed in one at home and in your intimate relationships, another at work or school, another at church, and yet another in sports and hobbies. Beck and

Cowan call these value "memes" or clusters, as discussed further in later chapters. Some of these systems and clusters overlap and share beliefs. Some have beliefs that differ widely from each other and may even be in conflict from time to time. Some of these systems are very rigid and expect you to play your part without question. Others insist that you take a lot of initiative and responsibility for your decisions. The values and worldviews you juggle in one day are probably more varied than those you will ever encounter in interspiritual work. Yet you balance their differing demands and likely have no difficulty in seeing each of them objectively in relation to each other. You can probably clearly see the structure each one forms and how its values and worldview within that structure are mostly internally consistent. As you travel across and through these varied belief structures, you can appreciate both their strengths and their weaknesses without having to adopt them unless you choose. You can bring this same sense of freedom, acceptance, and appreciation to your experience of interspirituality and blended traditions.

In summary, your interactions with physical reality and your experiences in the world help to shape the ideas you hold to be true. In turn, your beliefs also work to shape your experience of reality, as your beliefs act as a filter of that experience. Beliefs hold a great deal of power, and as they combine they create complex and intricate systems on which groups of people rely and take action. Beliefs are made visible and manifest in the religious, political, and social structures built from them. As powerful as beliefs are, however, they are no more so than your own power to examine and choose them, as their power derives from you.

Or put another way, beliefs are powerful because people empower them. Belief systems and structures, therefore, are human constructions, and they can be modified when people decide to modify them and take concerted action to do so. Individual belief systems are also constructions and can be viewed with objectivity if a person chooses and is not emotionally attached to the belief. People already tend to bring more flexibility to their interaction with belief systems than they realize, as the demands of the modern world require everyone to navigate multiple and competing belief systems every day. As we shall see in later chapters, interspirituality becomes possible when people are able to recognize the constructed nature of beliefs and systems, understand their power to shape experience and mobilize action, and appreciate their various contributions.

My Journal: Interspirituality and Blended Traditions

What is your opinion of interspirituality? What about interspirituality do you find to be positive? What do you find to be detrimental? Identify at least three or four points for each.

Are you comfortable or uncomfortable with interspirituality? With blended traditions? Why or why not? Would you ever get involved in interspiritual efforts and dialogue? Why?

Would you ever blend different religious practices into your spirituality? State your reasons.

Have you ever attended a service or ceremony in which different traditions were represented and shared their beliefs and practices? How did you feel about this experience?

Do you agree or disagree that beliefs and belief systems are constructed? Why? What effect do you think it would have on reality and your life choices if the opposite of your opinion were true?

An Inventory of Beliefs

This is an extension of the preceding journaling exercise, but it is more complex and we hope you will give it some time and thought. Reading the material in this book, perhaps even hearing the word *ChristoPagan*, is going to bring your own belief system into a state of alertness. You cannot help but react intellectually and emotionally at some level to these ideas, because you bring your own beliefs and values with you, and you interpret this material through your own filters. You may have strong feelings of either agreement or disagreement with what we are saying. This is only going to build as you go on in the book, because more provocative ideas lie ahead. You may think you will get around to evaluating all this against your own beliefs later, after you've finished the book, but we would rather you do it in smaller pieces as you go along. So we're going to begin by asking you to identify your own beliefs and some of the belief structures in which you operate every day. This will bring into the open what may be operating within you automatically. This is a good time and place to make conscious contact again with the ideas and values you have adopted in your life.

Identify the beliefs you currently hold about each of the following. If a question does not apply to you, or you have covered it in another answer, skip over it. There are a number of questions here. You may want to spread answering them over several days.

- Is there a god or goddess or other divine being(s) or principle(s)?
- What is the current nature of your relationship with your concept of the divine?
- What types of relationships generally are permitted with your concept of the divine, and what types are not?
- What does your concept of the divine expect of you, and what do you expect of it?
- What is and is not the spiritual nature of the physical world, and what role does the physical world play in spirituality?
- What is the nature of your relationship with the physical world, and what is it supposed to be? Is the physical world something that you can communicate with, participate with, or control, and if so, how? Does it relate back to you, and if so, how?
- Do supernatural powers exist? Are there other realms of existence, and if so, what is their purpose, nature, and relationship to you?
- How do these other realms and powers, if any, affect or influence your spirituality?
- Do you have a soul or spirit? What happens to you at death? Is there some form of afterlife?
- How does the existence, or nonexistence, of a soul and afterlife affect your spirituality and choices in your daily life?
- What beliefs are essential to your spirituality, and what beliefs should be essential to everyone's spirituality?
- What practices are essential to your spirituality, and what practices are required of you? Why?
- What is the purpose of spirituality in your life, what do you want it to accomplish for you, and how do you order your life around it?

If you enjoy creative writing, take your journal and answered questions and write a letter to yourself as though you were writing to us or a friend. In this letter, describe your spirituality as it exists now. What is your spiritual philosophy and how did you arrive at it? If you are studying this book with others, you may share and discuss parts of your letter and journal questions together.

Next, identify the belief systems and structures with which you interact regularly. These may include home, work, school, church, sports, hobby, social, political, or environmental groups, as well as corporations and government. How are these systems similar and how do they differ? For each one, identify between two and six values it holds or promotes, or by which you feel it operates. Do any of these values overlap? Are any in conflict? How do you move between these different systems throughout the day and keep your balance? Do you have to change any of your behaviors when you move from one to the other? How do you reconcile their differences? Do any of these differences make you angry or defensive? Are you conscious of these differences at the time, or do you navigate them automatically? Identify your philosophy about how you successfully interact with these various belief systems and how you balance their competing values.

The Rise of Blended Traditions

There has been a marked increase of interest in recent years concerning interspirituality and blended traditions. A few examples of this increased interest include interfaith dialogue, multifaith organizations, and cooperative projects and humanitarian efforts. It is also seen in the popularity of books and movies that look in and between the borders of accepted belief. We have noticed a general increase in awareness of diversity and of voices urging tolerance. This may be partially due to the fact that it is impossible to avoid coming face to face with different cultures and different belief systems anymore. The radio, television, and Internet bring the world into your home, and you receive large doses of intercultural and interspiritual information every day. The mythic literal worldview (covered in later chapters), which holds that its mythic perspective is the only one and all others must be destroyed, is now seen by many as toxic and unsustainable, though it was the cultural norm for centuries until the recent past. This is a major shift in worldview that is only getting started.

While political and economic necessity in a global environment may be driving some of this shift in worldview, it is raising issues for everyone. If you assume for a moment that global survival depends on societies being able to live peaceably together, and that such peaceful living might begin with some degree of tolerance or appreciation of differences in belief and culture, might this also apply to you personally? That is, to live peaceably, are *you* obligated to come to a tolerance and appreciation of different beliefs and cultures? If you cannot do so individually, how is society going to do so collectively? If religions cannot sustainably crusade, conquer, or blow each other up anymore, are *you* obligated to stop crusading, conquering, and blowing up other faiths in your mind? If you cannot stop blowing them up in your mind, will the blowing up ever stop in the world? When these issues are approached sincerely, a whole world of possibilities and ways of relating opens up. The energy once used to maintain an embattled mindset is now free to do other things.

Many people are no longer content to explore only one mythology for their entire lives. Pagans use the word "mythology" to refer to the religious story that informs and guides a faith tradition. While some may use this word to mean fictional, superstitious, or silly, Pagans do not. They do not use the word to belittle or ridicule. Most Pagans and many others, social scientists among them, use the word "mythology" to mean that grouping of concepts about how the world works that underlies a society or faith tradition. Sociologist James Fowler calls mythology a "shared narrative of meaning."[5] A religious mythology, then, is a collection of beliefs usually told as a history or story that forms a structure around which a religion is built. In other words, a mythology is a religious belief structure.

Many people are not content today to stay within only one religious belief structure. They are curious to see what the world looks like from other structures and to learn from this exploration. Why would they want to do this? Aren't they just being spiritual tourists? For some this might be the case, but for the majority we have met, it is based on a sincere desire to deepen themselves and increase their capacity to see and hold more of spirit. This is not always a comfortable experience—sometimes it is downright upsetting to their assumptions—but even so, it is a part of spiritual growth for many people.

In the following chapters we explore the structures, sacred years, and observances of both Paganism and Christianity, and study them as belief systems. We examine different mainstream scholarly views on how the New Testament came to be compiled, and then move on to less mainstream, non-historical perspectives of Christianity and ancient pagan Mystery religions. We end with a look at monotheism and the creation of the Old Testament from a variety of scholarly views. This study of "what's out there" in Paganism and Christianity will help clarify the landscape of belief that comes together as ChristoPaganism. We begin with an overview of the modern Pagan movement.

Chapter 2

AN OVERVIEW OF PAGANISM

The word *pagan* comes from the Latin word *paganus* and means "country dweller." It was used initially by the ancient Romans, and over time it acquired a negative connotation, much like our words "redneck" or "hick" have today. As Christianity spread first in cities and towns of the Roman empire, and beyond, the more isolated country people were the last to adopt the new religion. They clung to their old ways and practices and continued to venerate their own deities. Because the ancient pagans did not readily change to the new form of worship, *pagan* began to assume the meaning of someone who is "godless" or "without religion," a definition still found in dictionaries today, although the country people certainly did have their own gods and religion. Once this meaning became associated with *pagan*, it was natural for Christian missionaries to attach the word to any indigenous people who followed their native traditions. During the Crusades, Christianity applied the term to Muslims, and Muslims then used and still use the words *infidel* and *pagan* to refer to Christians and others in the West. We hear the term used in a derogatory sense now by some preachers who believe that *pagan* describes all the evils in the world.

As a word of insult, *pagan* has a long history that doesn't seem to be over. It is a word that attaches a negative value to being different, especially spiritually different, and declares these differences to be evil. It is a word whose intent is to divide and make people suspicious of each other. It distinguishes "our group" from "that other group" and declares "that other group" to be bad. Such labeling operates like a flashing danger sign, warning everyone away and raising their fear. No thinking is required. No listening is required. The label does your thinking for you and becomes a filter nothing can get through, and so a true understanding and appreciation of others under this label is brought to a halt.

Modern Pagans have adopted this word with an awareness of its bad history. They know that the "pagans" are whoever is feared and reviled at the moment—the religious minority, the spiritually oppressed, the stubborn, the misunderstood, the outsider and foreigner, the technologically primitive, and the indigenous. When the religious battle lines are drawn between "us" and "them," whoever the "pagans" of the moment are will be "them." They are the ones whose voices may be extinguished, whose history is sometimes rewritten but usually forgotten, whose wisdom is vilified, and whose writings and oral traditions are eradicated. Pagans accept this tarnished word and apply it to themselves in the belief that differences can be honored, that there is room for many views and perspectives, that a division into "us" and "them" is no longer healthy or sustainable in today's world. Paganism affirms that people can listen to each other and appreciate differences. Fear does not have to win the day.

Pagan Traditions

As used in the modern movement, *Pagan* is a broad term that encompasses many traditions. These traditions can vary widely in their beliefs and practices, just as Seventh Day Adventists and Catholics differ greatly from each other but are both considered a part of Christianity. According to the 1997 Jorgensen and Russell study, the largest of the Pagan traditions is Wicca, comprising approximately 47% of the movement.[1] Wiccans follow an earth-centered calendar of eight festivals a year, which we set out later on in this chapter, and venerate the divine as both masculine and feminine in the form of the God and the Goddess. Some Wiccans see the God and Goddess as symbolic representations of spirit and the way reality works, as in the polarities of day/night, male/female, and so on. Others see the God and Goddess as literal beings and deities. Either view is acceptable in Paganism and various Wiccan traditions may emphasize one view over another. Most Wiccans observe the ethic contained in the Wiccan Rede, which states, "If it harm none, do what you will." We explore the implications of this ethical system in greater depth in the last chapter of our introductory book, *Paganism: An Introduction to Earth-Centered Religions* (2002). There are a variety of paths and traditions within Wicca itself, including Gardnerian, Alexandrian, Dianic, Feri, Strega, Corellian, and Solitary, to name a few.

The next largest tradition in Paganism, according to the Pagan Spirit Gathering 1994 Tribal Survey results—the latest year available—at 27%,[2] is the Eclectic, which is another word Pagans use to describe blended or interspiritual traditions. Eclectic traditions cover a wide range of practices that may include ChristoPaganism but are not limited to it. An Eclectic Pagan is generally open to the wisdom of every religion and incorporates practices that speak to him or her most directly. An Eclectic's life experiences and personal encounters with the divine are what generally shape the direction his or her blended practice takes.

Other traditions within Paganism include shamanism, Asatru, Druidism, Celtic Traditionalism, ceremonial magick, and family traditions, among others. Shamanism is an ancient and often cross-cultural practice that involves the use of trance work and spirit guides or power animals to assist the shaman in performing a work such as healing or divination. The Asatru devote themselves to Nordic, Germanic, or Icelandic deities. Druidism is a revival tradition that desires to re-create the Druidic system, and may or may not combine with Celtic Traditionalism, in which groups or clans attempt to create a pre-Christian Gaelic religion and society. Strega is an Italian tradition of Wicca. Ceremonial magick draws on the works of Aleister Crowley and the Order of the Golden Dawn, a prominent occult society founded in Britain in 1887, and generally involves precise rituals, words, and the use of tools for gaining specific results. Family traditions include practices and beliefs handed down through a family for many generations, which are often informal and may contain no overt ritual, and in which the connection to Paganism is sometimes downplayed or combined with Christian elements.

You can find more detailed descriptions of all these Pagan traditions in chapter 1 of our introductory book. Despite their differences, all of these traditions are considered to be a part of modern Paganism. Paganism, then, is an umbrella term that includes a number of traditions, in the same manner that Christianity contains a number of denominations. To help our students visualize Paganism and its traditions, we created the Pagan umbrella shown in figure 2.1.

Paganism is a religion, and like other religions it addresses ultimate issues concerning the nature and purpose of life and the realm of spirit. It has ordained clergy and observes a liturgical year and religious holy days. Many Pagans organize themselves into groups, which may be called circles, churches, covens, or groves. They do not generally have missionaries or proselytize, nor is there one central hierarchy or dogma; some individual traditions, however, may adopt a hierarchical structure and promote specific teachings. Generally

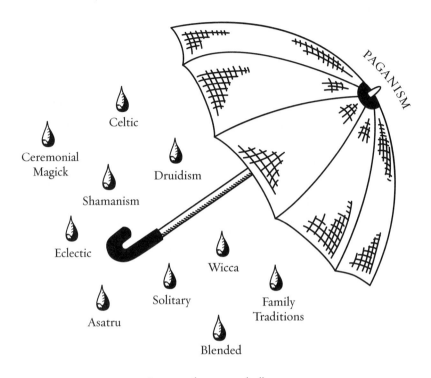

Figure 2.1. The Pagan umbrella

speaking, diversity is a hallmark of Paganism, and most Pagans would not find it appropriate to insist that all Pagans believe the same things or be organized under the same structure.

Paganism is recognized as a religion by social scientists, whose studies have already been referenced or will be examined in later chapters, and it is also recognized by the law. In 1986 the courts recognized Wicca as a religion in the landmark case of *Dettmer v. Landon*, 617 F. Supp. 592 (E.D. Va. 1985), affirmed on appeal, 799 F.2d 929. Paganism is also a spirituality and represents a way of living, worshipping, and connecting to nature and the divine. Spiritual practices among Pagans are quite varied and can be drawn from any source. Such practices include formal worship or ritual, meditation, singing, dancing, drumming, walking in nature, healing, gardening, divination, massage, and working with herbs.

Pagan Population

How many Pagans are there? This is a difficult question to answer because Pagans don't keep membership lists either in the United States or worldwide. It is also difficult because people may adopt aspects of Pagan philosophy or some of its practices, but not use the word *Pagan* to identify themselves. It is unclear how many people fall into this latter category.

The most recent population data concerning Pagans comes from a February 2008 survey conducted by the Pew Forum on Religion & Public Life called the U.S. Religious Landscape Survey. The results are available online and also by mail. The Pew researchers placed Paganism in a grouping they call "New Age," which includes the categories of Wiccan, Pagan, and Others. The total number of respondents in this category is 0.4% of the survey population. In addition to this number, Unitarian Universalists allow their membership to identify themselves as Pagan or earth-centered, among other categories, and the Pew poll found that Unitarians comprise 0.3% of the survey population. In attempting to discover how many of this 0.3% might classify themselves as Pagan or earth-centered, we learned that an in-house survey conducted by the Unitarian Universalist Association (UUA) in 1998 reveals that 19% of Unitarians so describe themselves.[3] Other categories in the Pew poll which could include Pagans are Spiritual But Not Religious at about 0.1%, Eclectic at approximately 0.1%, and Liberal or Other Liberal at approximately 0.2%.

Since Pagans might answer under a number of different categories, especially considering that "New Age" is not particularly accurate or descriptive of them, we think it is safe to say that the numbers of Pagans in the United States currently range between 0.4% and 0.5%. This range includes the 0.4% of the "New Age" category plus some leeway for Unitarians who answered as Unitarians even though they identify as Pagans (potentially up to 19% of that group), as well as other categories. If we extrapolate this range to the U.S. population as a whole, which is approximately 300 million at the time of this writing, then Pagans currently number between 1.2 and 1.5 million people. Interestingly, this means that Pagans now equal or exceed the number of Hindus at 0.4%, and are approaching the number of Muslims at 0.6% and Buddhists at 0.7%. Paganism has clearly come into its own as a religious presence in the United States.

Pagan Beliefs

Because the Pagan movement has not adopted an official dogma, it is not possible to identify what Pagans believe in a manner that will be true for all of them. As noted previously, some traditions adopt a set body of belief, and their position on certain topics is clear. Their beliefs, however, apply only to their members and not to the Pagan movement as a whole. Many Pagans recognize deities from one mythology or another, both male and female (as with the God and Goddess), but this is not a requirement. Most Pagans believe in some divine principle or spiritual force, but even this is not a necessity. We know of secular humanists who are comfortable in Paganism and identify or commune with the natural world only.

Most Pagans would agree that life is a beautiful and blessed thing, and that no part of reality is inherently flawed or damned if it is not saved by some means. While Pagans do recognize that people have the capacity to make poor choices, they do not equate this capacity with a flawed nature. Most Pagans also tend to believe that the universe is interconnected, and that this connection leads to possibilities for spiritual relationship and mutual exchange, described later on in this chapter.

From our years of listening to Pagans, we created what we call the Seven Principles of Paganism. They are not drawn from any one Pagan tradition but are our synthesis of common beliefs we have encountered throughout the Pagan community. These principles are not dogma, but statements concerning how Pagans typically approach the issue of spirituality. Although we have set out these principles in our other books, since we are not assuming a prior knowledge of Paganism here, we offer them again. Several of them will already sound familiar to you, as we discussed the basis for them in the prior chapter. The principles are as follows:

1. You are responsible for the beliefs you choose to adopt.

2. You are responsible for your own actions and your spiritual and personal development.

3. You are responsible for deciding who or what the divine is for you and forming a relationship with it.

4. Everything contains the spark of consciousness or intelligence.

5. Everything is sacred.

6. Each part of the universe can communicate with each other part, and these parts often cooperate for specific ends.

7. Consciousness survives death.

These principles presuppose the basic trustworthiness of the universe, both in its manifest and unmanifest forms, and the unflawed nature of life and consciousness. They envision a universe that is multidimensional, existing in realms both inside and outside of space-time, all parts of which contain a spark of intelligence or consciousness. They anticipate the ability of all parts of the universe to communicate with each other beyond the limits of space-time, beyond the notions of a mechanistic universe. These concepts take us into the realm of magick, which we will discuss later on in this chapter.

My Journal

Take out the list of spiritual beliefs you identified in the journaling exercise in the previous chapter. Look at each belief and see if you can determine its source. Where did this belief come from and how did you acquire it? If you can remember when you acquired it, make a note of when and what happened. If it seems you always had this belief, note that as well. If you can recall when you acquired the belief, did it replace an earlier one? If so, what was it? See if you can determine the source of this earlier belief also.

After finishing, take a look at what you have written. Have your beliefs changed a great deal over the years? What do you observe about the source of your beliefs? Is one source emphasized or represented more than another? Why do you think that is so? Do you notice any major shifts in your beliefs, and if so, what? Try to recall what brought on these shifts and what consequences they brought. How have these shifts impacted your life? Are there any beliefs you hold now that you wish you could abandon or change? Which ones and why? If you could change them, what would you change them to?

Next, for each of your beliefs, identify three ways in which it is life-giving, beneficial, or expanding for you. Does it have this same beneficial effect on others, such as your family, co-workers, or society?

How about on your environment and the natural world? The realm of spirit? Don't view this belief only in its ideal sense, but in how you actually live it day to day. If its beneficial effects for you differ from or are absent in the way others experience it, why is this so? For each belief, also identify three ways in which it is limiting, insulating, or even potentially detrimental to you. Also consider ways in which it may be so for your family, work, society, and the environment. Also include the realm of spirit. Every belief has limitations as well as benefits. Some of these limitations are obvious, some are not so obvious. Take your time with this and don't try to complete this part in one sitting. Give yourself a couple of weeks to work on it, and as things come to mind, add them to the list.

When you feel you are done, pick a time when you have half an hour to sit quietly. Take your list and read it through slowly—your beliefs, their sources, their benefits, and their limitations. What parts of the list feel really good to you? What parts raise strong emotions for you? What are these emotions? Do any parts of the list make you feel uncomfortable, angry, or resentful? Why do you think that is? What do you think it would take for your resentment to be resolved? Did any of your beliefs come as a surprise to you? How about the sources of your beliefs and events that formed them? Did any of the benefits and limitations of your beliefs surprise you? In what ways? How do you live out your beliefs? Is there something different you would like to do in terms of living them out? When you are finished, gradually relax your awareness and send gratitude and a blessing to yourself and all that you are now, and to all that you might become. Also send gratitude and a blessing to your concept of the divine, and then end your reflection.

The Sacred Year

Paganism is often called an earth-based or earth-centered religion. While this can refer to the fact that most Pagans honor the earth and the natural world, it usually refers to the fact that the Pagan sacred year is based on the cycles of the earth. Pagans observe a sacred or liturgical year, which unlike some faiths is not built around the life of a founder or great prophet. The Pagan sacred year, called the Wheel of the Year, is based on the cycles of the seasons and movements of the sun and earth. As with other experiences all humans share—such as day and night, birth and death—everyone shares the cycling of the seasons. People experience the solstices, the equinoxes, and the waxing and waning of the moon regardless of their ethnic and religious background, and without the requirement of any dogma or church membership. The earth is humanity's great common denominator.

As Pagans honor the seasons of the earth, they also honor the seasons of life. Honoring what is common to all of humanity brings a sense of solidarity with all of humanity. Honoring the waxing and waning of life, whether human, plant, or animal, helps increase awareness and respect for all of life. An earth-based sacred year takes many people, sometimes for the first time, beyond the boundaries set by race, ethnicity, culture, and faith-specific mythology, to encounter directly the unity they share with all humankind.

When Pagans honor the seasons, they honor aspects of spirituality in their life. A celebration for the arrival of winter is not just about winter, but those times in our lives that are hard and dark, when we have been stripped bare and move blindly forward. It's about the difficult times of death, depression, losing a job, illness, injury, and loss of relationships. It's about watching parents and friends age and saying goodbye to loved ones. It's about watching ourselves age and coming to grips with our mortality. Winter is also about rest, quiet, simplicity, recovery, and faith. One can say, then, that loss, faith, and change are some of the spiritual lessons of winter.

The celebration of spring, in contrast, is about those times in life when we have tremendous energy and enthusiasm, when we begin something new and everything is possible. It's about having confidence restored and pain lifted, taking a new job, and being healed. It's about starting life anew and being resurrected. Spring is also about falling in love and starting new relationships, watching our babies be born, and enjoying childhood. One can say, then, that hope, freshness, joy, and new beginnings are some of the spiritual lessons of spring.

The obvious correspondences between the seasons of the year and the feelings and spiritual issues they naturally raise have led some to say that the Pagan Wheel of the Year is "spiritually intuitive." If you want to give this a try yourself, especially if you are unfamiliar with Paganism, go through the Wheel of the Year and determine what personal,

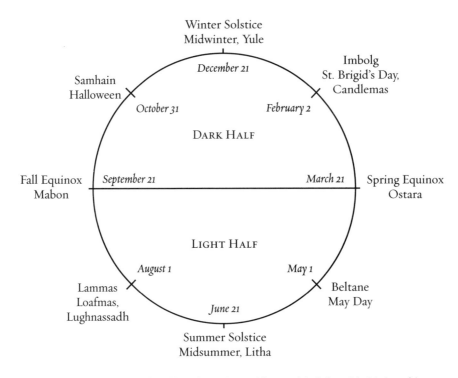

Figure 2.2. A wheel showing the eight Sabbats, their names and dates, and the light and dark halves of the year

communal, or spiritual themes the holidays might touch on. If you were going to design a ceremony to celebrate those themes at a religious gathering, what might you plan to do?

So it goes around the eight holidays, or Sabbats, of the Wheel of the Year observed by many Pagans (fig. 2.2). The year is marked first by the solstices and equinoxes, known as the Quarter Points, and these are divided again by what were originally Celtic agricultural holidays, known as the Cross-Quarter Points. The holidays are spaced fairly evenly, with one occurring about every six weeks.

In the Northern Hemisphere, winter solstice occurs around December 21 and is also called Yule or Midwinter. This day marks the longest night and the depths of the darkness of the season. Following winter solstice comes Imbolg, also known as Candlemas or St. Brigid's Day, on February 2. The increase of daylight is becoming more noticeable and is often celebrated by the lighting of candles. The recognition of this growing light (or its absence) can also be recognized in the secular observance of Groundhog Day, also on February 2. The next feast day is spring equinox, which occurs around March 21 and is also called Ostara, which is the root of the word *Easter*. The dark half of the year is left behind on this day, and life begins to bloom again. Following the spring equinox comes Beltane or May Day on May 1. This is a festival of fertility and the creative potential of life. Next comes the summer solstice, which occurs around June 21 and is also called Midsummer or Litha. Here the sun is at its peak, crops are growing, and life is full of bustling activity. Following the summer solstice is Lammas on August 1, also known as Loafmas or Lughnassadh. The first grain is ready to cut, and the gift of bread and the hope of a plentiful harvest is celebrated. Next on the Wheel is the Fall Equinox which occurs around September 21, and is also known as Mabon. This is a second harvest festival and marks the end of the light half of the year. Following the fall equinox comes Samhain (pronounced "Sow-un," "sow" rhyming with "cow"), or Halloween, on October 31. The dark half of the year has begun in earnest, the final harvest is brought in, decisions are made about the keeping or slaughtering of livestock for the winter, and ancestors are honored. This brings us back to the winter solstice, and the year begins again. The same holidays are observed in the Southern Hemisphere, but at the opposite times of year.

Pagans also celebrate life passages or rites of passage that honor the seasons or decision points of an individual's life. These include pregnancy and birth, baby welcomings, coming of age, handfasting or marriage, handparting, croning and saging, death, dedication to a path, and ordination. The themes of these life passages can also be correlated to the spiritual lessons of the Wheel of the Year, since an individual's life reflects many of the cycles experienced in the seasons.

How Pagans celebrate the Wheel of the Year and rites of passage varies considerably by tradition. Worship forms can be very formal and stylized, or fluid and informal. Some observe strict roles taken by an ordained priest and priestess, while others have no ordained clergy and trade roles as needed. Pagan worship services are frequently called "rituals," "ceremonies," or "gatherings," and they can be held indoors or out of doors. We have attended services with as few as three or four people and as many as several hundred. Rituals usually follow a prescribed order, which is set by those planning it. The most common ritual form is that of the Wiccan circle, which generally consists of the preparation of the people, the creation of sacred space, the invitation and honoring of the Quarters and the divine, the work of the ritual, and the dismissals and closing, all of which are explained in the following section.

Religious Ceremonies

During a service, participants usually do not sit in rows, but stand or sit in a circle so they can all see each other. The people might prepare themselves by singing, dancing, smudging, or quiet meditation. Since Pagans do not usually own churches, they tend to meet in someone's home, a rented hall, a park, or a backyard. They create sacred space for their ceremony and then let it go when they are done. "Casting a circle" is the most frequent means of creating a sacred space, and it is like energetically drawing the walls, floor, and ceiling of a portable church. It is visualized as an energy filter or container that keeps the static out and holds in the energy that is wanted. Circles can be cast by walking the perimeter one or several times, by pointing a finger, wand, or blade in the air to draw the circle, or by the entire group dancing in a circle or creating it with a wall of sound, among other ways.

The "calling of the Quarters" usually occurs next and is an honoring of the four directions—north, south, east, and west—and the four elements—earth, air, fire, and water. They are generally called as representatives of the Wheel of the Year and of life on the earth. The four directions can represent the four stages of life: birth and youth (east), maturity (south), elderhood (west), and death and rebirth (north); or aspects of being such as the mind, thinking, and communication (east), the will, passions, and spirituality (south), love, wisdom, healing, and the emotions (west), and the physical body and its health and needs such as food and shelter (north). The four elements represent all the forms matter can take in the physical realm: solid (earth), gaseous (air), plasmic (fire), and liquid (water). The directions and elements also typically correspond to each other, so that east and air are often paired together, south and fire, west and water, and north and earth. In figure 2.3 we show the correspondence between the four seasons, the stages of life, the directions, and the elements.

In addition to the four directions and elements, many Pagans also add the realm of spirit or center. The divine is also invited and honored, either as a part of calling center or separately. In a large or public ritual, a dozen or more traditions may be represented by those attending, bringing with them as many concepts of the divine. Sometimes several traditions of deities are called, but more frequently those planning the ritual decide which deities or aspects of the divine will be recognized. Most participants are comfortable with this, even if what is chosen is outside of their tradition or personal belief system. One tradition might be featured at one gathering and a different one at another gathering, with all present participating. Reading through this paragraph, we

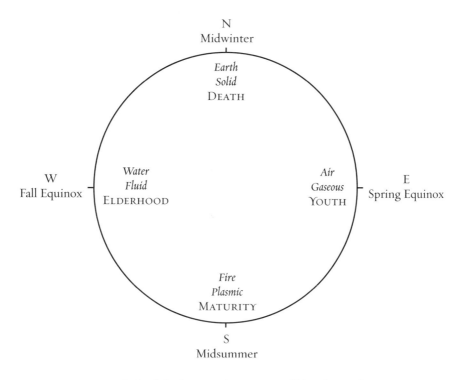

Figure 2.3. A wheel with the directions, elements, stages of life, and states of matter

realized that this description might not really convey what Pagans experience and the degree to which they are comfortable with variety. So to help illustrate the point better, we will put it in terms of a gathering of Christians.

Imagine, if you will, a gathering of a hundred Christians drawn from many denominations. Present are Baptists, Catholics, Jehovah's Witnesses, Presbyterians, Seventh Day Adventists, Quakers, Lutherans, Mormons, and Amish. This group has decided to get together periodically, perhaps once a month, and celebrate together. One month the Catholics plan the service and celebrate Mass, then teach everyone how to pray the rosary. Everyone participates, attempting to follow along in chant mode, genuflecting and using holy water. Another month the Mormons are in charge and they call on the angel Moroni (who delivered the golden plates to Joseph Smith) and share their personal testimonies. Everyone participates and sings Mormon hymns in four-part harmony as best they can. Afterward, most stay on for a potluck and end up in a philosophical discussion of doctrinal developments before and after the Reformation. A side group debates whether purple was always the color for Lent and Advent. No proselytizing or criticism of any of the denominations occurs. The Baptists ask the Catholics if they can borrow candles and incense for the next service, as they're planning something special and they don't keep such things on hand. Several of the women decide to spend a day at the mall with their kids, then change it to the zoo to accommodate the Amish. If you can imagine this happening, then you can imagine what public Pagan ritual and social life is like, and get a glimpse of the wide diversity of belief, practice, and cultural accommodation that a Pagan experiences.

Continuing with a description of a typical Pagan ritual, the working then occurs as determined by those who plan it. This may be a healing, a celebration of the season, a focus on a specific project or need, the energizing of a desire or goal, or a time of meditation. When the work is finished, the ritual ends with the dismissals. Generally going in reverse order, the divine is acknowledged and thanked, the four directions and elements are released, and the circle is taken down. The service is over and may be followed by visiting, food, dancing, and drumming.

A Magickal World

The Principles of Paganism affirm that all parts of the universe, large or small, contain a spark of intelligence or consciousness, are interconnected, and can communicate with each other. Some recent scientific findings, which we cover in some detail in our introductory book, also appear to support the view that all of matter contains information and conveys it to other parts of itself. The way particles appear to do this instantaneously in nonlocal phenomena, for example, may point to a form of interaction and connection beyond space-time. Some scientists have theorized that the universe is multidimensional and may enfold and unfold itself into physical existence millions of times per second. When matter enfolds, it may go into a state of potential in which time and space do not exist; the past, present, and future are found together simultaneously; and the whole is immediately accessible. In this state, consciousness has access to all of itself across the entire multidimensional spectrum.

Such theories do not conflict with the experience of mystics, who tend to report—regardless of religious background or historical period—similar experiences with multiple levels of reality. They describe a type of connectedness and relatedness to all that exists, usually arising from their tradition's concept of the divine or other ground of being. Many Pagans would agree that everything and everyone experiences the multi-dimensional flow of the universe, is interconnected, and participates in the sharing of information and potential ordering of events. This participation is part of a deep relationship and mutual exchange between all of matter, spirit, and consciousness. When Pagans purposefully interact with the multidimensional universe, they call it an act of magick. We define magick as *the actions of many consciousnesses voluntarily working together in an aware and interconnected universe to bring about one or more desired results.*

Magick as we define it generally takes one or more of the following forms in Pagan spirituality: communing, energy work, divination, and conscious creation. Together these comprise much of a Pagan's spiritual practice. *Communing* refers to prayer and meditation and the act of speaking and listening to one's concept of the divine. It can also involve listening and interacting with all the realms of consciousness. *Energy work* involves the sensing and directing of energies and intentions for a variety of purposes, such as healing, support, protection, and courage. Energies may derive from physical sources, such as electromagnetism, or from one's concept of the divine, or be more conceptual in nature, as with justice and forgiveness. *Divination* is the receipt of information from the realm of consciousness. A person may choose to work with a particular source of information, such as the divine or a spirit guide, or may be open to its receipt from across the multidimensional spectrum. *Conscious creation* involves the use of intention, prayer, projection, and hard work to manifest desires and goals into physical reality. These four expressions of magick may be combined in a given working, as they are not mutually exclusive. We discuss the four types of magick more thoroughly and give exercises for working with them for the purpose of spiritual growth in our book *Pagan Spirituality: A Guide to Personal Transformation* (2006).

We relate the four forms of magick to the four directions and the elements, placing divination in the east, energy work in the south, communing in the west, and conscious creation in the north. The philosopher Ken Wilber has also identified four quadrants of human experience which he calls the *Inner I*, *Inner We*, *Outer Its*, and *Outer It*.[4] The Inner I is a person's own private, interior, and subjective experience. The Inner We is the interior aspect of culture, such as language and shared values. The Outer Its is the realm of cultural expression in the world, as in a culture's institutions, buildings, legal codes, and churches. Since these physical things are built on the values (beliefs) of the collective, they are roughly equivalent to belief systems and structures. The fourth quadrant is the Outer It, which is the exterior physical world that can be objectively studied and

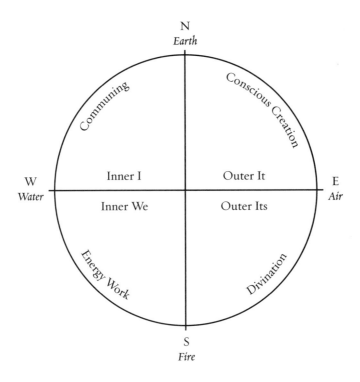

Figure 2.4. *A wheel including the forms of magick and Wilber's four quadrants*

examined. We have taken Wilber's quadrants and placed them into relationship with the four directions, elements, and types of magick, with the Inner I corresponding with the west and communing, the Inner We with energy work and the south, the Outer Its with divination and the east, and the Outer It with the north and conscious creation. We show these correspondences in figure 2.4.

Wilber notes that in the past people tended to merge the quadrants so that they were not readily seen to exist independently of each other. One quadrant may take the fore and try to merge the others into itself, insisting that all of reality be reduced to its perspective. An example of this merging was done by the church during Galileo's trial. Science was not allowed to be an entity separate from that of the church, and scientific findings were required to match the beliefs of the church or suffer the consequences. Much later this trend reversed itself and science became a primary, perhaps *the* primary, yardstick of truth. All phenomena that could not be scientifically observed and measured obviously wasn't real (usually meaning it was found in the realms of the Inner I and Inner We). The modern world is still experiencing the results of this reduction. Wilber instead encourages an "integral" approach in which all the quadrants are seen as valid, are free to express themselves in their own spheres, and together form a harmonious balance. This integral approach includes spirituality.

An "integral" spirituality is one that appreciates all four quadrants and allows them to exist independently. Such a spirituality, unlike in Galileo's time, would not try to force an individual's interior experience to match its belief system or insist that science limit its discoveries to those that support its beliefs. It allows room for the culture to express itself—as with artists and its institutions—creatively, in ways that are free of its beliefs, or in ways that may even be in conflict with its beliefs. A fully integral spirituality equally embraces the contributions of the inner and outer worlds, the individual and the collective. It strikes a balance between them that encourages the healthiest expression of each.

Since modern Paganism is a recent arrival and has not had to work to free itself from tangles caused by prior mergings of the four quadrants in its history, it is relatively free to try an integral approach from the start. This includes embracing an open and inter-spiritual approach. An integral approach to magick means that Pagans would learn how to integrate and balance the ways in which they connect to spirit in their *communing*, and the ways in which they support each other as with healing, forgiveness, and encouragement in their *energy work*. It would impact the ways in which Pagans act as an informing and prophetic voice in their *divination*, as they help guide the building of just and sustainable structures in the culture. In terms of *conscious creation*, an integral approach would help Pagans find balance in their relationships and interactions with the physical world, their bodies, and the realities of life shared by all.

My Journal

What was your reaction the first time you heard about Paganism? What did you think Pagans did and believed? Do you hold this view of Paganism now? Which of your views have changed and which have stayed the same?

What are your experiences with Paganism? Have you attended any Pagan rituals or festivals? Have you read any books by Pagans (other than this one)? How many Pagan friends do you have? Identify five ways in which Paganism as a religion and philosophy contributes positively to the world. Identify five ways in which you think it is detrimental or that make you uncomfortable.

Which season or time of the year is your favorite? Have you ever had any spiritual feelings concerning that time of year? What do you do in your spiritual practice to acknowledge the significance of this season for you, if anything?

What is your opinion of magick? How and when did you acquire this opinion? Identify eight events in your life that would qualify as magickal according to the Pagan view. Were these events spiritually significant to you? If so, why?

Do you agree or disagree that the universe is interconnected? Multi-dimensional? Conscious or intelligent? Describe your view of the universe.

Chapter 3

AN OVERVIEW
OF CHRISTIANITY

Writing an overview of Christianity presents a real challenge. So much scholarship is available concerning its history, early communities, theology, and the formation of its scripture, that we cannot begin to survey it all. At best we can hope to hit a few highlights. In this chapter we set out a basic overview of the structure of Christianity as it exists today in its denominations, worship forms, and liturgical year, as well as a bit of the history of its formation.

It was during the years of the Roman empire that the word *Christian* gradually came into use to describe those who followed Jesus of Nazareth. Ancient Rome was tolerant of monotheisms and even added Yahweh, the God of Israel, to its official pantheon as "Iao."[1] However, since a new Christian stopped going to the temples, did not participate in the state religious observances, and stopped worshipping the accepted gods, the Romans decided they were obviously "godless" and must be atheists.[2] Ironically, it is from this charge of atheism that Christians were considered treasonous and subject to punishment by death.

The early years of Christianity were marked by a great deal of variety in belief and practice. Each Christian group had its own idea about who Jesus was, what his ministry meant, and how best to emulate him. Some people today bemoan the number of Christian denominations and long for the early years of Christian "unity," when the faith was more "pure," when believers lived together, shared their goods, believed the same things, and worshipped the same way. According to biblical historian Elaine Pagels, this view of early Christianity is not accurate. She notes that even with its myriad denominations, the Christianity of today shows more uniformity than the Christian church of the first and second centuries.[3] It may be hard to imagine, but early Christian scriptures may have consisted of several hundred gospels, myths, poems, and teachings, of which only a fraction have survived. As New Testament scholar Burton Mack observes, most Christian literature of the first century has not survived, and what is set out in the New Testament is "only a small portion of what must have been a very rich and sizable production."[4] He notes that the range of literature circulated by the early groups was impressive, concurring with Pagels that it consisted of stories, gospels, hymns, instructions, prayers, treatises, polemics against the Greeks and Jews and Romans, commentaries, allegories, acts of apostles, martyrologies, and letters.[5]

Beliefs and practices differed greatly from one Christian group to the next. Modern Christians may be surprised to learn that not all early Christians accepted the resurrection of Jesus as a literal event, since today the resurrection is a foundational premise of Christianity. Early Christian groups also organized themselves in different ways, gave women equal participation, and did not necessarily recognize the authority of the developing orthodox hierarchy.[6] Many of the scholars we surveyed observed that the earliest Christians did not have a concept of Jesus as the "Christ," know about any disciples, or intend to begin a church. And this is just Christianity in the West. China had an active Christian population that believed in equality of men and women and had no concept of original sin. We explore some of these aspects of early Christianity in this chapter, not only because they are intriguing, but also because they pose an interesting question for interspiritual work.

The question is this: If ChristoPaganism is a blending of Christianity and Paganism, does that mean it incorporates only modern orthodox Christianity, or does it include all forms of Christianity experienced throughout history?

The Jesus People

New Testament scholar Burton Mack observes that the Gospel of Mark was written in the 70s CE, the Gospel of Matthew in the 80s, the Gospel of John during the 90s, and the Gospel of Luke and the Book of Acts in the early 100s.[7] Biblical scholar G. A.

Wells generally agrees with Mack's dating, but places the writing of Mark after 70 CE and the other three gospels closer to 100 CE.[8] We explore opposing views concerning the writing of the gospels in the next chapter. But before there were any gospels, many scholars believe there were collections of the sayings of Jesus that circulated among the people who followed him and used his sayings as teachings. Mack calls these followers "Jesus people" or parts of the "Jesus movement."[9] Scholars began to suspect the existence of a collection of Jesus sayings upon observing that Matthew and Luke contained large quantities of sayings that overlapped each other but were not found in Mark. This led scholars to the belief that Matthew and Luke had a similar source at hand as they were writing their gospels, which scholars then called the "source," or "Quelle" in German—Q for short.[10]

The existence of the Q source is not a new idea, being first advanced by Christian Weisse in 1838 and again in 1863 by H. J. Holtzmann. Bernard Weiss, a conservative Christian, demonstrated Luke's dependence on Q in 1907, and Adolf von Harnack published a book called *The Sayings of Jesus* in 1908, which contained an approximation of the Q sayings. In the 1920s, B. H. Streeter published a monumental study of the gospels that relied on Q, and his study became a classic among New Testament scholars. At this point, Q was seen as a missing sayings text that consisted of 225 verses.[11] With the discovery of the Dead Sea Scrolls, it became clear that there were a number of extracanonical (that is, outside of the canon of the Bible) writings that were unknown or lost, and so scholars accepted Q as a "document" in its own right. The Gospel of Thomas, discovered with the Dead Sea Scroll collection, was especially provocative, as it was also a "sayings gospel," and 35% of it parallels the sayings suspected to be in Q. After this finding, there was no question in many scholars' minds that this genre of writing existed in early Christianity.[12]

Mack identifies three levels in the development of the Q source. The first and earliest level is a collection of Jesus's sayings that portray him as an itinerant philosopher who says rather shocking and thought-provoking things, usually in the form of aphorisms. Mack believes that this early level of Q writing would have been compiled immediately after Jesus's death. Next comes a layer of material written between Jesus's death and 66 CE, in which Jesus is called Son of Man and is correlated to Sophia, or the wisdom of God, a concept we explore on the next section. In this layer of material, Jesus is cast in the role of prophet. In the third layer of material, developments that are becoming a part of orthodox Christianity are inserted, sometime after the end of the

Roman-Jewish wars in 73 CE. In this level, the view of Jesus is changed from a child or incarnation of Sophia to the Son of God. The destruction of the temple in Jerusalem (which had just occurred) is compared to the sovereignty of Jesus, and the authority of Jewish scripture is reaffirmed.[13] New Testament scholar Graham Stanton is skeptical of Mack's division of Q into three layers dependent on the timing of the writings. He agrees that Q consists of wisdom sayings and prophetic sayings but believes it is not "clear that one is earlier and more historical than the other."[14]

According to Mack, "the remarkable thing about the people of Q is that they were not Christians."[15] The Jesus movements were attractive as "arenas for social experimentation," as they questioned hierarchical social structures, ritual purity, ethnic taboos, taxation economies, and encouraged a view of the human family beyond cultural constraints such as social class, gender, or ethnicity.[16] He notes, however, that the Q group was not the only group within the Jesus movement. He outlines at least five others: those with allegiance to Jesus's family, Jews who resided in Jerusalem for a time, the group who designed the set of five miracle stories as their myth of origin, the movement of which Mark was a part, and the tradition in which Luke lived, in which a distinctly human view of Jesus (as opposed to divine) prevailed.[17] Over time other groups developed, of which the Gnostics are especially well known.

Given the materials that comprise Q, the people of the early Jesus movement did not know the story of Jesus as it would be developed in the gospels. Mack says that "they did not think of Jesus as a messiah or the Christ. They did not take his teachings as an indictment of Judaism. They did not regard his death as a divine, tragic, or saving event. And they did not imagine that he had been raised from the dead," nor did they worship in his name, regard him as a god, or praise his memory in rituals.[18] In addition, "Q's story puts the Jesus movements in the center of the picture as the dominant form of early group formations in the wake of Jesus, and it forces the modern historian to have another look at the congregations of the Christ. The congregations of the Christ will now have to be accounted for as a particular development within the Jesus movements, not as the earliest form of Christian persuasion."[19] These "congregations of the Christ" developed in northern Syria and Asia Minor. They viewed Jesus's death as a martyrdom and borrowed from a number of Hellenistic myths common to the Mystery religions in the area that concerned the destiny of a divine being brought to earth. (See the following chapter for more discussion of the relationship of Mystery religions to Christianity.) The congregations described in Paul's letters are of this type, although

Wells and other scholars date the letters believed to be written by Paul (1 Thessalonians, Romans, 1 and 2 Corinthians, Galatians, Philippians, and Philemon) at least a decade earlier than the writing of Mark.[20]

Mack notes that these congregations of the Christ formed a "cult of the resurrected or transformed Jesus whom they now referred to as Christ, or Lord, as well as the Son of God."[21] Only the "faintest suggestion" of having begun as a Jesus movement is discernible in these congregations, even though it must have been from the Jesus people who spread into Syria that they developed.[22] Perhaps there is a glimpse of these origins in the letters of Paul, as theologian Rebecca Merrill Groothuis notes, since in these letters "there arose for the first time a need for church leaders to exhort women to be properly submissive. Why? Did Christian women need to be told to submit because they were picking up some egalitarian notions from the secular society? No, the dominant cultural mentality at this time was still that a woman should stay out of public leadership roles and be submissive to her husband's authority. The idea of gender equality came not from society but from the gospel of Jesus Christ . . . Societal patriarchy, however, remained intact."[23] The Jesus movement, with its emphasis on social experimentation, could have brought more egalitarian practices with it to Syria, practices which the Christ congregations and the later orthodox church discouraged.

According to Mack, the view of Jesus that developed within the Christ congregations was that Jesus was a Jewish messiah who challenged the Pharisees, called for repentance, taught that the kingdom of God was about to begin, assigned disciples to be leaders, drove the moneylenders from the temple and announced its destruction, and was crucified and resurrected as part of the cosmic struggle between the Jews and God's plan for the kingdom. Jesus then appeared to his disciples after the resurrection, and they formed a church in Jerusalem and began missions to both Jews and Gentiles.[24] However, Mack observes that none of this story is reflected in the Q source. There is no baptism of Jesus, no encounter between Jesus and authorities, no plot to kill him, no last supper, no trial, no crucifixion, no resurrection, no transfiguration, no disciples, no reform of religion, no mention of a church.[25] As the new mythology became solidified into the gospels and was taught and explained by letters from church leaders to congregations, the concept of a chain of tradition and authority in the disciples and their successors was created. With this development, the teachings of Jesus became more symbolic and, as Mack notes, "instruction *about* Jesus was just as important as instruction *from* Jesus, and the instructions from Jesus needed a great deal of interpretation in order to clarify their importance for Christian faith, piety, and virtue."[26] Thereafter, Q faded from sight and was replaced by other writings and "later mythologies that had no room for [Q's] singular focus on the authority of Jesus."[27]

The Divinity of Jesus

Early Christians held a number of views on the nature of the divine, all of which would eventually be eliminated except for what would become the "orthodox" view. The Gnostics, for example, believed that God was a dyad consisting equally of male and female characteristics. Valentinus, a noted Gnostic leader, believed that God consisted of the Father, also called the Depth, and the Mother, also called the Womb, Grace, or Silence.[28] Pagels observes that some Gnostics treated this dyadic concept of God as literal while others treated it as a metaphor, believing that God is neither male nor female. Still others believed that God could be addressed as either sex depending on which aspect was being stressed at the time. Pagels notes, however, that most agreed that the divine is a "harmonious, dynamic relationship of opposites."[29]

Others saw the Mother aspect as residing in the Holy Spirit, based on the Hebrew word for spirit—*ruah*—which is a feminine word. The Gospel of Philip, for example, calls the Spirit the "Mother of many," and in the Gospel of Hebrews, Jesus mentions "my Mother the Spirit."[30] Every early Christian text that dealt with the divine as feminine was omitted from the canon that would eventually be called the Bible, and was declared heretical by the orthodoxy. Pagels notes that by the time the sorting of the writings ended around 200 CE, "virtually all the feminine imagery for God had disappeared from orthodox Christian tradition."[31]

Early Christians also held a number of views about the nature of Jesus and whether he was or was not divine. One school of thought believed that Jesus was a man—a very holy and wise man, chosen for a very special purpose, but a man nonetheless. Recall that Mack puts Luke's community in this category. The other school believed that Jesus was divine, that he was not a "creature" in the sense that people and animals are "creatures," but that his nature proceeded directly from God and could be equated with God. This perspective was found in the congregations of the Christ, as Mack identifies them. They looked to the surrounding Jewish and Hellenistic cultures for images to express their ideas about Jesus, and over time they built a mythology from themes familiar to the cultures around them. Noted biblical archaeologist William F. Albright, a conservative Christian, observes that the mythology developed in the gospels contains "many striking parallels with more ancient Near Eastern religious ideas, such as the virgin birth of a god, his astrological associations, birth among cattle, imprisonment, death, descent to the underworld, disappearance for three days, resurrection, [and] exaltation to heaven." [32] Albright says that the "underlying dramatic forms" that touched the emotions of the Near East for three thousand years apparently held the same appeal for Christians of the first century, which may explain how "the messianic framework of the Gospels came to bear such a striking . . . resemblance in details to the corresponding framework of the cycles of Tammuz, Adonis, Attis, Osiris, etc."[33] We leave a deeper discussion of these issues for the next chapter.

As noted by Mack, the first shift in the nature of Jesus is observed in the second layer of Q, in which Jesus is identified with Sophia, or the wisdom of God. Sophia was already well known to the Jews. Theologian Elizabeth Johnson explains that Sophia was a personification of Wisdom, who in Jewish literature had been variously portrayed as an attribute of divine intelligence, a patron goddess of Hebrew schools and the Torah, an entity who mediates between God and the world, and a feminine personification of God.[34] Many of Sophia's powers and deeds were the same as those ascribed to Yahweh, and Johnson notes that female images of deity would not have been considered unusual as Judaism was surrounded by cultures that honored the feminine divine. Judaism was itself still developing into a monotheism, as we explore in depth in chapter 5, and it reconciled Sophia with monotheism by equating her with the God Yahweh. As Johnson puts it: "Sophia is Israel's God in feminine imagery."[35] Scriptural historian Marcus Borg says, "thus the language about Sophia is not simply personification of God in feminine form. Sophia *is* a feminine image for God."[36]

Johnson notes that much of Christology (equating Jesus with God) was built upon identifying Jesus with Sophia. By way of example, the Gospel of John adapts or assigns many of Sophia's behaviors and imagery found in Jewish literature to Jesus, as when Jesus calls out in a loud voice in a public place (7:28, 7:37), engages in long discourses and "I am" statements (6:51, 10:14, 11:25), is identified with the Torah and themes of seeking and finding (1:38, 1:41, 7:34), with the idea of right instruction and a revealer of mysteries (14:6), and in the view that whoever loves Jesus is beloved of God and is his friend (14:23, 15:15).[37] In Luke 7:33–35, the gospel writer has Jesus identify himself as a child of Sophia.

Johnson comments that because of his linkage to Sophia, Jesus was also linked to God and then became the incarnation of God.[38] As Borg notes, Jesus was increasingly spoken of as having "all the qualities of God" and came to be experienced as the "functional equivalent" of God.[39] The link to Sophia was pivotal to the arguments leading to the success of making Jesus into a christological figure. In the fourth century, the Arians, who believed Jesus to be only a man, downplayed his divinity by denying Sophia's divinity. According to the Arians, since Jesus is linked to Sophia, then if Sophia isn't divine, neither is Jesus. The christologists were then forced, ironically, to insist on Sophia's divinity and Jesus's equation with her, and "argued for the Son's divinity from Sophia's identity with divine presence and activity."[40] Mack observes that the linking of Jesus to Sophia was used to "shift from a characterization of Jesus as a teacher to one that imagined Jesus first as an envoy of the divine agent in Israel's history and then as a kind of prophet."[41]

According to Mack, the third layer of additions that were added to Q transformed Jesus from a child of Sophia to the Son of God, in keeping with the views of the congregations of the Christ. The use of the word *Christ* in the writings signals this change. In this transformation, Jesus is recognized as the rightful heir to God's kingdom. As Mack notes, "the idea of the son of god as heir to his father's kingdom was available in many hellenistic mythologies,"[42] as you will see in the next chapter, and perhaps even earlier as discussed in chapter 5 concerning the story of Akhenaten. While the shift to Son of God seems a simple one, Mack observes that its effects were "stupendous." As he puts it, "The move turned a prophet-teacher into a divine sovereign. . . . He would now be a king who would execute his authority over the congregation in the present, and since resurrection meant ascending into heaven, the Jesus people came to think of Jesus as a god. The Christ was installed as ruler of God's world and lord of God's people."[43]

Theologian Albert Nolan can find no evidence that Jesus ever claimed christological powers and authority for himself, and believes that Jesus was unique in his time for being able to "overcome all authority thinking."[44] He says that Jesus did not "expect his audience to rely upon any authority at all—either his own or that of others. Unlike the scribes, he never appeals to the authority of the rabbinical tradition nor even to the authority of scripture itself . . . he does not even lay claim to the authority of a prophet."[45] Nolan further notes that when Jesus "is faced directly with the question of what authority he might have, he refuses to answer the question (Mark 11:33). People were expected to see the truth of what he was doing and saying without relying upon any authority at all."[46]

Borg notes that the main sources used by the christologists to support Jesus's divinity, namely the Gospel of John and the birth stories of Matthew and Luke, are not historical accounts. The versions of Jesus's birth in Matthew and Luke differ so markedly from each other that biblical scholars have concluded they are not historical accounts, but are "symbolic narratives created by the early Christian movement."[47] Borg observes that the Gospel of John, written during the period of debate over Jesus's divinity, is also not seen as a historical narrative according to many scholars. If these writings are not historical accounts, Borg notes, then Jesus never actually spoke of himself as Son of God or as one with God, as the light of the world, or as the way, the truth, and the life; that is, he "never spoke the words of John 3:16."[48] Mack agrees, and states that all the events in the gospels added onto the original Q material should be "accounted for as mythmaking," and that the gospels are "imaginative creations."[49]

As a historical figure, Borg calls Jesus a "spirit person," a teacher of wisdom, a social prophet, and a movement founder.[50] Borg notes that "there is a major difference between what Jesus was like as a figure of history and how he is spoken of in the gospels and later Christian tradition,"[51] and also that in the gospels "it is very difficult to discern the voice of Jesus from the voice of the church."[52] He identifies a "spirit person" as one who has "vivid and frequent subjective experiences of another level or dimension of reality," experiences that involve "momentary entry into nonordinary states of consciousness and take a number of different forms,"[53] such as visions or shamanic journeys. Borg's studies of religion worldwide brought him to the conclusion that spirit persons are found in all religions and cultures. The cross-cultural existence of such persons "undermines a widespread Christian belief that Jesus is unique, which most commonly is linked to the notion that Christianity is exclusively true and that Jesus is the 'only way.'"[54] Instead, Borg characterizes Jesus as "one of many mediators of the sacred."[55]

Authority in the Early Church

The resurrection is often considered the pivotal event of the Christian faith, yet initially there was no uniformity of belief about it. The gospel accounts themselves are not clear what to make of the resurrection. Did Jesus really rise in the flesh, or was his rising more metaphorical, more spiritual? Some biblical stories put Jesus in the flesh, but Luke and Mark say he appeared "in another form," not a physical body (Mark 16:12, Luke 24:13–22). So while some stories portray the resurrection as literal, others suggest a different view. As mentioned earlier, Mack points out that none of the Q material contains any mention of a resurrection. Church officials also held differing opinions. In the second century Bishop Irenaeus taught that Jesus was not crucified or resurrected and that he lived to be an old man, that this teaching was received directly from St. John, and that many church fathers believed this to be true.[56]

What is known for sure is that the gospels describe a resurrection and state that certain disciples claim that it occurred, and that Peter thereafter took charge of the group as its leader. Peter and the remaining eleven apostles adopted the position that their witnessing of the resurrection and the risen Jesus conferred authority on them to govern the church. While the gospels state that others also witnessed the resurrection (most notably women), by the second century orthodox churches claimed that authority to govern was conferred only on Peter and the eleven apostles.[57] Luke, written by orthodox writers during the period of debate on this issue, confirms the position of the orthodox church that only the eleven and Peter count as "official" witnesses[58] (see Luke 24:48).

Pagels notes that the theory that authority be given only to the male apostles who experienced the resurrection carried enormous implications for the structure of the early church community.[59] This position limited power to a small group who were also the only ones who could appoint their successors. While this position was certainly favored by the orthodox priests and bishops of the first two centuries, not everyone agreed with the idea. The Gnostics, for example, believed that the resurrection was not a past event but one that happens every day. When the apostles and others "saw" Jesus, they were simply experiencing him in a new way. As Borg puts it, they experienced Jesus in that moment as a "spiritual reality" that transcended his physical life, a reality that could be "experienced anywhere and everywhere."[60] Pagels says that the resurrection symbolized for them a moment of enlightenment, a "migration into newness"[61] that everyone can experience right now. Several of the writings circulated among early Christians contained accounts of people "encountering" the risen Jesus in this manner. According to the Gnostics, whoever "sees" Jesus and encounters him personally has spiritual authority equal to the apostles. Many of the writings rejected by the orthodox hierarchy contained stories of appearances by Jesus to others, including the Gospel of Mary, the Apocryphon of John, the Letter of Peter to Philip, and the Wisdom of Jesus Christ.

In the second century, Bishop Irenaeus declared these other writings to be fraudulent and only the four gospels to be valid since, he said, the four gospels were written by the apostles themselves. Modern biblical scholarship knows that his assertion concerning authorship is not true, as we will explore in more detail later on.

The controversy of the resurrection greatly influenced the development of Christianity as an institution. One question facing the early Christian was, who has spiritual authority? Two answers were given. A number of scattered, unorthodox, and Gnostic groups believed that whoever has a personal experience of Jesus has authority. Pagels says that according to this view, "the structure of authority can never be fixed into an institutional framework: it must remain spontaneous, charismatic, and open."[62] The second answer was given by the developing orthodoxy, which stated that the apostle's testimony is more trustworthy than one's own experience, and that priests and bishops are the only persons who have authority to succeed the apostles.

These two approaches to the issue of spiritual authority were reflected in the styles of worship and organization of the groups. The non-orthodox communities were charismatic and free-flowing. When the Gnostics met, they would draw lots and one person took the role of priest, another offered bread and wine, another read scripture, and another offered instruction.[63] This resulted in a very different type of structure than that experienced in the orthodox church, which had very distinct groups playing defined roles. The clergy—namely priests, bishops, and deacons—had authority and the laity had none. The Gnostics refused to recognize such distinctions, and since they chose roles each time they met, they never established permanent ranks of power as did the orthodox.

Furthermore, the non-orthodox groups shared power with women. Women were allowed to engage in priestly functions and teaching while the orthodox allowed no priestly, prophetic, or episcopal roles to be played by a female. This was a remarkable development considering that in its earliest years, the Jesus movement was quite open to women, and Jesus himself openly violated Jewish conventions concerning women. Historian Riane Eisler notes that Jesus taught that so-called "feminine virtues," such as compassion, gentleness, turning the other cheek, and loving one's enemies, should be given primacy.[64] She says that "time and time again we find that he was preaching the gospel of a partnership society."[65] Such a society included the involvement of women at all levels. Pagels notes that within ten to twenty years after Jesus's death, women held leadership positions in the churches.[66] Paul greets a woman as an apostle in Romans

16:7. But by the second century, men and women were segregated at worship services and women held no roles in orthodox churches. In 190 CE, Tertullian wrote in horror that in the non-orthodox groups women "teach, they engage in discussion, they exorcise, they cure."[67] The orthodox reinforced its position concerning women by producing letters "written" by Paul that urged their view, and as noted earlier, encouraged women to be submissive and no longer take prominent roles in the community. Mack observes that letters were a common way for the bishops of the early church to give instructions. They were often written anonymously or ascribed to certain persons whose word carried authority.[68] Biblical scholars now acknowledge that the letters from Peter were not written by Peter, and that Ephesians, 1 and 2 Timothy, Colossians, Hebrews, and Titus were not written by Paul. They were written by bishops and, naturally enough, give the orthodox position on issues of authority and require obedience to the bishops.[69]

Not everyone was convinced or pleased by these developments. Orthodox bishop Irenaeus complains that many highly placed members of the church and the church hierarchy agreed with non-orthodox views.[70] Among them was the theologian St. Clement of Alexandria who wrote in 180 CE that God is "both father and mother," that "men and women share equally in perfection . . . for the same 'humanity' is common to both men and women; and for us 'in Christ there is neither male nor female.'"[71] His position on this point, however, met with little support among orthodox clergy. Even so, theologian Elisabeth Schüssler Fiorenza notes that the elimination of women's participation did not happen without opposition. Orthodoxy had to overcome existing practices and the theologies that supported women in these roles. The issue continued to be debated into the third and fourth centuries, but things finally progressed to the point where a woman in leadership was equated with heresy.[72] In fact, St. Jerome eventually states that women are not only the root of all sin but also of all heresy.[73] Eisler muses that by the year 200 CE, "the model for human relations proposed by Jesus in which male and female, rich and poor, Gentile and Jew are all one was expurgated from the ideologies as well as the day-to-day practices of the orthodox Christian church," which "was well on its way to becoming precisely the kind of hierarchical and violence-based system Jesus had rebelled against."[74]

The Canon of Scripture

By the fourth century, many of the issues of belief, especially those concerning the resurrection, the nature of God, and Jesus as divine, had been decided and were set out in the Nicene Creed. In roughly the same period, the canon of scripture was chosen by the orthodox church. Out of a vast quantity of material, only a small number of selections were chosen to be "official" scripture. Mack points out that the materials that would become the New Testament were not an ad hoc collection, but a highly select and carefully arranged set of writings that were representative of several streams of Christian thought that the bishops hoped to fashion into a universal church.[75] The synoptic gospels were chosen for inclusion, according to Mack, because they provided a historical point of origin supporting the institutional claims of the church. "This means that their primary function as narratives was to create the illusion of a chain of tradition that not only linked Jesus with the epic traditions of Israel but also with the disciples as the apostles of the church."[76] In addition, because the early Christians were aware of their recent beginnings and were troubled by the resemblance of their myth to that of other Near Eastern mythologies, Mack notes that they saw their myth as history.[77] They distanced themselves from these other cultures and distinguished their "myths from the others only by emphasizing the recent historical setting of their myths and the impression given by the narrative gospels that the myths really happened."[78] This issue will be addressed further in the next chapter.

As Fiorenza notes, the canon of the New Testament was chosen by the historical winners, but the debates surrounding the choices give us glimpses into some of the egalitarian and inclusive practices of the early Christians.[79] Because the orthodox majority chose the canon of scripture, all books that contained references to a feminine divine were omitted. Those in which women played prominent ecclesiastical roles were not included. Those that urged the authority of personal experience over the authority of priests and bishops were left out. Essentially, the books that supported the orthodox view and the power of the institution were kept while those that did not were rejected. But they were not only rejected; they were collected and destroyed, their ideas vilified and their proponents driven away or persecuted.

As Pagels states, so successful were the efforts of the orthodox majority "to destroy every trace of heretical 'blasphemy'" that until the discoveries at Nag Hammadi, all information on alternative forms of Christianity came only from orthodox records of attacks against them.[80] This was a tremendous loss for Christianity, as the fifty-two writings found at Nag Hammadi offer "only a glimpse of the complexity of the early Christian movement. We now begin to see that what we call Christian—and what we identify as Christian tradition—actually represents only a small selection of specific sources, chosen from among dozens of others."[81] Fiorenza echoes this sentiment when she says that the texts accepted into the New Testament are only "the tip of the iceberg indicating a possibly rich heritage now lost to us."[82]

Organizationally, the Gnostics and other early groups were no match for the large and efficient system of the orthodox church, which according to Pagels "expressed a unified religious perspective based on the New Testament canon, offered a creed requiring the initiate to confess only the simplest essentials of faith, and celebrated rituals as simple and profound as baptism and the eucharist."[83] Without these elements, Pagels wonders if Christianity would have survived, since "ideas alone do not make a religion powerful."[84] She notes that equally important are the "social and political structures that identify and unite people into a common affiliation."[85]

Early Christianity in China

Onto this brief summary of the development of Christianity in the West must be added the story of the church in China. Records from the third century CE recount that the Apostle Thomas went to the Chinese, as chronicled in the extracanonical writing called the Acts of Thomas. Archaeologist Martin Palmer says that by the fifth century CE, church records document the existence of the church in China.[86] There are detailed records of a mission established at Da-Qin, just outside the ancient city of Chang-an and near the temple of Lou Guan Tai in 635 CE. Local Chinese records say the Da-Qin monastery was built in 650 CE.[87] According to Palmer, these records tell of a Bishop Aluoben of the Eastern church, who approached the city of Chang-an with his entourage and was greeted by the emperor. The emperor entered an edict that the Christians were to be welcomed, an edict found engraved on a *stela*, or *stele* (a carved stone slab), in 1625.[88] The Chinese gave the religion a name using characters that mean "luminous" and "religion."[89] Palmer says that the size of the church in China and the East is one of the best-kept secrets of Christian history. At its peak in the eighth century CE, it was larger than all the Christian populations in the Western church combined. Unlike the church in the West, the East was dealing with highly literate and civilized people and had to adapt itself to them in ways the West did not.[90] Because it was a different world, the East produced a different church and a variety of forms of Christianity.

In the year 1005 CE, a copy of the Chinese Christian scriptures and a number of Buddhist, Confucian, and Taoist texts were sealed in a cave at Dunhuang, perhaps due to civil unrest in the region. The cave remained sealed and undisturbed for eight hundred years, when it was discovered by a Taoist priest in the late 1800s.[91] After their discovery, the scrolls were unfortunately removed by explorers by the sackful. Some were taken to Paris, others surfaced at Chinese antique dealers. Many were not handled properly and disintegrated. The Christian scrolls, which describe themselves as *sutras*, meaning a sacred teaching, were sold to collectors in Beijing in the 1920s.[92] These sutras say they are translations of writings brought by Bishop Aluoben, and they also make reference to texts that are known to have been destroyed between the eighth and eleventh centuries CE, such as certain Sanskrit texts likely kept by Indian Christian communities.[93]

The sutras present a different picture of Christianity, as in the first sutra, known as the "Sutra of the Teachings of the World-Honored One," in which the divinity of Christ is denied in verses 12–13, when it says, "The Messiah is not the Honored One [God]. Instead, through his body he showed the people the Honored One" (4:12–13). It also presents a different view of women and the resurrection in 5:29–32, when it says, "The women went to tell all his other students what they had witnessed. As the first woman caused the lies of humanity, so it was women who first told the truth about what had happened, to show all that the Messiah forgave women and wished them to be treated properly in future, for he appeared and confirmed all they had said."[94]

Another sutra, called the "Sutra of Returning to Your Original Nature," offers the concept of "original nature" rather than "original sin." Original nature says that human nature is essentially good, although it can be distorted.[95] Palmer reminds us that the Eastern church separated from the Western church before St. Augustine formulated the concept of original sin, so in this sutra it is possible to see what Christianity might have been like otherwise.[96] Palmer believes that Christianity is consistent with a notion of original goodness, which is reflected in the following text found carved on a stone stela at the long-abandoned Da-Qin monastery. It reads, "He gave to them the original nature of goodness and appointed them as the guardians of all creation."[97]

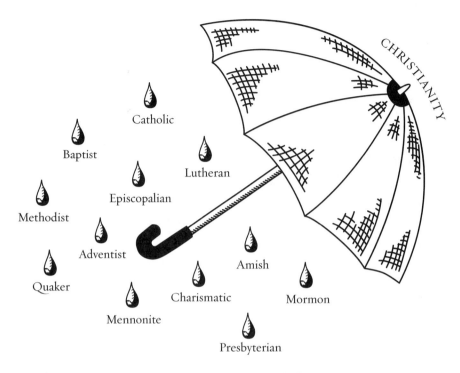

Figure 3.1. The Christian umbrella

Modern Christianity

According to the 2006 *Time Almanac*, Christians number 2.1 billion people worldwide, representing 33% of the world population.[98] In the United States, the largest denomination of Christians are Catholics at nearly 68 million, or 23% of the U.S. population. The next largest denomination are Baptists at 29 million, then Methodists at 9 million, Lutherans at 8.5 million, and Presbyterians at 4.5 million. There are an estimated 250 Protestant sects in the United States as of 2006.[99] Christianity, then, is also an umbrella term that encompasses a variety of denominations. Although the denominations differ from each other in various beliefs and practices, most accept the Bible as their scripture, believe in the Trinity, believe that Jesus is the Son of God and that he came to earth with a redemptive mission, and believe that Jesus died and was resurrected. We illustrate the Christian umbrella in figure 3.1.

Some of the ways in which the denominations differ from each other on matters of belief and practice include the necessity of baptism; the appropriate age and manner of baptizing; whether there is scripture in addition to the Bible (such as the Book of Mormon); the style and order of worship; the use of candles, statues, or relics; the necessity, style, and frequency of communion; whether women can be ordained; whether the sabbath is observed on Saturday or Sunday; whether medical treatment can be obtained and which types; permitted hairstyles and clothing; requirements for dating and marriage, the frequency of church services, and attendance; the nature and manner of observance of sacraments; whether sexual preference and lifestyle is an issue either in the membership or the clergy; and whether tithing is required. This list is not complete, but it gives some idea of the variety found within Christianity today, even with its general adherence to the core beliefs established by orthodoxy, which were examined earlier.

My Journal

If you were raised Christian, what have your experiences with Christianity been? Have you belonged to more than one denomination in your life? What have you found most positive and enriching about Christianity? What has disappointed you or made you uncomfortable? Do you agree or disagree that early Christianity was more diverse in its core beliefs than those that are found today? What ideas or emotions does a discussion of early Christianity and orthodoxy raise for you?

Identify three beliefs that *modern* Pagans and *early* Christians seem to share. Identify three beliefs that *modern* Pagans and *modern* Christians seem to share. Identify three to five values you think modern Pagans and modern Christians might agree on.

What do you see as the biggest obstacles facing people blending Christianity and Paganism? Why are they obstacles? How did they become obstacles? Is there any way to resolve them? If a pre-orthodox Christian were to be included in this discussion, what might his or her thoughts about these obstacles be?

Spirituality without a Mythology

This is an extended journal exercise you may wish to do over the course of several days or weeks. For this exercise, you will be working with the following question: *If you were to strip away all the mythology from your spirituality, what would be left?*

Set aside half an hour when you will not be disturbed, close your eyes, and clear your mind. Imagine your spirituality as it exists in your life right now. See it walk across the stage of your mind in whatever form it wants to take. What does it look like? What are its characteristics? How would you describe it? If you were to place it in one spot and walk all the way around it, what would you see, feel, and experience? Take several days to get in touch with this image of your current spirituality.

When you are ready, go back to the question that's been posed. Given your spirituality as it exists right now, if you stripped all mythology out of it, what would be left? Remember that when we use the word *mythology*, we are not meaning something derogatory. We mean those stories that inform your religious belief and practice. If there were no saints, no Bible, no shepherds, no guiding stars, no Moses with the stone tablets, no stories of heaven and hell, no disciples, no gods or goddesses, no Mount Olympus, no demons, no karma or original sin, what would be left of your spirituality?

Take your time with this. Set aside fifteen or thirty minutes here or there to contemplate this question. Don't rush to an answer. Give this several weeks or even months if you like. This is not a test you will be graded on; this is about you becoming more familiar with yourself and the foundational messages you have built your spirituality and your life upon. As part of this process, ask yourself how much of your spirituality, beliefs, and practices are tied up with a mythology. Make a list. Identify everything you can think of. Are you surprised by your answers?

When you're ready to move on, you might want to ask the following questions: Without mythology, what would you believe in? How would you define your values? What would those values be, and why would you pick them? What would be important to you? What would your spirituality consist of? What would your beliefs and practices be, and why would you choose them?

The Sacred Year

While the Pagan sacred year is entirely earth-centered and follows the cycles of the earth's seasons, the Christian sacred year is a combination of an earth-centered and a Christ-

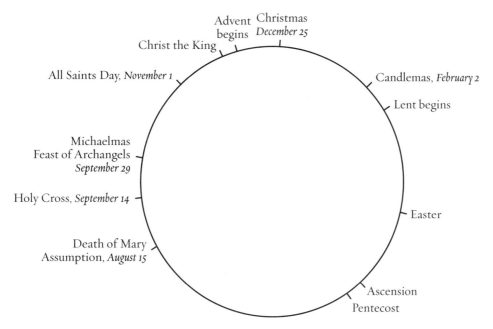

Figure 3.2. Christian Wheel of the Year

EASTER: *first Sunday following first full moon after the spring equinox*
ASCENSION: *forty days after Easter, now moved to the next Sunday*
PENTECOST: *fifty days after Easter*
CHRIST THE KING: *Sunday before Advent begins, marks end of the liturgical year*
ADVENT: *starts four weeks before Christmas, begins the liturgical year*
LENT: *starts six weeks before Easter*

centered cycle. The sacred year begins with Advent, approximately four weeks before Christmas, then proceeds to Christmas on December 25, and moves into Lent six weeks before Easter. This is where the calendar becomes earth-centered, as Easter is calculated anew each year as the Sunday following the first full moon after the spring equinox, and is moved if it coincides with Passover.[100] The week immediately before Easter Sunday is called Holy Week, which includes the observances of Holy Thursday, Good Friday, and Holy Saturday. After Easter, the liturgical year continues with Ascension and Pentecost and ends with the feast of Christ the King. Not all Christian churches follow the liturgical year with this detail. Some recognize certain dates and not others, but most Western Christians observe Christmas on December 25 and Easter at its calculated time. Because

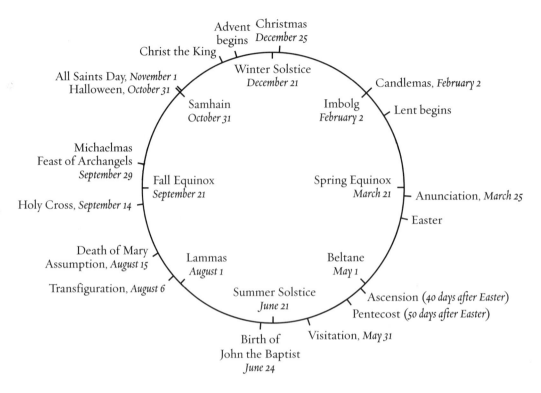

Figure 3.3. Christian and Pagan calendars compared

many of the dates vary with the cycles of the earth and moon, we cannot show an exact calendar on a Wheel of the Year, but the Christian sacred year looks something like the illustration in figure 3.2.

For an interesting comparison, we have set the Christian sacred year next to the Pagan one as shown in figure 3.3

Christians also observe special moments in the lives of individuals, either personal moments or ones that are part of the faith journey, known as sacraments. They vary somewhat among denominations but generally consist of baptism, confirmation, confession or reconciliation, marriage, ordination, extreme unction (also called laying on of hands or blessing of the sick), and Eucharist or communion.

We also compare rites of passage in Paganism and the Christian sacraments as follows:

CHRISTIAN SACRAMENTS	PAGAN LIFE PASSAGES
—	Pregnancy and birth
Baptism	Baby blessings, Wiccanings
Confession, Reconciliation	—
Confirmation	Coming of age ceremonies
Marriage	Marriage, handfasting
—	Handpartings
Ordination	Ordination
Taking vows	Dedication to a course of study or community levels of initiation
Communion	Cakes and Ale (served during services)
—	Croning, saging
Laying on of hands	Laying on of hands, healing ceremonies
Last Rites	Crossing-over ceremonies

Christians experience variety in their forms of worship but typically meet on Sunday mornings (some meet on Saturday) at a church or in someone's home, and may meet on other days of the week for prayer meetings and classes. The Sunday service can take a number of forms, from the highly formal and stylized to the informal and charismatic. Most services involve singing and other music, prayers, and a sermon or talk on some subject, frequently scripture. The Quaker service, by contrast, is often held in silence and may or may not have any music and generally no sermon. Some groups take communion every Sunday, some once a month or even more infrequently. Additional services may be held at special times of the year, like Christmas pageants and Holy Week observances.

We have not discovered teachings, in either our studies or personal experience of Christianity, that are opposed to Paganism's magickal view of the universe. We have found no theological pronouncement that prohibits a view of the universe as multidimensional or interconnected at all its levels, or prohibits human beings from interacting with it. Our reading of Christian mystics, both Protestant and Catholic, indicates that mystics in fact frequently report experiencing the divine and the universe as multidimensional. They often go to different spiritual realms and levels of reality and directly experience the interconnectedness of all creation. The meaning given to these experiences and the terminology used to describe them may differ depending on historical period and denominational affiliation, but in substance appear to be similar to what Pagans experience.

Honoring the Voices

As noted at the beginning of this chapter, the Christianity of today—despite its seeming variety—exhibits a uniformity scholars tell us it did not have in its early years. What should we make of the early Christians? Did they just not get it, or was their perspective valid?

With few exceptions, the Christian denominations today accept the Bible as their official canon of scripture. Many people are unaware that other books of scripture existed and that some have survived to the present. Even fewer have read these books. Nor are people generally aware that many of the New Testament books were written by church leaders rather than those to whom they are credited, for the purpose of addressing issues and disputes of the time.

Most Christians today accept the Nicene Creed or substantial portions of it, and are unaware that some early Christians saw God not only as the "Father Almighty," but also as "Mother." Many people may not know that Jesus was not always identified as "true God from true God, begotten not made, one in being with the Father," but that his divinity was long in dispute, and some arguments in its favor were based on equating him with a feminine aspect of the divine, or Sophia. Nor do they know that the early church in China altogether rejected the concept of Jesus as divine.

Most Christians today accept the physical resurrection of Jesus as a literal truth and may be unaware that many fervent early Christians did not see the resurrection as literal, but as only a metaphor for a spiritual event. The early Jesus movement as contained in Q appears to have had no concept of a resurrection at all. Nor do many Christians realize that part of the reason the literal interpretation of the resurrection was urged by the orthodoxy was to secure its authority and power, a power based on the identity of male persons who "witnessed" an actual resurrection.

Many people today assume that the doctrine of original sin is foundational to Christianity, but the experience of communities insulated from its development in the West show this not to be the case. Their scriptures show instead that Christianity can embrace and co-exist with the concept of original goodness.

We have covered this material to raise this question: if ChristoPaganism is a combination of aspects of Paganism and aspects of Christianity, which Christianity would that be? The one that calls God Father, or the one that calls God Mother? The one that became a patriarchy, or the one that involved women at the highest levels? The one that placed authority within the individual or the one that placed it in an ecclesiastical hierarchy? The one that believes in original sin or the one that believes in original goodness? These have all been valid perspectives within the Christian landscape at one time or another and must be considered a part of Christianity, if only historically. Since Pagans frequently feel a kinship or sense of honoring for peoples whose beliefs and histories have been lost or silenced, would this not also apply to those voices within Christianity that have been lost or silenced? To include these voices in the Christian landscape now changes that landscape. Perhaps Christian experience taken in its totality is not as opposed to ChristoPaganism as one might first assume.

Chapter 4

MYSTERY RELIGIONS AND CHRISTIANITY

In the previous chapter we presented an overview of Christianity from the perspective of mainstream scholarship. Even though these scholars debate issues concerning the early Christian community, the authorship and dating of writings, and which words Jesus might or might not have actually said, they at least agree that their investigations rest on historical truth. That is, they believe that Jesus existed as a historical person, as did the other characters in the New Testament, and that the New Testament describes events that occurred in history. For the purposes of the discussion that follows, we call these scholars the "historical" group or camp.

There is a body of research, however, that directly challenges the historicity of Jesus. In the nineteenth century, only a handful of books were available on this issue. These books were hard to find and understandably unpopular except among "freethinkers." By the 1950s, a few more authors had appeared on this topic, often at the cost of their employment or clerical office. This cautious trend continued through the 1970s, but lately this body of research has generated significant attention from scholars, philosophers, and theologians. Given the number of books published on this topic since the 1990s, we have a feeling it is not going to go away. This body of research has raised issues that have never been dealt with in a particularly satisfying manner by Christianity since the first century CE. No one from the historical group of scholars that we surveyed addresses the issues raised by the non-historical camp. In our research, we were unable to discover any response by a historical scholar in a mainstream publication to the body of non-historical work, which is unsettling at best. The implications of this material can be disturbing, and its impact on the increasingly rational Christian milieu now current in the United States seems worthy of a response from the historical camp. We discuss what we mean by an "increasingly rational" Christianity in Part II. We ourselves found this material disturbing, despite our years in Paganism and interfaith efforts, so we can imagine its effect on others. This is fair warning that the material presented in this chapter is not for the faint of heart. We have carefully documented our sources so you can determine their credibility for yourself.

Setting the Stage

To understand what we call the "non-historical" body of research regarding Jesus and early Christianity requires a basic knowledge of the world in which Christianity developed. For help with this, we turn to Charles Guignebert, a Professor of Christian History in Paris in the 1920s and 1930s. It should be noted that Guignebert is actually in the "historical" camp when it comes to Jesus's existence, but he can set the cultural stage for us.

Guignebert notes that all around the Jewish world of Palestine was a pagan milieu.[1] To the north, west, and southwest were the Syrians and Phoenicians, from whom came a mixture of beliefs and worship forms. In the east was Mesopotamia, where influences from India and Persia combined with Babylonian culture. This region was the "parent of many ancient myths current throughout the Semitic world" of the time.[2] To the south was Egypt, where ancient religious practices were universalized under the influence of Greek thought. Also to the north was the Hellenistic world, which was a crossroads of religious thought and practice. From here flowed Greek myth, philosophical theories, and pieces from the other milieus, including the Jewish, where they blended together in a syncretic manner.

Guignebert notes that as people travel, they take their religious ideas with them, and in this region travelers encountered religions whose myths and rituals were similar to their own. Their similarities aided exchanges between them, and in the end the religions of this entire region all share a "striking family likeness."[3] There were a number of popular deities who so closely resembled each other that they were occasionally confused, such as Attis, Adonis, Melkhart, Tammuz, Marduk, Osiris, Dionysus, and Mithras.[4] The religions which grew up around these various deities were often called Mysteries—the Mysteries of Dionysus, the Mysteries of Attis, and so on.

It may be of interest to note that in Tarsus, the place from which Paul is believed to have originated, the Mystery schools were well established. Guignebert states that "the syncretistic tradition that mingles, confuses, or combines deities whose appearance or functions seem more or less similar" had been clearly present in Tarsus before Paul's time.[5] Tarsus boasted a university of Stoic philosophers, and a person could attend their public lectures without being enrolled as a student. Guignebert observes that this influence may explain why the Pauline epistles in the New Testament set out some of the fundamentals of Stoic philosophy.[6]

All of the Mystery religions were similar in theme. Many of their deities died at a certain time of year to be restored to life later, either in connection with solar or agricultural cycles. Their Mysteries, in other words, were tied to the seasons, and in their stories of death and rebirth gave "visible expression to the great mystery of human destiny."[7] Every one of these religions, Guignebert tells us, offered their followers the hope of immortality and promised the means to attain it.[8] For several thousand years, Egyptians also had a strong belief in eternal life and the immortality of the soul. Concerning this belief, historian James Bonwick takes an example from the Book of the Dead, which says, "Thy soul rests among the gods, respect for thy immortality dwells in their hearts."[9]

Guignebert tells us that in the Mystery religions, as the god suffers and dies, so too does humanity, but the god's restoration "is a sign of his triumph over suffering and death."[10] To be connected to this immortality, the believer would go through a series of rituals or initiations, often ones through which the god himself had passed. These outward observances would assure an inner assimilation with the god, which guaranteed that the believer's future would be like the god's—eternal. In case we doubt the truth of this, Firmicus Maternus, a Christian writer of the fourth century, describes the assurances given to Mystery initiates in which the priest anoints the throat of each person with holy oil, and says, "Take confidence from the fact that the God is saved; you shall be, you also, saved at the end of your trials."[11]

Guignebert comments that the rituals of the Mysteries are much more than mere rites, that "the issue here concerns a certain idea of human destiny and of salvation, of trustful confidence in a divine Lord," who "has consented to live and suffer like a man, so that man may sufficiently resemble him to be able to effect a union with him and be saved by casting in his lot with him, as it were."[12] This description should sound familiar to us today, as it remains the primary source of most religious sentiment. Guignebert agrees that this spiritual relationship and identification with the divine "is exactly St. Paul's doctrine" concerning the mission and role of Jesus. "Not even the weighty moral element implied in Paul's teaching—I mean the injunction to live a life not merely pious, but pure, charitable and lofty—is peculiar to him, for the Mysteries too," he observes, "made demands of the same nature upon their initiates."[13]

Out of this environment, then, which was already being organized into "syncretistic combinations," Christianity arose.[14] It was surrounded by Mystery religions whose purpose was to align believers with the immortality of the gods. As the god overcame death and enjoyed eternal life, so would the believer. These Mystery religions also freely borrowed concepts from each other and lent themselves "indefinitely to all kinds of exploitation. For the future of Christianity, therefore, it constituted an almost inexhaustible reserve."[15]

The Inexhaustible Reserve

The non-historical body of research examines the content of ancient religions in order to explore their impact on the development of Christianity. Most of the researchers in this area have come to the conclusion that the Christian mythos is directly borrowed from its pagan neighbors and is not based in historical events. Occasionally historical figures appear in the Christian story, but these historical tie-ins are more the exception than the rule. According to the scholars we survey, Jesus did not exist as a historical person, nor did John the Baptist, Mary and Joseph, or the disciples. The virgin birth, Jesus's ministry, death, and resurrection were not historical events. The position of these scholars is that all of Christianity was borrowed from religions already in existence or created afresh from ideas already made popular in these other religions.

These scholars point out that most religions are based on a story of a divine or heroic figure who goes into a lower world (either literally or by incarnating into a body), experiences victories over enemies, performs miraculous deeds, suffers, dies, rises and returns to his native upper world, and then celebrates his triumph by being enthroned on high. While the pagan stories were treated as symbolic, the Christian story quickly lost its symbolic character by treating its mythos as historical fact and making Jesus into a historical figure. The process of how this happened, according to these scholars, is the primary focus of this chapter.

Isn't this is a preposterous claim for these scholars to make, especially in light of the centuries of teachings by the church and the seamless history that Christian scripture portrays? What kind of people would make such outrageous claims? Our review of these scholars reveals a wide range of people from ardent freethinkers and humanists, to those who are neutral about religion, to those who are fervent Christians. Those who are strongly Christian definitely struggle with the evidence and the conclusions, but seem to prefer the struggle over being at ease in their faith while ignorant of the evidence. Some even stated their belief that Christianity would be stronger and more persuasive if it could acknowledge its origins and the symbolic nature of its mythos.

While this material could be presented in a number of ways, such as by culture (Babylonian, Greek, etc.) or by deity (Attis, Mithras, etc.), we have decided to treat it by topic as it relates to the story of Jesus.

THE VIRGIN BIRTH. Many Mystery religions that existed in the regions surrounding first-century Palestine included a miraculous virgin birth. For example, in Asia Minor, Attis is born of the virgin Cybele; in Alexandria, Aion is born of the virgin Kore; in ancient Egypt, Neith brought forth the sun god, Ra, without a male partner; and in Greece, Dionysus's mother is Semele, who is impregnated by a lightning bolt from Zeus.[16] Likewise, Jesus is born of the virgin Mary, who is impregnated by the Holy Spirit sent from God.

Mithras, Dionysus, and Adonis all celebrate their birthdays on December 25, along with Jesus. In Rome, this day was known as Natalis Solis Invicti ("Birth of the Invincible Sun").[17] The ancient Greek historian Plutarch notes that the birth of the Younger Horus (as opposed to the Elder Horus) was celebrated at the winter solstice,[18] and mythologist Joseph Campbell notes that in those times the winter solstice was observed on December 25.[19] St. Justin Martyr quotes an unidentified ancient Syrian commentator, who wrote that "it was in fact customary among the pagans to celebrate the festival of the Sun's birthday on 25th December and to light bonfires in honor of the day. They even used to invite the Christian population to these rites. But when the teachers of the Church realized that Christians were allowing themselves to take part, they decided to observe the Feast of the true Birth on the same day."[20] Regarding the role that veneration of the sun played in Christianity, Professor Alvin Kuhn observes that until the fifth or sixth century CE, Christians addressed their deity as "Our Lord, the Sun,"

Figure 4.1. Isis and Horus

Figure 4.2. Mylitta and Tammuz

but in later centuries this was changed to "Our Lord, the God."[21] In the second century, Tertullian remarks that "You [pagans] say we worship the sun; so do you."[22]

Isis, the mother of Horus, is frequently shown with Horus sitting on her lap (fig. 4.1). So greatly do some of these images resemble Jesus and Mary that some statues of the Black Virgin, which were venerated in France during the Middle Ages, were later shown to be statutes of Isis made from basalt.[23] Isis and Horus were not the only madonna and child portrayed in art. Figure 4.2 is an example from Babylon of the fertility goddess Mylitta and her son Tammuz, the god of vegetation. Titles that were given to Isis include Our Lady, Star of the Sea, Queen of Heaven, Governess, Mother of God, Intercessor, and Immaculate Virgin.[24] Any Catholic will recognize these titles as belonging to Mary as well. Isis was shown standing on a crescent moon with twelve stars surrounding her head, an image frequently used for Mary.[25] A similar version of this is shown in the image of Juno, Queen of Heaven (fig. 4.3).

The question of the genealogy of Jesus provides a good example of how a historical event may have been blended with story. Kuhn states that there are references in the Jewish Talmud to a person who lived in 115 BCE by the name of Jehoshua ben Pandira. According to the Talmud, his birth was accompanied by supernatural manifestations. Later he traveled to Egypt where he studied the magickal arts and then returned to Palestine and worked a number of miracles. He aroused the hostility of the orthodox priesthood, was arrested for practicing sorcery, tried, and condemned. He was then

Figure 4.3. Juno, Queen of Heaven

held for forty days to see if anyone would speak for his release, and when no one did, he was stoned to death and his body hung on a tree as an example to others.[26]

This story was well known in the region, even into the early centuries CE when the church father Epiphanius gave Jesus's genealogy as follows: Jacob (called Pandira), Mary, Joseph, Cleopas, then Jesus. In the mid-second century, Origen states that James, the father of Joseph, the foster father of Jesus, was called Panther (a translation of Pandira), apparently to explain why Jehoshua (a derivative of Jesus) was called ben Pandira in the Talmudic legend, thus equating Jehoshua and Jesus. In the fifth century, Gregontius, Bishop of Africa, states that Jesus was put to death because he was a sorcerer, again referring to the legend. In the eighth century, John of Damascus gives Mary's genealogy as Joachim (her father), Bar Panther (his father), and Levi before him.[27] None of these genealogies are found in either Matthew, chapter 1 or Luke, chapter 3, but then those two genealogies also differ so much from each other that they cannot be reconciled.

TITLES. The Egyptian god Osiris, who accompanied the dead to their resurrection, was called "the soul that lives again," "the first-born of unformed matter," and "the lord of life for all eternity."[28] The Egyptian god Horus, also involved with the guiding and resurrecting of the dead, was called Savior and is identified in inscriptions as "the second emanation of Amon, the son whom he begot."[29] The Egyptian god Serapis was called the Savior as well, as was Dionysus, who also carried the titles of the Slain One, the Sin Bearer, the Redeemer, and Only Begotten Son. The god Attis, whose worship came into Asia Minor from the Phrygians, considered by some historians to be one of the most ancient cultures in the area, was called Savior and Only Begotten Son. Mithras was also called Savior and Mediator Between God and Man.[30] All of these titles have been applied to Jesus.

You will notice the frequent use of Only Begotten in connection with several deities discussed here. This was a common title in Mystery religions of the time, perhaps made popular by the Egyptian use of the scarab beetle in the incarnation of certain gods, since this beetle was believed to be self-produced, requiring no female. Like the beetle, incarnations of gods were also seen as only-begotten or self-begotten. For example, the god Amon, or Amun, later combined with the god Ra into Amun-Ra, is described as the one who "existed from the beginning, none knew his emergence. No god existed before him, no other was with him who could tell his form. He had no mother to name him, no father to beget him and say 'This is I.' He shaped his egg himself. Force, mysteries of birth, creator of his own beauty, God Divine One, self-created."[31] The Gospel of John appears to draw on this tradition when, in John 1:18, the writer refers to Christ in some versions (see the Jerusalem Bible for a notation) as the "only begotten God" or "God, only begotten." The identification or equation of Jesus with the only-begotten Egyptian gods, and then later, the only-begotten gods of the Mystery religions, was still so well known that even centuries later St. Ambrose calls Jesus "the good scarab" who "clung to the cross as a good scarab and as a good scarab shouted from the wood, 'Lord, do not count this sin against them.'"[32]

John's gospel gives the title of Logos to Christ. The idea of the Logos was first articulated in the writings of the Greek philosopher Heraclitus, who lived from 535 to 475 BCE.[33] As used by Heraclitus, Logos referred to both speech and reason. The Greek philosopher Zeno described the Logos as the arranger of the universe and of the established order of things; or as Lactantius said, "the spirit of God which he named the soul of Jupiter."[34] The Stoic philosophers believed that certain gods were personifications of the Logos, in particular Hermes, or Mercury.[35] The Jewish philosopher Philo believed the Logos to be a parallel of Sophia, the Wisdom of God, who acts as a mediator between god and the world.

The title of Good Shepherd was one shared by several deities of the time, including Horus, Apollo, and Mercury. Jesus was given the title also and in early art is shown carrying

Figure 4.4. Apollo

Figure 4.5. Etruscan illustration

Figure 4.6. Christian Good Shepherd

a lamb over his shoulders, which is typical for the other deities as well. Mercury often carried a ram over his shoulders and so was called the Ram Bearer. So frequently was Mercury depicted in the role of the Good Shepherd that the art historian Jameson notes that "in some instances [it] led to a difficulty in distinguishing the two."[36] Apollo was also shown as the Good Shepherd in his role of Apollo Agreus, or Aristeas (fig. 4.4). And yet the concept may be even older, as can be seen in an early Etruscan drawing (fig. 4.5). For comparison, figure 4.6 shows a typical Christian rendering of Jesus as the Good Shepherd.

The concept of the Trinity was also not unique to Christianity. Many religions have deities with triple aspects, forms, or emanations. Neo-Pagans reading this will be able to think of several such examples that are familiar to them. To give one example from the Egyptians, we read, "Three are all the gods, Amon, Ra, Ptah; there are none like them. Hidden in his name as Amon, he is Ra, his body is Ptah. He is manifested in Amon, with Ra and Ptah, the three united."[37]

JESUS'S MINISTRY. Jesus's period of ministry officially begins with his baptism in the river Jordan by John. Mythology scholar Joseph Campbell notes that the rite of baptism has been traced to ancient Sumeria and the practices surrounding the water god Ea, the "God of the House of Water."[38] Ea's symbol was Capricorn, an animal that is part goat and part fish, and it is his zodiacal sign that in that period of history rises on the horizon at the winter solstice. Campbell notes that during the Hellenistic period Ea was called Oannes, which in Greek was Ioannes, in Hebrew Yohanan, in Latin Johannes, and in English John.[39] So we have John who leads the way before Jesus, baptizing. Some scholars believe that John and Jesus represent the dual aspects of the solar and lunar cycles—as one increases, the other decreases. John echoes this in John 3:30 when he says of Jesus, "he must increase but I must decrease." Campbell notes that some scholars maintain there never was a historical John or a Jesus, but that they were instead metaphors for a water god and a sun god.[40]

The correspondences with Oannes appear to go further than John the Baptist. Berossus was a third-century BCE Chaldean priest who wrote a three-volume series on the history and culture of Babylonia. In his work, he sets out the myth of Oannes and recounts that Oannes would come out of the sea every day and go among men, teaching them wisdom and crafts. He would eat and drink nothing while with them, and then return to the sea at night. Berossus says that Oannes was accustomed to pass the day among men; but took no food at that season; and he gave them an insight into letters and sciences, and arts of every kind. He taught them to construct cities, to found temples, to compile laws, and explained to them the principles of geometrical knowledge. He made them distinguish the seeds of the earth, and showed them how to collect the fruits; in short, he instructed them in every thing which could tend to soften manners and humanize their lives. From that time, nothing material has been added by way of improvement to his instructions. And when the sun had set, this Being Oannes retired again into the sea, and passed the night in the deep; for he was amphibious. After this there appeared other animals like Oannes.[41]

In the same manner, Jesus, the Icthys or fish, instructs men by day but at night often retires to the lake of Galilee or into a boat. The Gospel of John also tells that the disciples tried to get Jesus to eat but he refused, saying, "I have food to eat you know not of. My food is to do the will of him who sent me" (John 4:32–34).

Baptism was a requirement in many Mystery religions. Initiates to the Mysteries of Isis and Dionysus were baptized, as were those in the Mysteries of Mithras. Zoroastrians took their children to the temple after they were born, and the priest either sprinkled water on the child or immersed the child in a vase filled with water. After this ceremony, the father named the child.[42] One form of baptism in Mithraism, called the taurobolium, was performed by slaughtering a bull on a perforated platform, under which the initiate stood in a pit. The blood of the sacrificed bull poured down on the one to be baptized, and he or she was considered to be washed free of their sins.[43] Poorer people who could not afford a bull made do with a sheep in a ceremony called the criobolium, in which the sheep was slaughtered in like fashion. In this case, the initiate was literally "washed in the blood of the lamb,"[44] a description that would later be applied to Jesus's sacrifice. An inscription of gratitude to Mithras proclaims, "Thou hast saved us by shedding the eternal blood."[45] The last taurobolium was performed in Rome in the late fourth century CE, on the site now occupied by St. Peter's Basilica.[46]

The number twelve was commonly found in neighboring religions. Just as with the twelve disciples of Jesus, Mithras was accompanied by twelve personages who corresponded to the twelve signs of the zodiac. In the celebration of the Mysteries of Mithras, the initiate would be surrounded by twelve people dressed as these zodiacal signs.[47] Kuhn states that twelve was chosen for the number of disciples because it was a mystical number used frequently in both pagan and Jewish religions. The following are some of the examples he gives: the twelve powers of intelligence of the sun god Ra, the twelve signs of the zodiac, the twelve dungeons of the soul in the Egyptian Book of the Dead, the Twelve Reapers of the Golden Grain, the Twelve Rowers of the Boat with Horus, the Twelve Sailors in the Ship of Ra, the twelve sons of Jacob, the twelve tribes of Israel, the twelve stones set by Joshua in the riverbed, the twelve pieces of the concubine's body (Judges 19), the twelve tables of stone, and the twelve Urim and Thummim stones on the breastplate of the High Priest.[48]

Jesus is recorded as performing a number of miracles. The scholars surveyed here find parallels from other miracle workers in the region, some of whom were legendary and some of whom were historical. There is too much material on this topic to cover more than a few examples here. We have already mentioned the Talmudic story of Jehoshua ben Pandira, who apparently was a historical figure in the second century BCE. Biblical skeptic Joseph Wheless and others note that many of the men revered as wonder workers in this period were also considered gods or sons of god.[49] The historian Charles Waite quotes St. Basil as saying, "Every uncommonly good man was called the Son of God" in that era.[50] Names of some these "uncommonly good men" are Apuleius, Alexander, Iamblichus, and Appollonius of Tyana. The course of Appollonius's life mirrors that of Jesus in many details—Appollonius healed the sick, cast out devils, prophesied, and raised the dead. He was considered a man of extremely upright character and pure morals. Wheless notes that pagans of the time and some later historians believed that Appollonius was used as a pattern for Jesus.[51] In 98 CE, the Roman historian Tacitus recorded stories concerning the miracles of a man named Vespasian, who was born in 10 CE. In one of them, a blind man came to Vespasian for a cure. Vespasian rubbed his spit on the man's face and eyes, whereupon the man could see again. Tacitus also records Vespasian healing a man who had a withered hand.[52] Similar miracle stories are told of Jesus.

Perhaps the most moving and dramatic of Jesus's miracles is that of raising the dead. It should be noted that each of the scholars surveyed here provides numerous stories of other miracle workers who supposedly did the same. However, this may demonstrate no more than that such stories were common at the time. In the Egyptian Book of the Dead, Horus calls to the mummies and commands them "to come forth."[53] In like manner, Jesus cries "Lazarus, come forth" (John 11:43). Authors Thomas William Doane and J. P. Lundy both discuss the bas-relief carving on the sarcophagus now in the Museo Gregoriano Etrusco in Vatican City, which shows Jesus raising Lazarus. On this carving, Jesus is shown as a beardless young man pointing a wand at Lazarus, while Lazarus

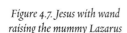

Figure 4.7. Jesus with wand
raising the mummy Lazarus

Figure 4.8. Horus raising the dead

is wrapped as a mummy (fig. 4.7). Horus frequently uses a wand, often in the shape of the ankh, while he raises the dead[54] (fig. 4.8).

SYMBOLS. The discussion of religious symbols could fill a volume in and of itself, but we will limit our discussion to the Christian symbol for Jesus, the X bisected with an upright line (✳) or P (☧). Lundy observes that this symbol was first discussed by Plato in his *Timaeus*. When explaining why the earth is round, Plato says that God made it that way because the circle is the most perfect shape and most like himself. God then placed the soul in the center of the world. When God decided to express himself in physical form, "he decussated in the form of the letter X."[55] Proclus, a commentator on Plato, explains this by saying that the world is two circles, one the circle of the equinoxes and solstices, which remain always the same, and the other of the zodiac, which is always changing. These two cross each other in the form of an X "for the equinoctial circle does not cut the zodiac at right angles."[56] Indeed, if you lay out the wheel of the zodiac in its proper alignment, with Aries in the first house, the dates of the solstices and equinoxes connect with each other in an X shape rather than a + or plus sign. On such a wheel, the spring equinox falls at eight o'clock and the fall equinox at two o'clock; the summer solstice is at four o'clock and the winter solstice is at ten o'clock. Speaking metaphorically, then, the X represents the points where what is always changeable and what never changes intersect, the connection point between the heavens (zodiac) and the earth (the seasons). Understanding this, we can grasp Plato's meaning when he says that the X represents the divine expressed in the physical world—that is, the point where the earth and heavens meet or cross. So when the early church father St. Justin Martyr says that the X symbol is "the Son of God placed crosswise in the world," we understand his meaning—Jesus as the X represents the eternal intersecting the temporal—as well as the pagan system on which his comment is based.[57]

Lundy says this form of the cross is not solely Platonic, but also Egyptian in origin, which should be no surprise considering that Plato studied in Egypt. Pictures of the Egyptian god Amon show this symbol on his breast. Lundy says that Christians added the upright line to represent Jesus, but this form of the symbol is also found on coins and medals before Jesus. Even the X-P (☧), which Lundy thought to be exclusively Christian, is found on coins of the Ptolemies and Herod.[58]

THE PASSION, RESURRECTION, AND ASCENSION. Dionysus is pictured in inscriptions as riding a donkey on the way to his death. At his festival, an image of him was set in a basket on the donkey, while the crowds shouted his praises and waved bundles of branches. In a similar manner, the festival of Attis began on March 22 with the entry of the reed-bearers, followed by the entry of the tree, on which an image of Attis was tied.[59] Likewise, Jesus entered Jerusalem riding a donkey or ass while the crowd cast reeds, palms, or branches before him. The pine tree on which Attis was tied was then buried in a tomb and left. But on the third day, after night had fallen, the tomb was opened and Attis was proclaimed to be risen from the dead. The priests of Attis touched the lips of each person present with balm and spoke the glad news of salvation to them. On the morning of March 25, which was reckoned as the vernal equinox, Attis's divine resurrection was celebrated with great joy. In Rome this celebration eventually took the form of a carnival and became the *Hilaria*, or Festival of Joy.[60]

In Euripedes' play, *The Bacchae*, written five centuries before the birth of Jesus, Dionysus is imprisoned and brought to the king to be tried. The guards tell the king wonderful things about Dionysus and say, "Master, this man has come here with a load of miracles." The king interrogates Dionysus, who replies, "Nothing can touch me that is not ordained" and "You know not what you are doing, nor what you are saying, nor who you are."[61] Jesus's trial and Passion contain similar characters and dialogue.

The followers of Mithras also celebrated communion, which consisted of water mixed with wine, and bread or wafers marked with a cross.[62] On a temple inscription, Mithras says, "He who will not eat of my body and drink of my blood, so that he will be made one with me and I with him, the same shall not know salvation."[63] The church father Justin Martyr accused the Mithraists of mimicking the Eucharist, as their rites used the phrases "This is my body . . . this is my blood . . . do this in commemoration of me."[64] It is unclear who might have been mimicking whom. But apparently it wasn't the only mimicking going on, as the Christians adopted the shepherd's crook of the Mithraic bishops, and their hat known as the "mitre" or "mithra," named after Mithras. Also, the highest initiatory grade in the Mithraic mysteries was called the *Pater*, or Father, and one who reached this grade acted as head of the congregation and supervised the offerings made in the temple.[65]

The theme of resurrection was a common one in the religions of the area. The resurrection festival of Osiris was spread over three days, with his death being mourned on the first and his resurrection on the night of the third. The priests would herald his resurrection with the shout "Osiris has been found!" New Testament scholar G. A. Wells refers to an image of Osiris as a mummy with a stalk of corn growing from his mummified body, indicating that new life would spring out of death.[66] The feast of Adonis also observed a three-day resurrection period. An image of Adonis was first washed, anointed with spices, wrapped in linen or wool, and then laid in a coffin. This coffin was carried to his grave. The pagan writer Lucian records that "they make offerings to Adonis as to one dead, and the day after the morrow they tell the story that he lives."[67] According to the Phoenician version of this story, on the third day he was resurrected and ascended to heaven.[68]

Historian James Bonwick explains the connection to three days for the resurrection period in this way:

> But the sun appears to die and rise again at the solstice. For instance, on our shortest day, December 21st, the sun descends its lowest on the southern side. It is our depth of winter, our death of the sun. For three days the sun appears to stand still; that is, rising each morning at the same place, without advancing. Then it exhibits sudden vitality, leaves its grave December 25th, re-born, and progresses upward day by day towards us in the northern hemisphere. At the equinox—say the vernal—at Easter, the same phenomenon occurs. The sun has been below the equator, and suddenly rises above it, to our natural rejoicing. It has been, as it were, dead to us, but now it exhibits a resurrection.[69]

The followers of Mithras also celebrated his resurrection, after which Mithras ascended to heaven in a sun chariot and was enthroned as ruler of the world. It was believed that he waits in heaven for the end of time, when he will return to wake the dead and pass judgment.[70] Concerning the last judgment, James Bonwick suggests that "a perusal of the 25th [chapter] of Matthew will prepare the reader for the investigation of the Egyptian notion of the Last Judgment," so closely are they related.[71] Bonwick notes that the idea of an atonement was well established in Egyptian religion for several thousand years. Four gods of the dead accompanied the deceased to a trial before judges. Sometimes these gods present offerings to the judges on behalf of the deceased, and sometimes the gods are themselves sacrificed for them. Jesus also is seen as the sacrifice that atones for sins and allows the sinner to pass successfully through his or her judgment. Bonwick notes that the dead were called the "justified ones," even as early as the sixth Egyptian dynasty. Frequent reference is made to the "crown of justification," and a "robe of righteousness," which is given to the dead and is symbolized by the wrappings of the mummy. Horus, who raises the mummy to its resurrected life, is called the "justifier of the righteous."[72] Similar titles and descriptions are given to Jesus in the New Testament.

Thoughts on Pagan and Christian Similarities. Professor Guignebert gives his opinion on the similarities between Christianity and ancient paganism by saying that Christianity "could meet and overcome the entire pagan syncretism, because it had itself become a syncretism in which all the fertile ideas and the essential rites of pagan religiousness were blended. It combined and harmonized them in a way that enabled it to stand alone, facing all the inchoate beliefs and practices of its adversaries without appearing their inferior on any vital point."[73] Furthermore, "it is sometimes very difficult to tell exactly from which pagan rite a particular Christian rite is derived, but it remains certain that the spirit of pagan ritualism became by degrees impressed upon Christianity, to such an extent that at last the whole of it might be found distributed through its ceremonies."[74] Spiritual commentator Edward Carpenter observes that Christianity "has managed to persuade the general public of its own divine uniqueness to such a degree that few people, even nowadays, realize that it has sprung from just the same root as Paganism, and that it shares by far the most part of its doctrines and rites with the latter."[75]

But perhaps it should not be surprising that so many similarities existed between Christianity and the Mystery religions, since *all* of the early church fathers up to the time of Constantine were pagans who had been trained in one or more Mystery religions. The only exception to this was Origen, who comes late in the list of church fathers and was the first to be born of Christian parents. And except for Clement of

Alexandria, all the church fathers were Greek and wrote in Greek, so they would have been very familiar with the religious syncretism so common in the Hellenistic world of the time.[76] Wheless notes that not one of these church fathers mentions the New Testament, or quotes from a book in it, although they do quote extensively from the Old Testament and the oracles given by the pagan Sibyls, prophetesses they believed foretold the coming of Jesus.[77] Wheless identifies these church fathers as Clement of Rome, 30–96 CE; St. Ignatius, 50–98 or 117 CE; St. Polycarp, Bishop of Smyrna, 69–155 CE; Papias, Bishop of Hieropolis, 70–155 CE; St. Justin Martyr, 100–165 CE; St. Irenaeus, Bishop of Lyons, 120–c. 200 CE; Tertullian, Bishop of Carthage, 160–220 CE; Clement of Alexandria, head of the catechetical school in Alexandria and teacher of Origen, c. 153–c. 215 CE; Origen, c. 165–254 CE; and Lactantius, ?–330 CE.[78]

Lundy, a Christian art historian, expresses his amazement that in order to study early Christian art he had to study paganism, for as he says, "the ancient Christian monuments, from which I have drawn my facts and illustrations," several of which are set out in this chapter, "reveal so many obvious adaptations from the Pagan mythology and art, that it became necessary for me to investigate anew the Pagan symbolism."[79] Lundy almost apologizes to his readers for having to spend so much time on paganism, for "it is a most singular and astonishing fact sought to be developed in this work, that the Christian faith, as embodied in the Apostles' Creed, finds its parallel, or dimly foreshadowed counterpart, article by article, in the different systems of Paganism here brought under review. No one can be more astonished at this than the author himself!"[80]

What does Lundy mean when he says that the Creed is foreshadowed in the pagan religions? Carpenter has some thoughts to share on this point. The Nicene Creed, which was written during the reign of Constantine in the fourth century, is still professed by millions of Christians today. It states:

> We believe in one God, the Father, the Almighty,
> Maker of heaven and earth, of all that is seen and unseen.
> We believe in one Lord, Jesus Christ, the only Son of God,
> Eternally begotten of the Father, God from God,
> Light from Light, true God from true God,
> Begotten, not made, one in Being with the Father.
> Through him all things were made.
> For us and for our salvation he came down from heaven:
> By the power of the Holy Spirit he was born of the Virgin Mary and became man.

For our sake he was crucified under Pontius Pilate;
He suffered, died, and was buried.
On the third day he rose again in fulfillment of the Scriptures;
He ascended into heaven and is seated at the right hand of the Father.
He will come again in glory to judge the living and the dead,
And his kingdom will have no end.
We believe in the Holy Spirit, the Lord, the giver of life,
Who proceeds from the Father and the Son.
With the Father and the Son he is worshipped and glorified.
He has spoken through the Prophets.
We believe in one holy catholic and apostolic Church.
We acknowledge one baptism for the forgiveness of sins.
We look for the resurrection of the dead,
And the life of the world to come. Amen.

Carpenter explains what he sees to be the similarities between the Creed and paganism as follows:

Here we have the All-Father and Creator, descending from the Sky in the form of a spirit to impregnate the earthly Virgin-mother, who thus gives birth to a Savior-hero. The latter is slain by the powers of Evil, is buried and descends into the lower world, but arises again as God into heaven and becomes the leader and judge of mankind. We have the confirmation of the Church (or, in earlier times, of the Tribe) by means of a Eucharist or Communion which binds together all the members, living or dead, and restores errant individuals through the Sacrifice of the hero and the Forgiveness of their sins; and we have the belief in a bodily Resurrection and continued life of the members within the fold of the Church (or Tribe), itself regarded as eternal.

One has only, instead of the word "Jesus," to read Dionysus or Krishna or Hercules or Osiris or Attis, and instead of "Mary" to insert Semele or Devaki or Alcmene or Neith or Nana, and for Pontius Pilate to use the name of any terrestrial tyrant who comes into the corresponding story, and lo! the Creed fits in all particulars into the rites and worship of a pagan god . . .[81]

Early Membership Structures

The ancient Mystery schools were divided into at least two groups, the greater and lesser Mysteries. The lesser Mysteries were open to the public. Here stories would be enacted and teachings imparted, but generally the inner meaning of the rites and symbols was not shared. The greater Mysteries were private, and to be admitted to them required long periods of probation and training.[82] Once a person completed the training, he or she could be "initiated" into the full meaning of the Mysteries. The philosopher Sallustius explains the rationale for this when he says, "For one may call the world a myth, in which bodies and things are visible, but souls and minds are hidden. Besides, to wish to teach the whole truth about the Gods to all produces contempt in the foolish, because they cannot understand, and lack of zeal in the good; whereas to conceal the truth by myths prevents the contempt of the foolish and compels the good to practice philosophy."[83]

So the Mystery schools took the approach of "concealing the truth by myth," as Sallustius puts it. The myth, or story about the gods and their doings, was not what was "true," and it was not "the truth" in and of itself, but it was the carrier for a deeper hidden truth. One might say that the story of the myth was an allegory, or a metaphor perhaps, the underlying meaning of which was given only to the initiated. The uninitiated may never have realized this to be the case, which ultimately is unfortunate, since the metaphorical teachings were kept secret and therefore have been lost.

The Christian historian Johann Lorenz von Mosheim states that the Mystery religions were highly respected and regarded. He says that "the highest veneration was entertained by the people of every country for what was termed the Mysteries; and the Christians, perceiving this, were induced to make their religion conform in many respects to this part of the heathen model."[84] One simple example of the influence and reputation of the Mystery schools can be seen in the New Testament where Lundy notes that the words *mystery* or *mysteries* appear twenty-eight times.[85] Like the Mysteries, the Christians also created a tiered structure of membership, which consisted of three classes: the Catechumens, the Competentes, and the Illuminati. The Illuminati were also called the Faithful or the Mystae, the latter term being the name given to the initiated members of the the Mysteries of Eleusis.[86]

Like the Mystery religions, the Christians held their meetings at night and kept their inner teachings secret. Only the Illuminati class, for example, were allowed into the Mysteries of the Eucharist.[87] St. Basil the Great says that the Christian rites were "guarded in reverent silence and dignity from all intrusion of the profane and uninitiated, so that they might not fall into contempt."[88] Both of the church fathers Clement of Alexandria and Origen supported this doctrine of reserve as late as the third century, and believed that the inner mysteries of the faith should not be declared publicly, but only to the initiated.[89] Origen writes that "certain doctrines [are] not made known to the multitude," which is "not a peculiarity of Christianity alone," since the Mystery traditions and some philosophical systems teach "certain truths which are exoteric and others esoteric."[90] *Exoteric* here means discernible by the senses, on the exterior, public, and literal. *Esoteric* means hidden, private, and metaphorical. Clement of Alexandria, who was Origen's mentor, wrote that "mysteries have been inserted into the Scriptures in the first place to exercise the minds and wits of intellectual Christians and in the second to disguise the deeper and more up-setting doctrines from the simple Christians."[91] This makes one wonder what mysteries were supposedly inserted into the scriptures, and by whom. Origen and Clement's views on the doctrine of reserve, however, would soon be abandoned by the church. The Mystery school structure continued in Christianity into the third century, after which it began to be dismantled.

The Shift to Literalism

As noted earlier, the Mystery schools were very highly regarded, but they were also very exclusive, requiring extended training and probationary periods that not everyone could commit to or master. The Christians quickly sensed that there was a need to be filled here, and so began to look for ways to make their religion more accessible and thereby more popular. Kuhn explains that "a movement began to take form to drag the arcana of the Mysteries out to common knowledge and to make the emblems and rites 'under-standable' to the people."[92] Christianity could become more accessible if it eliminated its own tiered system of training and made membership faster. Unfortunately, just as with the Mystery schools, what took so long to teach were the hidden, metaphoric meanings of the myths. When the intensive training was dropped, so were the esoteric, metaphoric teachings. What this left were the stories and their outer literal meanings. Kuhn notes that it is at this same time that the gospels began to be composed.[93]

A school of literalism, as Professor Hanson calls it, began to grow in Christianity. It taught that Jesus was a historical person and the events set out in the gospels were his-torical fact and literally true. Many of the church authorities who supported the literal approach were also those who supported the abandonment of tiered membership and teaching the symbolic and esoteric meanings of the scriptures. Origen did not care for the literalists. He says of them that "they attack allegorical interpretation and want to teach that divine Scripture is clear and has nothing deeper than the text shows."[94] As an example, Origen believes that the story of the resurrection is a metaphor and does not involve a resurrection of the flesh as the mythic literalists taught. Origen called the resurrection of the flesh a "crude" doctrine, despite the fact that it was becoming "the resurrection as it is believed in the Church."[95]

Even though the levels of training had been dropped and myth had begun to be treated as fact in order to attract the masses, there seems to be a sort of contempt for the masses expressed in the writings of the period. Take the letter of St. Jerome to St. Gregory Nazianzen, where Jerome says "nothing can impose better on a people than verbiage; the less they understand the more they admire . . . Our fathers and doctors have often said, not what they thought, but that to which circumstance and necessity forced them."[96] Or this passage by Synesius, Bishop of Alexandria, in the fourth century: "In my capacity as bishop of the Church I shall continue to disseminate the fables of our religion; but in my private capacity I shall remain a philosopher to the end."[97] How nice for him that he could stay with philosophy's deeper meanings while he taught "fables" as literal truth to the masses. In the second century, the pagan writer Celsus complained of Christians that "while there are a few moderate, reasonable and intelligent people who are inclined to interpret its beliefs allegorically, yet it thrives in its purer form among the ignorant."[98]

Origen believed that the literal sense of scripture should only be taught to people initially, to attract them to study the Bible so they may eventually venture into a deeper and more metaphoric understanding of it.[99] And yet Origen also said that "it is true that those who have no way of abandoning their livelihood in order to learn philosophy we instruct to believe without examining the reasons for their belief."[100] We wonder if it is truly necessary for people to abandon their livelihoods in order to be instructed with sound reasons for belief. We suspect it may be possible to use one's reason, examine one's beliefs, and remain employed. But Origen was apparently unable, from his historical perspective, to make the connection between his own attitude and the ultimate success of the mythic literal approach he so disliked. Origen tried valiantly to maintain his allegorical approach to scripture in the face of encroaching literalism, but failed. He was the last church father to argue against mythic literalism and for his troubles was declared a heretic after his death.

The problem with telling people to believe without examining the reasons for their belief is that eventually the reasons are forgotten. By the year 529 CE, under the edict of Justinian, all the schools of philosophy were finally closed.[101] The tiered structure of Christian teaching and membership was abandoned, no hidden or esoteric truths concerning the scriptures were taught, and the mythos was presented as historical fact.

Accusations and Responses

Once the change to mythic literalism was complete, what had once been seen as a symbolic mythos was treated as literal fact, and any knowledge of the teachings being otherwise was rapidly lost. Nineteenth-century writer and Egyptologist Gerald Massey asks us to imagine how perplexed the Christians of the third and fourth centuries must have been, who "had started from a new beginning altogether, which they had been taught to consider solely historic, when they turned to look back for the first time to find that an apparition of their faith was following them one way and confronting them another."[102] This apparition was the pagan and symbolic origin of their beliefs and practices. "Then," Tom Harpur, professor of Greek and the New Testament, says, "the charge of the pagan enemies and critics of Christianity was sounded. You have stolen all our beliefs and rites, they claimed, and by making them out to be concrete, historic events, you have claimed them as your own."[103]

The pagan Celsus, for example, writes in the second century that the Christians "are really very dishonest, borrowing even their incantations from other religions in their magic acts."[104] In discussing the Christian view of heaven, he states that the fact that "their system is based on very old teachings may be seen from similar beliefs in the old Persian Mysteries associated with the cult of Mithras."[105] Celsus also says, "It is clear to me that the writings of the Christians are a lie, and that your fables have not been well enough constructed to conceal this monstrous fiction."[106] No one bothered to respond to Celsus for seventy years, long after he had died. It was then that Origen wrote a lengthy response to Celsus called *Contra Celsum*, in which he sets out about 70% of Celsus's text as he responds to it. This is a fortunate thing, since Origen's quotes are all that are left of Celsus's works, all the rest being burned by the Christians.

Beginning in the third and fourth centuries and continuing for some time, the Christians destroyed all the pagan writings they could find. Bishops ordered books to be burned, popes ordered books to be burned, and eventually, so did the Roman (now Christian) emperors. Anything that was found about Mystery religions was destroyed, as were pagan commentaries, critiques of Christianity, the works of the gnostics, the philosophers, Plato, and the writings of the Essenes. Entire libraries were burned to the ground, including the incomparable and irreplaceable library at Alexandria. When the Christians came to the Egyptian monuments, they sometimes hacked away at the figures and at other times covered them with plaster. Eventually the need to do this faded, as no one knew how to read the hieroglyphs anymore. It was not until the Rosetta stone was discovered at the mouth of the Nile River by Col. Broussard of Napoleon's army that the world of Egyptian religion opened again.[107]

Kuhn offers a dramatic rendition on the effect of finding the Rosetta stone when he says,

> The pick that struck the Rosetta Stone in the loamy soil of the Nile delta in 1796 also struck a mighty blow at historical Christianity. For it released the voice of a long-voiceless past to refute nearly every one of Christianity's historical claims with a withering negative. The cryptic literature of an old Egypt, sealed in silence when Christianity took its rise, but haunting it like a taunting specter after the third century, now stalks forth like a living ghost out of the tomb to point its long finger of accusation at a faith that has too long thriven on falsity.[108]

As Harpur says, it may never be known to a certainty if Christianity plagiarized from the pagans, "but judging by the utter ferocity of the reaction of the Church of the third and fourth centuries, we can conclude that this accusation was regarded by the Church authorities as a highly embarrassing, even lethal, rebuke."[109] "All the signs," he says, "point to a guilty, fearful conscience at work."[110]

How did church officials respond in their writings to these accusations? At first, they ignored them, then they attempted to demonstrate that paganism and Christianity were essentially identical so that Christianity would not seem strange or threatening. Of course, such statements of identity can be seen as admissions that the pagans are correct in their accusations. Remember Tertullian's response to the pagans that "you say we worship the sun; so do you."[111] This is such a statement of identity. As another example, St. Justin Martyr explains to the pagans that "in saying that the Word was born for us without sexual union as Jesus Christ our teacher, we introduce nothing beyond what is said of those called the Sons of Zeus."[112] He is referring here, of course, to the stories of other virgin births celebrated in the Greek Mystery religions. In a letter to Servianus, the Emperor Hadrian wrote that "those who worship Serapis are likewise Christians; even those who style themselves the Bishops of Christianity are devoted to

Serapis,"[113] thereby professing that the worship of Serapis (also virgin-born, killed, and resurrected) to be essentially the same as the worship of Jesus. And later, St. Augustine writes, "That which is known as the Christian religion existed among the ancients, and never did not exist; from the very beginning of the human race until the time when Christ came in the flesh, at which time the true religion, which already existed, began to be called Christianity."[114] Apparently, before it began to be called Christianity, it was known by other names, like paganism.

As the literal position of the church hardened and the church gained temporal power after Constantine, this approach to answering the pagans was heard no more. Instead, the church realized that what had really happened was that the devil had gone back in time and planted all of Christianity's themes, characters, stories, and rites into the pagan Mystery religions ahead of time. Justin Martyr can explain it best in his own words:

> For when they tell that Bacchus, son of Jupiter, was begotten by [Jupiter's] intercourse with Semele . . . and when they relate, that being torn to pieces, and having died, he rose again and ascended to heaven; and when they introduce wine into his mysteries, do I not perceive that he [the devil] has imitated the prophecy announced by the patriarch Jacob and recorded by Moses? . . . and when he [the devil] brings forward Aesculapius as the raiser of the dead and healer of all diseases, may I not say in this matter likewise he has imitated the prophecies about Christ? . . . And when I hear that Perseus was begotten of a virgin, I understand that the deceiving serpent counterfeited this also.[115]

Once the church articulated this position, it used it frequently. The resemblances between the feasts in honor of Jesus's and Attis's resurrections were so striking, for example, that it led to conflict in the fourth century, with the followers of Attis claiming that the resurrection of Jesus was a "spurious imitation" of Attis's resurrection, while the followers of Jesus claimed that Attis's resurrection was a "diabolical counterfeit" of Jesus's resurrection.[116] In a similar vein, Tertullian observes that the cult of Mithras (which practiced baptism, offered forgiveness of sins, celebrated a communion of bread, and promised a resurrection) is obviously the work of the devil, who implanted such things in the Mystery religions before Christianity came along.[117]

A related argument we have heard, which might be called the "fulfillment" argument, goes something like this: whatever truth the pagans had was only partial, whereas Christianity represents God's full and perfect revelation to mankind, which replaces all the partial and imperfect ones that came before. Christianity, therefore, is a *fulfillment* of what the pagan religions point toward imperfectly. This argument expresses an opinion that Christianity is better, more complete, and more perfect than other religions. This is certainly an opinion a person can hold. You may hold it yourself. But it's not an answer to the charge of whether or not Christianity borrowed or plagiarized from paganism.

Let's take the church's arguments completely out of a religious context in order to see them from another perspective, to remove them from a venue that may be highly emotional. Let's see how these arguments sound in a different context, such as education. Imagine a teacher saying to her student, "Johnny, I am very concerned because the paper you handed in greatly resembles Suzi's paper from last semester. I can see you changed some bits here and there, but the majority of it is just like Suzi's." Johnny says, "Teacher, the serpent of evil went back in time to last semester and implanted my paper into Suzi's mind in order to create this problem for me today." If you were the teacher—or Johnny's parent—what would you say to his answer? What do you think is the reason Johnny's paper is so much like Suzi's? The teacher replies, "Johnny, that's not an adequate answer, and I will not accept it." So he says, "But teacher, Suzi's paper is imperfect. The one I turned in is a full treatment of the subject; in fact, it should be the standard by which all other papers on this subject are judged. It is obvious that Suzi's paper falls short while mine completes what she was trying to do with hers." If you were his teacher, how would you respond to this answer? Has Johnny satisfactorily explained why his and Suzi's papers resemble each other?

Jesus and Historians

According to biblical scholar G. A. Wells, the writings of Paul are earlier than the gospels, and yet Paul is curiously silent about the life and ministry of Jesus. Wells says that "the most striking feature of the early documents is that they do not set Jesus's life in a specific historic situation."[118] There is no ministry in Galilee, and there are no miracles, parables, Passion, time, places, or circumstances mentioned. Several of the scholars surveyed for this book noted the same curious lack of reference to Jesus in Paul's writings. Even when discussing the resurrection, Wells states that Paul depicts Christ only as an "archetype of a universal resurrection (1 Cor. 15:22–23)."[119] Wells echoes the sentiments of a number of other scholars when he says that "my view is that Paul knew next to nothing of the earthly life of Jesus."[120] The first biographical material one can find about Jesus is located in those writings that are contemporaneous with or later than the gospels.

Regarding non-Christian ancient historians, Kuhn notes that only four mention Jesus. These are Pliny, Tacitus, Suetonius, and Josephus. Together they amount to no more than a couple of paragraphs.[121] In regard to Josephus, a Jewish historian who wrote during the first century, there is a section in his *Antiquities of the Jews* (18.63–64) where he discusses Jesus, including the information that he was crucified by Pilate and then raised from the dead. Josephus also calls Jesus the Messiah. Writing in the third century, Origen—who, despite his later problems with the orthodox church, is universally considered a conscientious historian of the church—is clear that there is no mention of Jesus in Josephus. It is not until the fourth century that Bishop Eusebius appears with the new version of Josephus's writings. The scholars we surveyed agreed that this section is a forgery, and they tend to date it to some point in time between Origen and Eusebius, or even to Eusebius himself. Kuhn notes that the writings of the other three historians mentioned—Pliny, Tacitus, and Suetonius—are also considered to be forgeries by nearly all scholars, Protestant and Catholic alike. He says, "It is so rare a thing to find unanimous consensus of opinion on such matters among scholars that their practically complete agreement in this case enables the layman to accept the academic verdict with assurance."[122] Conservative Christian scholars would not necessarily agree, and so it appears the debate on this issue will continue.

The Gospels

In the previous chapter we explored what mainstream scholarship has to say about the formation and content of the gospels and New Testament. This includes efforts to date writings and, as with the Q material, to sift through layers of writing in order to understand how the character of Jesus developed. This chapter presents another perspective on the creations of the gospels. As with all the material presented in this chapter, we leave it to you to examine the sources, weigh the evidence, and make your own decisions.

The common view of the creation of the gospels and New Testament holds that the writings occurred over the course of many years. Paul's writings may have come first, but meanwhile the gospels existed in fragmentary form—collections of the sayings of Jesus (as in Q), recollections of those who knew Jesus or had heard stories about him and so on. These pieces and fragments were then gathered up, according to the common view, and were compiled into the four gospels over time, perhaps over a span covering fifty or more years. But what if the gospels were not produced in this fashion?

Historian Charles Waite surveyed twenty-six Christian writers up to the year 170 CE and notes that in none of them is there a single mention of the gospels.[123] This seems strange for a collection of writings that had supposedly been circulating in bits and pieces among the Christian community beginning shortly after Jesus's death. Waite notes that none of the gospels are mentioned in any other book of the New Testament nor in any work of art before the latter part of the second century, not even in the Christian catacombs in Rome.[124] The earliest extant fragment of a gospel has been dated only to the mid-to-late second century, and the first definitive mention of the gospels is made by Bishop Irenaeus in his book *Against the Heretics* in approximately 185 CE.[125] This indicates that the gospels may have been created much later than is assumed, and could have been more or less simultaneous.

The second century was a pivotal time in the church, because the Gnostic Marcion had just assembled his own group of scriptures. Marcion came to Rome and converted to Christianity in 138 CE. However, he soon became a Gnostic and was expelled from the church in 144 CE. Within ten years he established his own Gnostic church, which attracted large numbers of people and spread over much of the empire. Among other things, Marcion rejected the Jewish scriptures and believed that Christ had completely freed humankind from Jewish law. In response, Rome moved in the opposite direction and claimed Jewish scripture as Christianity's own heritage. Marcion established a canon of scripture that consisted of ten epistles and an early form of what would become the Gospel of Luke, later greatly expanded by the church.[126] Marcion adopted Paul's epistles because they supported his Gnostic views. This appropriation of Paul is what author Earl Doherty believes spurred the church to establish its own canon of scripture, which included the creation of the expanded Luke and the composition of the Book of Acts, so that "Paul would be rehabilitated and rescued from the gnostics" and "a wider apostolic base of authority would be established."[127]

Even after the second century, the gospels circulated in a number of versions that often differed significantly from each other. The New Testament scholar Graham Stanton notes that in the third century, Origen lamented the state of the Book of Matthew when he said, "It is an obvious fact today that there is much diversity among the manuscripts, due either to the carelessness of the scribes, or to the perverse audacity of some people in correcting the text, or again to the fact that there are those who add or delete as they please, setting themselves up as correctors."[128] Stanton picked chapters 10 and 11 of Mark at random, studied all the early manuscripts that still exist of these chapters, and found forty-eight differences among them.[129]

The New Testament scholar Burton Mack states that the majority of scholars agree that the only books in the New Testament written by those whose names are attached to them are the Book of Revelation and seven of the letters of Paul.[130] He says that "most of the writings in the New Testament were either written anonymously and later assigned to a person of the past, or written later as a pseudonym for some person thought to have been important."[131] He goes on to say that over the course of the second and third centuries—the crucial time period for the appearance of the gospels and epistles and also, as noted earlier, the first biographical material about Jesus—the church authorities "were able to create the impression of a singular, monolinear history of the Christian church."[132] Therefore, the view modern readers have of the New Testament as a "charter document" for Christianity is understandable, according to Mack, since this is precisely what the church intended.[133]

My Journal

What do you think about the material presented in this chapter? How does it make you feel? Do you agree or disagree with the findings of these scholars?

Think back to the journal exercise in the previous chapter where you imagined what would remain of your spirituality if the myth and story surrounding it were removed. Review what you wrote about the essentials of your spirituality that would remain—your values, your ethics, your beliefs, and why you would adopt them. If Jesus and the events and characters in the New Testament are not historical, would that impact what you identify as the essentials of your spirituality or not? Why?

If you did not do the journal exercise in the previous chapter, ask yourself to what extent your spirituality is dependent on Jesus and the New Testament being historically true. What would happen to your spirituality if their historicity were suddenly disproved beyond any doubt? Identify the essentials of your spirituality that you believe would remain. Are there any essentials you would lose? What would your ethics be before such a change? What would they be after?

Make notes for one or two weeks of how much time you spend studying and discussing the details of your faith's mythos, either with others of your faith or those who are not. If your faith values proselytizing or witnessing to others, include the time spent in these activities. Over the course of a year, how much time does this add up to? If these activities suddenly stopped, what would you do with this time?

History contains one type of truth because it claims to recount events and facts accurately. This is temporal truth. Myth contains another kind of truth that speaks outside of history, without concern for events, cultures, time, and place. This is eternal truth. Can you identify some of the eternal mythic truths of Christianity? Identify at least five. Do the same for Paganism. Study your two lists of Christian and Pagan truths. What differences do you observe? What similarities? What do you see as the causes or origins of the differences, and what are the causes or origins of the similarities? If you were to lay these two lists down in front of another person after eliminating all faith-specific references in them, could this person identify which list is for Christianity and which for Paganism? Why or why not?

Harmony in Difference

If there is one overriding theme among the scholars surveyed here, it is that what had been meant to be taken symbolically became historical. This development cut Christianity off from its pagan beginnings and estranged it from the deeper universal meanings or metaphors to which myth, as symbol, points. It set up an adversarial mindset between Christianity, paganism, and other religions, and led to cruelties, destruction, and needless human suffering on all sides over the centuries. Many of the scholars surveyed here believe that Christianity needs to accept its pagan origins and the gradual transformation of symbolic myth into historical fact. As Kuhn puts it, "One wonders how long it will be ere the minds that go so far toward the truth, will not go the few additional steps to the goal of the full truth—that, far more than were the first and second centuries, the entire ancient period was transfused with the spirit of poetic and mythic representation of wisdom, and that the entire Gospel content was a formulation of this nature, and of immemorial antiquity."[134] And further, "the tragedy is that so few can go beyond the symbol to the deeper plummeting. Erroneous tradition presses so heavily in upon them that they are afraid to let go of the symbol as fact itself and reach for the wondrous grace of the miracle of meaning beyond it."[135]

If Christianity were able to move beyond this fear, what then? For one thing, Harpur believes that the energy being spent on ferreting out the historical Jesus could be freed for other activities. As Harpur says, "No amount of archaeology can ever prove a myth."[136] Such a change could also open doors to interfaith dialogue and understanding that now are closed, including a greater appreciation of blended spiritualities such as ChristoPaganism. Harpur notes that by allowing Jesus to be "deeply true in the mythical sense rather than literally as God, the vast theological offense currently given to the majority of other faiths . . . is entirely removed. Thus lies open a way to interfaith understanding that otherwise can never exist."[137] He also believes that taking such a step may also increase the emphasis on personal responsibility, as it would move people away from what he calls "the current idolatrous cult of a 'personal Jesus,'" and into a space where everyone is expected to assume complete responsibility for his or her own moral struggle.[138] The problem with a literal, historical Jesus, according to Harpur, is that most people see him as a type of celestial Superman who will "transform each of us by some remote magic and thus save us from the evolutionary task of transfiguring ourselves. . . ."[139]

A small example of this came up for us as we were working on our next book, an interfaith Book of Hours, which is a volume of interfaith daily prayer in a morning-and-evening prayer format. In writing the petitonary prayers for each day, we occasionally consult other sources for inspiration. We have been discouraged to see that most Books of Common Prayer put the responsibility for peace, justice, and the solution of many problems onto God or Jesus. It is Jesus or God who is asked to see to it that food is equitably distributed, that the naked are clothed, that someone is paid a fair wage, that the sick are comforted, and that wars end, while there is almost no mention of *each of us* making these things occur. So habituated was our own thinking in this regard that despite our years in Paganism and its emphasis on personal responsibility, we found it difficult to word petitions in such a way that they leave room for divine guidance while keeping the responsibility for acting where it belongs. If you want to test this for yourself, find a Book of Common Prayer or an Office of the Hours, and try rewording the petitions to reflect this balance. The fact that this difficulty existed, for us at least, may give some credence to Harpur's concerns.

Harpur also believes that letting mythology be symbolic allows it to be more spiritual as it moves away from a reliance on the literal, which is often embodied in something material (such as words, clothing, gestures, observances, foods, colors, times of day, amulets, or relics). Sociologist Richard Potter, for example, believes that fundamentalism as experienced today "ironically, is materialistic religion. Fundamentalism replaces myth, mystery, and consciousness with reading a book."[140] When the focus on the literal goes away, what is left is the something that is "more spiritual," as you may have discovered in the earlier exercise of stripping your spirituality of mythology and looking at what was left.

Professor Vittorio D. Macchioro, an expert on Orphic religion, suggests that "the only way to deliver Christianity from this imposition [of turning myth into history] is to transform theology into mythology, that is, to cease to consider it from a religious viewpoint as a sort of knowledge and to view it in the light of the history of religion as a complex of symbols by means of which man realizes his faith."[141] This means that "the dogma-concept may be replaced by the dogma-symbol, which permits harmony in difference."[142] The shift in view from the dogma-concept to the dogma-symbol is the shift from the mythic literal view to the mythic global view, and is an example of an expanding concept holon, ideas which we explore in later chapters. When concepts expand, they tend to become more universal, thereby permitting Macchioro's "harmony in difference." When one can attain this perspective, the door to interspiritual experience and understanding begins to open.

In the next chapter, we continue our examination of "what's out there" in the exterior landscape of belief by looking at the issue of monotheism, often given as a primary reason why any mixture of Paganism and Christianity is impossible. Since the development of monotheism in Jewish history is indelibly tied together with the Old Testament, we also examine its creation.

Chapter 5

MONOTHEISM AND
THE OLD TESTAMENT

The overview of the landscape of belief is not complete without a look at the history and development of monotheism in Western religion. This is particularly true for interspiritual work, since the issue of monotheism is often seen as a major stumbling block between Paganism and Christianity. This stumbling block rests upon a couple of assumptions, the first of which is that Paganism is always polytheistic and Christianity is always monotheistic. This distinction, however, does not hold up under scrutiny.

Some Pagans, for example, conceive of the divine as a "oneness" or singularity, and believe that the names given the divine by various cultures are simply ways of describing this oneness. Is this polytheism? Some Christians assign power to angels, saints, or prophets, and pray to them in lieu of or in addition to God. Is this monotheism? Some Pagans do not believe that the God and the Goddess are actual beings, but are a metaphor for the creativity of the universe, which frequently expresses itself in polarities such as light and dark and male and female. Is this polytheism? The doctrine of the Trinity divides the divine into interdependent and co-equal pieces. Is this monotheism? The fact that some Christian denominations reject the doctrine of the Trinity and veneration of angels and saints seems to indicate that they, at least, sense a difficulty here. The point of these examples is to show that the dividing line between "polytheism" and "monotheism" that many assume solidly exists between Paganism and Christianity cannot be so clearly drawn.

The second assumption comes from the place held by monotheism in the history of Christianity. The gospels present a story of Jesus that shows him to be the fulfillment of Old Testament history and a long line of prophecy. Many events and characters of the Old Testament are directly linked by the gospel writers to the life and destiny of Jesus. A first-time reader of the gospels may not be able to grasp all the allusions and references made about Jesus without having a copy of the Old Testament at hand.

In addition, the gospel writers tie the spiritual purposes of Jesus's mission to the Old Testament. The salvific aspects of Jesus's life have no context without it. The bondage from which Christians believe Jesus frees people is the bondage begun by Adam and Eve. The story of the Fall is one of innumerable falls highlighted again and again in the Old Testament—a turning away from covenant, "relapses" in worship, ignoring prophetic warnings, being conquered by foreign armies—which are followed by rescue, release, forgiveness, and a re-gracing of the people. In one sense Jesus continues this story, which can be viewed as a single thread woven through the Bible from beginning to end. In another sense Jesus ends the story, according to the gospel writers, by breaking the pattern once and for all.

For these and perhaps other reasons, Jesus is forever linked to the Old Testament and the version of Jewish history that it gives. Because Jesus is linked to the Old Testament, so also is orthodox Christianity. Orthodox Christianity adopted the view of monotheism presented in the Old Testament and the characterizations of Yahweh found there. At least historically this has been so, but we wonder if it must be so. Is there anything in the words and actions of Jesus that *require* a monotheistic view of deity? Perhaps the doctrine of the Trinity and the veneration of angels and saints bring unease to some Christians because Christianity has existed quite well with these beliefs for centuries, which suggests that strict monotheism may not be a requirement in Christianity after all.

But how did Judaism, and then Christianity by extension, arrive at monotheism to begin with? In our own childhoods, monotheism was such a foundational belief that it was assumed. It was so deeply assumed, in fact, it did not have to be mentioned or discussed. Monotheism had simply always been, springing up fully formed, as it were, and delivered to Moses directly by God (Yahweh) in a time so ancient it is hard to imagine now (but perhaps in the twelfth century BCE). It certainly was not a belief system that developed over time or in stages, or worse, recently. In fact, it was not a belief system at all, it was simply The Truth. It was divinely ordained, not created by kings or scribes, and therefore constituted an eternal concept, magnificent and unassailable. These perceived qualities of monotheism add to the belief that Paganism and Christianity are irreconcilable and that dialogue between them is difficult. These qualities put monotheism beyond the reach of debate, if you will, because it does not seem to share the conditions of other belief systems whose construction can be more clearly observed. There is a mysterious or forbidden quality surrounding monotheism that makes it difficult to discuss. And yet it must be discussed if interspiritual efforts are to be truly authentic.

For the rest of this chapter, then, we explore the world that created the literature of the Old Testament, especially as it concerns monotheism. We begin with the earliest recorded experiment in monotheism and proceed to the completion of the Old Testament as a collection or canon of writings that came to be viewed as scripture. In the material that follows, we present the ideas of mainstream scholars, historians, and archaeologists, and include opposing views.

Akhenaten

The first recorded experiment in monotheism occurred during the reign of King Akhenaten, pharaoh of Egypt in the fourteenth century BCE. Archaeologist Donald Redford states that Akhenaten was born Amenophis IV and succeeded his father as pharaoh.[1] Amenophis's wife was the famed Nefertiti. From correspondence we know that Amenophis suffered from physical deformities. He had an elongated skull, long earlobes, a prominent jaw, narrow shoulders, a potbelly, large hips and thighs, and spindly legs. Medical experts today postulate that he may have suffered from an endocrine disorder that causes secondary sex characteristics to fail to develop.[2]

Amenophis's father was working on several building projects at the time of his death, and for the first years of his reign Amenophis continued them. He completed, for example, the finishing work at the Amun complex at Karnak. Images of Amenophis are found on the gates of this complex. In the third year of his reign, Amenophis declared a jubilee, an unusual act, as jubilees did not usually occur until a pharaoh's thirtieth year of reign. For the next two years Amenophis engaged in building projects at Thebes, the capital city, but then suddenly abandoned them and announced he was moving the capital to an empty plain in Middle Egypt. This area was a desert waste and had little access to water. We can imagine how unpopular this move must have been to his subjects. After working for several years to build a new city in this wasteland, Amenophis moved into it even though it was not yet completed, and erected boundary *stelae* (stone markers) at its borders, swearing an oath that he would never cross them again.[3] Until the move to the new capital, which occurred during his fifth year, Amenophis's reign had been tolerant of a variety of gods.

In his fifth year, however, Amenophis prohibited the worship of Amun-Ra, the central deity of Egypt, and closed his temples. Anyone whose name was compounded with Amun—including Amenophis himself—was required to change his name. Amenophis changed his name to Akhenaten, which means "the beloved of Aten." The famed King Tut was Akhenaten's son-in-law and would follow Akhenaten as pharaoh upon his death. Tutankhamun came under this edict also and changed his name to Tutankhaten in order to comply with it.[4]

Akhenaten then declared that the only god who would be worshipped in Egypt was Aten, a word that literally means "disc." Aten was a male deity and the god of light, lifted above all humans, and the creator and sustainer of the whole earth.[5] In a carving Akhenaten says that Aten is "one who built himself by himself, with his [own] hands—no craftsman knows him."[6] Notice how the theme of the only- or self-begotten deity is already in use here. Akhenaten proclaimed Aten his father and declared Aten to be a divine king deserving the reverence due a king. Akhenaten states that as Aten's son he occupies Aten's throne on earth. As his father's image in this world, Akhenaten alone knows his father's mind and will, and he only can teach and interpret it for humankind.[7]

Akhenaten not only closes all other temples but destroys and desecrates the names of other gods wherever they appear. Redford notes that this was accomplished so thoroughly that it must have taken a small army circulating through the country to bring it about. As part of this defacement, the plural word "gods" was erased from inscriptions and was never used again for the remainder of his reign.[8]

Few texts are left from the Aten cult; in fact, only two hymns have survived. They are called the Great Hymn and the Shorter Hymn. Since these texts were discovered, scholars have been struck by the resemblance between Psalm 104 and the Great Hymn.[9] A number of the scholars we surveyed for this chapter mention the similarity, if only in passing. While the resemblance between these documents appears to be more than accidental or coincidental, the connection between the two remains unclear. We set out two examples from Psalm 104 and the Great Hymn here. Interested readers can find the entire text of the Great Hymn in Jan Assmann's book referenced in the bibliography.

GREAT HYMN
When you set in the western lightland
Earth is in darkness, in the condition
　of death.
The sleepers are in chambers,
Every lion comes from its den, all the
　serpents bite.
At dawn you have risen in the light-
　land
And are radiant as the sundisk of
　daytime.
Humans awake, they stand on their
　feet, you have roused them.
They wash and dress, their arms in
　adoration of your appearance.
The entire land sets out to work
(lines 13–16, 19, 20, 24, 25, 28–31)[10]

The earth comes into being by your
　hand as you made it,
When you dawn, they live,
When you set, they die;
You yourself are lifetime,
One lives by you.
(lines 111–114)[11]

PSALM 104
You make darkness and it is night,
And all the beasts of the forest creep
　forth.
The young lions roar after their prey
And seek their meat from God.
The sun arises, they gather themselves
　together
And lay down in their dens.
Man goes forth to his work
And to his labor until the evening.
(verses 20–23)

When you give them, they gather;
You open your hand, they are filled with
　good.
You hide your face, they are troubled;
You take away their breath, they die,
And return to the dust.
You send forth your spirit, they are
　created,
And you renew the face of the earth.
(verses 28–30)

In the eleventh year of Akhenaten's reign, a series of plagues began, which swept through the Near East, raged for at least twenty years, and were the worst epidemics experienced by the region in antiquity.[12] Akhenaten may have lost several of his children to these plagues. Akhenaten himself died in 1359 BCE after only a seventeen-year reign. For the next ten years, the cult of Aten continued in a relaxed form with other gods being allowed to be worshipped again. The first thing Tutankhaten did upon his rising to power was to change his name back to Tutankhamun, thereby again claiming a connection to the god Amun.[13]

Many people of that time believed Akhenaten caused Egypt's woes by ignoring the gods. The people wanted nothing to do with his enforced monotheism and iconoclasm. The prolonged series of plagues, combined with the destruction of temples and temple practices, and the introduction of monotheistic intolerance, made this period a traumatic one for Egypt. As historian Jan Assmann states, it was a time of "sacrilege, destruction, and horror for the Egyptians."[14] This mood is clearly captured in the "Restoration Stela" of Tutankhamun, a large granite stela that documents the re-establishment of the traditional state religion. Notice the mention of "grave disease," a reference to the plagues sweeping the area, and also the reluctance to mention Akhenaten's name in the last sentence.

> The temples of the gods and goddesses were desolated
> From Elephantine as far as the marshes of the Delta,
> Their holy places were about to disintegrate,
> Having become rubbish heaps, overgrown with thistles,
> Their sanctuaries were as if they had never been,
> Their houses were trodden roads.
> The land was in grave disease
> The gods have forsaken this land.
> If an army was sent to Syria to extend the borders of Egypt,
> It had no success at all.
> If men prayed to a god for help,
> He did not come.
> If men besought a goddess likewise,
> She came not at all.
> Their hearts had grown weak in their bodies,
> Because "they" had destroyed what had been created.[15]

Tutankhamun reopened the temples Akhenaten had closed and reinstated their religious observances. King Tut died at a young age, however, and after only the briefest reign. He was succeeded for a period of four years by the aged vizier Ay, and then by one of his military generals, Pa-aten-em-heb, who dropped his connection to Aten and changed his name to Horemheb, as his chosen patron was Horus. Horemheb imposed an edict of reform to counteract the lawlessness and corruption into which he claimed Egypt had fallen under Akhenaten. Horemheb closed the temples established by Akhenaten and suppressed the worship of Aten. Texts began to be produced that denounced monotheism and demonstrated how Akhenaten's doctrines had been in error.[16]

Horemheb then began a systematic dismantling of Akhenaten's desert city and temples. Buildings were taken apart stone by stone, and remaining items such as stelae, offering tables, and statues, were smashed. Then the walls were set on fire until the remnants crumbled away. Horemheb took the masonry stones or blocks and used them as structural fill in other building projects, many of which have been found by archaeologists at sites in surrounding areas. Archaeologists began to collect these blocks as they were found, and by 1965 had acquired forty-five thousand of them.[17]

Horemheb also ordered Akhenaten's name to be chiseled out of all records and inscriptions.[18] Even the king list was changed so that Akhenaten's name was permanently removed from it. Horemheb was shown as coming after Amenophis III, thereby eliminating both Akhenaten's and Tutankhamun's reign from the record. Akhenaten is rarely mentioned again, but when he is it is with words like "the reign of that damned one Akhenaten."[19] Akhenaten's reign gradually faded from memory, leaving only a sense of trauma behind. Assmann notes that within eighty years, Akhenaten's reign came to be completely forgotten. The troubling and traumatic memories remained, but since they could not be located in any official record—all traces of him having been so carefully destroyed—the memories became "free floating," susceptible of being associated with and even producing "legendary traditions."[20] With this in mind, we now turn to a legendary tradition that some scholars believe may have been influenced by the traumatic memories of Akhenaten.

The Story of Moses

The Egyptian historian Manetho, who served as a priest in the reign of Ptolemy II in the early third century BCE, recorded various legends and stories circulating in Egypt during his time. Unfortunately, his work was later destroyed, but it is known today because he was extensively quoted by Josephus. Manetho recounts two stories that are of interest to our discussion here. The first sets the stage by telling the story of the Hyksos, or Palestinian invaders who conquered Egypt and ruled for five hundred years, until the

King of Thebes expelled them. The Hyksos then emigrated to Syria and settled in the area of Judea. Manetho dates this story to the seventeenth century BCE. The Hyksos period did exist and is documented by archaeologists and historians, who speculate as to whether the Hyksos are the beginnings of the Jewish peoples.[21] A historical time-line provided by historian William Albright identifies the Hyksos period as 1710–1550 BCE.[22]

The second story tells of a King Amenophis who one day decides that he wants to see the gods directly. He consults an oracle who tells him his wish will be granted if he expels all the lepers from the land. So King Amenophis rounds up the lepers and their priests and expels them into the desert. They find their way to the city of Avaris, which is the old capital of the Hyksos. There they choose Osarsiph to be their leader. In a sort of reaction against those who expelled them, Osarsiph makes laws that forbid doing what is permitted in Egypt and allows the doing of what is forbidden in Egypt. Manetho particularly mentions laws relating to food restrictions and the worshipping of gods. Osarsiph also forbids his people to leave the city and surrounding area and associate with people outside it.[23]

Osarsiph then forms an alliance with the Hyksos and invites them to join forces with him in a revolt against Egypt. They do so and succeed, ruling Egypt with cruelty for thirteen years. During this time the temples are laid waste, holy images are destroyed, sanctuaries are turned into kitchens, and sacred animals are cooked and eaten. Oh, and by the way, Manetho mentions as an afterthought, Osarsiph is also called Moses. After thirteen years of rule, Amenophis and his son Ramses finally reassemble their forces, return, and drive Osarsiph and his people from Egypt.[24]

A number of versions of the Lepers Story circulated in the region over the next several centuries, but Manetho's is the earliest known. Here, in a nutshell, is a very early form of the story of Moses and the Exodus. This story has several remarkable features. It begins with a king by the name of Amenophis, who sets events in motion because he desires to change his interaction with the gods in a notable way. To accomplish this, he rounds up those considered to be unclean (the lepers) and expels them, along with their priests. This part of the story might describe the dramatic change in relationship with the gods sought by the real Amenophis IV, or Akhenaten, and echoes his expulsion of the "unclean" priests of Amun and their religious practices.

Then the story shifts to those who are expelled, who leave the king's city and relocate to a desert waste where they build upon an abandoned city and capital. This desert city becomes their new capital and they elect Osarsiph/Moses as their leader. Although the characters shift in the roles they play (not uncommon in oral traditions), one can still see the sequence of events in Akhenaten's rule at work. Akhenaten also left his acknowledged circle of civilization in Thebes and began anew in a desert location, which to many seemed an uninhabitable wasteland, and turned this city into his new capital.

Osarsiph/Moses then prescribes laws that fly in the face of everything the people knew in Egypt. In fact, his laws dictate the opposite behaviors of those the people were accustomed to observing. This was also the experience of those under the rule of Akhenaten, who saw their normal religious practices reversed. Osarsiph/Moses even goes so far as to prohibit his people from leaving the city and not to associate with others. We are reminded of Akhenaten setting boundary markers around his capital city and swearing upon an oath that he will never cross them. Osarsiph/Moses leads a successful revolt against Egypt and together with the Hyksos rule it cruelly for thirteen years. This bears a close resemblance to Akhenaten's seventeen-year rule. Manetho particularly notes that the "cruelty" of Osarsiph/Moses and the Hyksos centers around the destruction of temples and desecration of their images and sacred animals. We know that Akhenaten took similar actions.

Finally, the story ends when Amenophis and Ramses return and drive out the evil Hyksos and Osarsiph/Moses. Recall that Horemheb changed the king list so that he followed immediately after Amenophis III. The Ramses pharaohs come after the Amenophis line by fifty years, more or less. If Horemheb was eventually forgotten or overlooked, the story could align Amenophis III (Akhenaten's father), who was not ill thought of, with the Ramses pharaohs who would follow in the succession. Together they are credited in the legend with doing the things Horemheb actually did, that is, eliminating Akhenaten's presence from the land.

Assmann believes, along with many mainstream scholars, that Moses is a figure of memory. Despite the biblical description of Moses's long life, his impact on Egyptian history, and his wide-ranging adventures, there is *no* historical or archaeological evidence that he ever lived.[25] In contrast, even though Akhenaten was carefully eradicated from Egypt's history, significant archaeological evidence has been collected regarding him. Akhenaten did what is ascribed to Moses: he abolished polytheism, he forcibly established monotheism, and he removed himself and his people to a desert wasteland.

The parallels between Akhenaten and Moses in this as well as later versions of the Lepers Story are too numerous to be dismissed. Assmann considers the Lepers Story "extraordinary," as he believes it gives us a direct view of Akhenaten re-entering the literary tradition of Egypt in the guise of Osarsiph/Moses. He says, "The story of the lepers can thus be explained as a conspicuous case of distorted and dislodged memory. In this tradition Egyptian recollections of Akhenaten's monotheistic revolution survived."[26]

The rule of Akhenaten was startling and traumatic, because it took place in a world that was thoroughly polytheistic. Akhenaten's attempted changes were so shocking that even his immediate successors could not erase his memory fast enough. This is hard to imagine today, in a generally monotheistic Western world.

Polytheism and Israel

Whether or not "Israel" existed as a tribe, nation-state, or ethnic identity before the writing of the Old Testament literature remains in dispute among historians and archaeologists. According to archaeologist William Dever, in the area believed to be the region of "Israel," there arose about three hundred small agricultural hilltop villages in the thirteenth and twelfth centuries BCE. These villages were small, no larger than four or five acres, sat on hills near water and fertile valleys, and were unwalled, without defenses. Most were located in the central hill country north of Jerusalem. Dever points out that there is a notable absence of pig bones in the excavations, unlike those of Assyrian settlements. No temples or shrines were discovered, however, except for one in the Samarian hills containing a bronze bull figurine of the deity El, whom we discuss later on in this chapter.[27]

Historian Philip Davies believes that "Israel" was not known by that name until the late eleventh century BCE.[28] Dever responds that the "Victory stele" of pharaoh Merneptah, dated 1210 BCE, celebrates the pharaoh's victories over enemies, including "Israel," which "is laid waste." He believes this reference to "Israel" is to a political or ethnic entity, and not a reference to a person or place.[29] Davies counters with the observation that on an Assyrian stela, the only relevant reference is to the "House of Omri," Omri being one of the kings of the region identified as Israelite in the Old Testament. Jehu, also a king, is called a "son of Omri."[30] The only capital city for this region mentioned in Assyrian historical records is Samaria, and it is this kingdom which fell to the Assyrians in 722 BCE, referenced in the Old Testament as the fall of Israel.[31] And so the debate among scholars continues.

The book of Joshua tells the stories of numerous battles waged by the "Israelites" against the "Canaanites" as the Israelites conquered over forty cities in the region in order to claim their "promised land." However, Dever notes that the conquest history of Joshua is not supported by archaeology.[32] Of the supposed forty cities, only two or three are even potential candidates for some form of conquest, as most of the other cities either didn't exist in that period, or if they did, show no destruction.[33] Most are new sites, in an area that was essentially unpopulated, so there was no need for conquest. However, during the twelfth century BCE there was a dramatic population increase in this central hill country, though none of the hill villages were built on earlier sites. Dever believes that Israel was initially formed by displaced Canaanites; in fact, "most of those who came to call themselves Israelites . . . were or had been indigenous Canaanites."[34] What might have happened to displace a large number of Canaanites and cause a population shift to the hill country?

Interestingly, Dever notes that in 1500 BCE there began a long, slow decline in the entire Mediterranean region, including Canaan, Egypt, and Greece. This decline involved increased lawlessness, corruption of officials, burdensome taxation, and increased poverty. Eventually the Canaanite government collapsed, and the region regressed to political anarchy for at least two centuries. During this period, urban populations decreased significantly. This time period includes the reign of Akhenaten. Dever sets out the content of several letters written to Akhenaten, which were found in 1887. These letters complain of corruption among Egyptian officials, their conspicuous wealth, and the increasing poverty of the populace.[35] Akhenaten apparently did nothing to correct these problems, and so they continued to worsen. The situation was likely aggravated by the series of plagues that afflicted the region during and after his reign. Recall that general Horemheb enacted an edict of reform when he took power in order to counteract the lawlessness that had taken hold.

Even after Akhenaten's death, the situation in Canaan continued to collapse, and by the twelfth century many Canaanite cities were abandoned. The Egyptian empire in Asia disappeared by 1160 BCE. Dever proposes that conditions in the Canaanite heartland became so miserable that people moved to the hill country to find relief, that "withdrawing was prudent, if not necessary."[36] This migration brings to mind the Lepers Story. It is interesting that the Hyksos are considered by many scholars to be the beginnings of the Jewish peoples, and in the Lepers Story they combine with Osarsiph/Moses to form their own society that dramatically "changes the rules" concerning dietary laws and worship.

Perhaps those who continued to favor monotheism after Akhenaten's death were part of this "exodus" to the hill country—they certainly would not have been welcome to stay during Horemheb's eradication of their sect—thus beginning the thread of monotheism in Jewish history.

According to Dever, the settlers in the hill country were probably composed of several different groups including refugees, those escaping corruption or plague in the cities, and some bandits and local nomads. There was a group of roving bandits called the 'Apiru, who were complained of in the time of Akhenaten and are mentioned in letters sent to him, who caused disruption in the region for some time.[37] Some of the scholars we encountered believe that the word 'Apiru is the root word for Hebrew, while others disagree.

The hill country settlements continued only to the tenth century BCE, however, at which time they were abandoned for larger towns, although a few grew into large fortified cities such as Dan, Hazor, Megiddo, and Ta'anach.[38] Dever believes that the displaced Canaanites who settled in the hill country are the people who would eventually call themselves "Israelites" and would later be identified by the Assyrians as the House of Omri.

The religion of the early Israelites most likely grew out of the Canaanite religion. Dever notes that the Israelite sacrificial system and liturgical year was Canaanite. Even the Hebrew language of the Bible is a Canaanite dialect and some of the early Hebrew was written in a Canaanite script. He observes that some of the Psalms and poems in the first five books of the Bible (the Pentateuch) are very close to Canaanite poetry. Biblical historian Professor Bernhard Lang notes that during the years of the Israelite monarchy, identified in the Bible as 1020 to 586 BCE, the Israelites continued to be indistinguishable from their neighbors in terms of worship.[39] According to Lang, the Israelites, Ammonites, Moabites, Edomites, Tyrians, and others all participated in similar West Semitic polytheistic cults.

Like its neighbors, the kingdom of Omri/Israel had a clan god, each city in the kingdom had a city god, and each family adopted a family god. The Ammonites worshipped Milcom as their national god, the Assyrians worshipped Ashur, the Egyptians worshipped Amun or Amun-Ra (except during Akhenaten's reign), the Moabites worshipped Kemosh, the Philistines worshipped Dagon, and the Israelites worshipped Yahweh.[40] While Yahweh was Israel's national god and was charged with the protection of the king and the kingdom, he was not considered to be the creator god. According to biblical scholar Richard Friedman, both Israel and most of its neighbors believed that the world was created by the god El. El was portrayed as a young bull, and he was sometimes referred to as Bull El.[41] El is also referred to as Elohim, which some scholars believe to be a plural form of his name, meaning something akin to "all the gods."

Even Genesis tells us that El created the world, as in Genesis 14:19: "Blessed be Abram by El, the Most High, creator of heaven and earth." The worship of Yahweh and El appears to have co-existed quite peacefully for some time. Biblical historian Morton Smith notes that the Temple of El, or Beth-El ("beth" means "house" in Hebrew), became a center of worship for Yahweh without changing its name, and with no evidence that the worship of El was banned there.[42] El and Yahweh may have been viewed over time as the same or very similar deity, and eventually Yahweh was equated with and transplanted El in Jewish literature. Bernhard Lang believes this did not occur, however, until after the Babylonian exile ended in the sixth century BCE.[43] At least one biblical passage, Genesis 2:7, clearly shows the equating and eventual supplantation of El by Yahweh, when it says, "Then Elohim (that is, Yahweh) formed man."[44] How, when, and why Yahweh came into prominence is explored in the next section.

As discussed in some detail in the previous chapter concerning Mystery religions, the blending of spiritualities in a syncretic way was common throughout this period in the regions surrounding Palestine, continuing through the last days of Solomon's temple. Smith notes that an archaeological find, which some think may have been Solomon's temple, contains images of other deities and a room in which incense was burned to them. At the northern gate of this temple, women kept observances to the god Tammuz, and in the inner court, men were allowed to worship the sun god Shamash. Archaeologists have found evidence of the worship of Shamash in a number of holy sites around Jerusalem dating from the eighth and ninth centuries BCE.[45] Smith observes that the fact that these practices occurred in the temple indicates that the priests of Yahweh did not see the worship of Yahweh as exclusive, and that it could co-exist with the worship of other deities. These practices could not have occurred without "the consent and cooperation of the priests of Yahweh."[46] While there may have been priests who saw the worship of Yahweh as exclusive, they were not in the majority at this time.

Dever gives a further example of a temple/shrine in the city of Ta'anach, dating to the tenth century BCE, in which was discovered a mold for making terra cotta goddess figurines, a collection of knuckle bones for divination, and a four-tiered offering stand showing a winged sun disc carried on the back of an animal, a doorway into an empty temple (which may depict that the god inside is invisible), a row of cherubim, and lastly, a nude female standing between two lions. The goddess Asherah was known as the Lion Lady, and was often depicted nude and riding a lion. Dever believes this offering stand depicts a combination of Yahweh—as a sun disc—and Asherah worship.[47] If Akhenaten's supporters and priests fled into the hill country after his death, they would have taken their image of God as a disc with them. Since Yahweh is here portrayed as a disc, this may be one example of the connection between Akhenaten and Yahweh. Such a connection may also explain the similarities between Akhenaten's hymn to Aten and Psalm 104.

Syncretic or polytheistic practices were also common at home. Most homes had altars and shrines to a number of deities.[48] Numerous goddess figures have been excavated in Israelite cities,[49] and you will recall that the shrine found in the Samarian hills had a mold for making terra cotta goddess figurines. A jar found at Kuntillat 'Ajrud dating to the ninth century BCE states, "I bless thee by Yahweh and by his Asherah."[50] Dever discovered a tomb at Khirbet el-Qôm that contained an inscription invoking "Yahweh and his Asherah." This inscription is dated later, to the eighth or seventh century BCE.[51] Asherah was frequently symbolized by a carved pole or a living tree set up near temples or shrines. Smith notes that during their polytheistic years, Israelites venerated Asherah as Yahweh's consort and most of Yahweh's temples had an Asherah sacred tree near them.[52] Biblical stories concerning the removal of trees or carved wood from temple areas refer to the removal of this symbol of Asherah. Dever notes that "archaeology is literally forcing us to revise our basic notion of what ancient Israelite religion was," and that "most biblical scholars now agree that true monotheism . . . arose only in the period of the Exile and beyond."[53]

The Yahweh-Alone Movement

Dever's comment highlights the fact that while at one time scholars believed Judaic monotheism started in the time of Abraham or Moses, most biblical scholars now agree that it occurred much later. Monotheism most likely arose in the ninth century BCE as a minority movement (perhaps brought forward by survivors of Akhenaten's religion) and grew until it became the standard in the sixth century BCE.[54] The story of monotheism in Judaism as presented by many scholars, then, is the story of the emergence and eventual success of what Bernhard Lang terms the "Yahweh-alone" movement.[55]

According to Lang, this was a movement of priests and scribes who not only promoted the worship of Israel's national god, Yahweh, but prescribed that Yahweh was the *only* god who could be worshipped.

Mainstream Old Testament scholars currently accept the events described in the Old Testament as actual historical occurrences that took place on the dates given for them, just as mainstream New Testament scholars believe Jesus was a historical person and the events told about him actually occurred. Old Testament scholars also generally date the writings in the Old Testament to the period of the events being described. So as an example, if the Old Testament describes events occurring in the eighth century BCE, conventional scholarship accepts that the event did occur, that it occurred in the eighth century BCE, and that the writing of it was created shortly thereafter. Other scholars are more skeptical and do not assume the Old Testament to be history. According to these scholars, the Old Testament is a collection of stories or oral traditions that were assigned dates and a chronological order later for a variety of reasons. Some scholars accept biblical dates for some events while dismissing dates for other events that have been proven to be non-historical, often based on archaeological findings or the lack thereof.

If the first group of scholars were asked how they know, for example, that King Josiah lived between 641 and 609 BCE, and that he did and said certain things, they would answer "Because the Old Testament says he does." Other scholars are not content with this answer and want to know if archaeology and other literature of the period supports this as a fact. Some scholars approach the Old Testament as a collection of literature subject to the same concerns as other literary creations. Even where the Old Testament mentions historical personages known from other sources to have existed, such as Ahab and Jehu, they still urge caution. Professor Philip Davies, for example, who is a biblical scholar in the non-historical camp, observes that while Shakespeare wrote about Julius Caesar, we do not assume that Caesar actually did and said the things Shakespeare attributes to him.[56] We understand that Shakespeare's Caesar is a literary construct. As Davies puts it, "There are no *literary* criteria for believing David to be more historical than Joshua, Joshua more historical than Abraham, and Abraham more historical than Adam. An additional problem, in fact, is that there is no *non-literary* way of making this judgment either, since none of these characters have left a trace outside the biblical text!"[57]

With this background we now proceed through the development of monotheism in the Old Testament. We present findings of scholars from both the historical and non-historical perspectives, just as we have in prior chapters. Again we document our sources carefully so that you can study the arguments for yourself and make your own decisions about them.

BEGINNING OF THE YAHWEH-ALONE MOVEMENT, 841–722 BCE. Many scholars say that the story of the Yahweh-alone movement begins in the ninth century BCE. According to the Old Testament, after King Solomon died, his kingdom split into two pieces, the north and the south. Philip Davies, a biblical historian of the non-historical school, cautions readers to remember that there is no archaeological evidence that the empires of either David or Solomon existed.[58] Dever counters that there is an inscription on a stone found at Tel-Dan in the region of Galilee dated to the ninth century BCE, which mentions "the House of David," although otherwise he agrees that there is no archaeological evidence that either the reigns of David or Solomon existed historically. However, he believes that conditions were such in the tenth century BCE that they *could* have supported a kingdom such as Solomon's.[59] After Solomon's kingdom divided into two pieces, the northern territory was called Israel and the southern was called Judah. In the northern kingdom there arose for the first time a faction of priests who urged the worship of Yahweh alone.

The first Old Testament stories of the Yahweh-alone movement appear to occur in the ninth century BCE in the northern kingdom, when the prophet Elijah incited a mob to riot and murder priests of Baal.[60] In approximately the same time period in the southern kingdom, the Old Testament recounts that King Asa (who died in 875 BCE) and his son Jehoshaphat (the first king to have a name compounded with Yahweh) briefly promote the worship of Yahweh alone. Smith notes that no prohibition to worship other gods can be found in the Old Testament before the ninth century BCE, and that prohibitions that seem to be dated earlier were edited into the Old Testament writings later.[61] Examples he gives of such editing include Exodus 20 and 34, Genesis 35:1–5, Judges 6:25–32, 1 Samuel 7:3, 1 Kings 11:33 and 14:9, and Numbers 25:1–5. We will discuss issues of editing in more detail later.

In the following generation, King Jehoram (852–834 BCE) of the northern kingdom restricts Baal worship, and King Jehu (841–813 BCE) is credited with eliminating it. However, Lang cautions that these reforms were political, not religious, and that the biblical record indicates that Jehoram and Jehu were not monotheists and did not worship Yahweh exclusively.[62] There is then a gap in the Old Testament writings with no more Yahweh-alone stories appearing until the eighth century BCE in the book of Hosea, who was a prophet active in the northern kingdom. Lang notes that most of the knowledge of this era comes from Hosea, as no independent historical sources for it have been found.[63] It is in Hosea that the reader finds the first statement that worship of Yahweh-alone is required, as in Hosea 13:4: "Yet I am the Lord your God from the land of Egypt, and you shall know no god but me, for there is no savior besides me." While this may sound like language borrowed from the Ten Commandments, the sequence is actually reversed. As we shall see, Lang and a majority of biblical scholars believe the story of Moses and the Ten Commandments were written much later than Hosea.[64]

Both Smith and Lang agree that the Yahweh-alone movement was quite small at this point.[65] Hosea notes that exclusive worship of Yahweh is not the common practice, and the temple priests are not interested in it (Hosea 11:2). As we noted in an earlier section, polytheistic practices continued well into the sixth century BCE. According to Smith, during the monarchic period the Yahweh-alone movement was comprised of a small number of independent groups from differing social backgrounds. One such group was found in the royal court of the southern kingdom, another in the Jerusalem temple, another among the followers of the prophets, and a few among sects such as the Rekabites.[66]

Hosea refers to all gods other than Yahweh as "the Baals," or "Baalim," a plural form of *Baal*, and rejects any cults promoting them. Yet, interestingly, one meaning of the word *ba'al* is "husband," and Hosea uses that meaning in the second chapter of his book when he identifies Yahweh as the "ba'al," or the husband, of the land and people. It becomes clear that Hosea believes Yahweh to be the husband of the people *literally*, and so equates the worship of other gods with adultery. Yahweh loves his people, but they are "unfaithful," therefore Yahweh is filled with anger and metes out punishment. Smith comments that the theme of adultery gives the writings of Hosea and later prophets an unusual power that alternates between love and hatred, and is full of sexual metaphor and violence.[67] The association of polytheism with adultery also created an unfortunate identity between other views of divinity and being immoral. The association lingers to this day and contributes to making discussions difficult between monotheists and those they suspect of not being monotheists. The "adultery" of polytheism provokes rage and jealousy in Yahweh. These emotions are such a central theme in the prophetic literature that eventually jealousy becomes Yahweh's outstanding feature. Furthermore, the "imitation and execution" of this jealousy are identified as peculiar virtues of Yahweh's followers, and were "without parallel in the Near East," according to Smith.[68]

It is not as clear what effects the Yahweh-alone movement had in the southern kingdom. The Old Testament literature is silent on this point until the story of the reforms of King Hezekiah (739–699 BCE). His reforms were very modest and consisted of cutting down one Asherah sacred tree and destroying Moses's bronze serpent.[69]

The end of this period brings us to 722 BCE, at which time historical records note that the House of Omri fell to Assyrian control. According to the Old Testament, the southern kingdom of Judah continued on for more than another hundred years, until it fell to the Babylonians in 586 BCE. Davies points out that the existence of a southern kingdom called Judah in the ninth and eighth centuries BCE is entirely theoretical and exists only in Old Testament literature. However, he notes that beginning in the 700s, the Assyrians created a small state in that region called Yehud and made Jerusalem its administrative center. After the Assyrians took Omri in 722 BCE, it is possible that some of its residents fled south into Yehud.[70]

KING JOSIAH, 641–609 BCE. The Old Testament writings fall silent again until the story of King Josiah. In the year 622 BCE, a scroll is brought to the king, who was about twenty years old at the time, by the high priest of Jerusalem, who was named Hilkiah. Hilkiah told Josiah that the scroll was discovered during the restoration of the temple. This scroll, which would become chapters 12 through 26 of the book of Deuteronomy, contained a code of law that no one had ever seen before and that overthrew previous ritual practice.[71] The scroll commanded that only Yahweh be worshipped, imposed a duty of pilgrimage to Jerusalem, consolidated power in the priesthood at Jerusalem, and ordered all shrines outside of Jerusalem to be closed. It also advocated the destruction of non-orthodox shrines and worshippers.[72] King Josiah instituted the reforms contained in this scroll and agreed to rule from it. The Old Testament recounts that he destroyed temples outside of Jerusalem and put non-orthodox priests to death. (See 2 Chronicles 34 and 2 Kings 23.) However, Josiah's reforms were short-lived, lasting only as long as he did. As soon as he died, in 609 BCE, the story says that the people returned to their prior polytheistic and syncretist ways. The Yahweh-alone movement continued as a minority.

Davies uses this story as an example of what concerns him about conventional biblical scholarship. He notes that the *only* evidence for this story is the Bible itself. No historical or archaeological evidence has been found to support the existence or reign of a King Josiah or any of the events that occur in the story, despite the fact that Josiah would have been king in or near the Assyrian province of Yehud, and the Assyrians kept good records. The evidence aside, Davies asks if the story makes sense for this region in the age of monarchy. Would a king adopt a book of rules which is silent concerning the powers and responsibilities of kings? Would a king who has been on the throne since he was eight years old happily and eagerly abdicate his authority by agreeing to rule from a book? Even if Josiah had been willing to do so, Davies doubts his courtiers would have allowed it, as their livelihoods depended on the monarchy. Given all these considerations, Davies finds the truth of this story to be highly improbable,[73] though several of the scholars we studied credit Josiah with being the creator of Jewish monotheism.

THE FALL OF JERUSALEM AND THE BABYLONIAN EXILE, 586 BCE. In 587 or 586 BCE, the Babylonians under King Nebuchadnezzar captured and destroyed the city of Jerusalem, the Jewish monarchy came to an end, and Yehud became a province subject to tribute. Some of the people fled to Egypt as refugees and others were forcibly exiled to Babylon. Davies notes that the historical record tells little about the Babylonian exile, but it is known that deportation was a common practice in that period after a conquest.[74] Deportation was used not only for control and punishment, but also to move labor where it was needed throughout Mesopotamia. Records of other deportations note that temple furnishings, statues, and archives were generally confiscated. Deportees were intentionally cut off from their religious artifacts and documents, since the idea of deportation was to "alienate the people from their homeland."[75]

Lang comments that beginning with the fall of Jerusalem, the "hour of the Yahweh-aloneists [had] come."[76] Members of this movement portray the fall of Israel in 722 BCE and the destruction of Jerusalem in 586 BCE as Yahweh's punishment for polytheism. Lang notes that these Yahweh-alone voices are now known as the Deuteronomic school among conventional scholars, and that they wrote the books of Deuteronomy, Joshua, Judges, Samuel, and Kings. These writings present a rather bulky history that goes back to the time of Moses and reinterprets events from their perspective.[77] Smith calls this work a "single system" containing history, laws, customs, and prophecies that demand the worship of Yahweh alone.[78] Smith notes that the Deuteronomists also set out to make Israel a separate and unique people by banning intermarriage, promoting customs not followed by their neighbors, and requiring the teaching and reciting of the law.[79]

Abstention from work on the seventh day also became mandatory, perhaps from the sixth century BCE on. Lang points out that Ezekiel's writings show no knowledge of a sabbath, but a later editorial addition to Ezekiel adds a reference to it (see Ezek. 46:1).[80] The idea of a sabbath day was not new, as such a day was observed by many religions in the region. Historian James Bonwick notes that even the ancient Egyptians consecrated the seventh day of the week to Amun-Ra, and that they observed this day by visiting the temples and praying. No business was allowed to be conducted.[81] Wheless observes that the fifth tablet of the Babylonian *Epic of Creation* tells of the god Marduk that "On the seventh day he appointed a holy day, and to cease from all work he commanded."[82] Hosea calls these days the "days of the Baalim" (see Hosea 2:13–15). There was also a law that gave agricultural workers one day off in every seven during plowing and harvesting seasons, when the work was heaviest. This was not a year-round observance, however (see Exod. 23:12 and 34:21). Babylon had a similar rule, although it was year round, giving its workmen a day off every ten days.[83] The Deuteronomist writers determinedly worked to rededicate the sabbath concept, obviously of ancient origin, to the worship of Yahweh alone.

The Deuteronomists also made religious intolerance a requirement. Only Yahweh could be worshipped. Even a suggestion to recognize or worship other gods was punishable by death. This extended to one's own family, for if such a suggestion were made by a spouse or child, "you shall have no pity on him, you shall not spare him or shield him" (Deut. 13:9). To the requirement of the sole worship of Yahweh was added the declaration that Yahweh is, in fact, the only god (see Deut. 4:39 and 1 Kings 8:60). Lang notes that this is a new requirement of belief.[84] Even so, Smith observes that the period of the exile saw the continued co-existence of Yahweh worship with other syncretist or polytheistic practices.[85] One notable example is the Jewish military colony on the island of Elephantine in Egypt during the fifth century BCE, which preserved polytheistic practices even after the exile ended and monotheism became the standard elsewhere. Assmann recounts that this colony built a temple to Yahweh, where records show that offerings were made not only to Yahweh but three other deities as well.[86]

AFTER THE EXILE, 538–458 BCE. In the year 538 BCE, the Persians swept in with their armies and conquered the entire region, and the exile came to an end. Archaeological data indicates that the repopulation of the Yehud region may not have been the beneficent permission to return that is portrayed in the Old Testament. Rather, the record indicates that the Persians forcibly transported subjects to regions that were sensitive or underpopulated in order to support imperial and economic policies.[87] The population that was settled in Yehud most likely came from all parts of Palestine. A chain of fortresses was built across this region in the mid-400s BCE, probably to protect trade routes. Davies notes that the Judean resettlement appears to be part of a larger Persian reorganization plan, which included creating new cities, funding the restoration of temples, and establishing legal codes.[88] Jerusalem was rebuilt with Persian funds and a new temple was dedicated there in 516 BCE.

Smith notes that the period following the rebuilding of the temple appears to be one of syncretist control.[89] According to the Old Testament, when Nehemiah came to Jerusalem from the Persians in the mid-400s BCE, he began sweeping reforms to reintroduce or enforce Yahweh-alone worship, some of which had to be implemented by force. Polytheism and blended practices were eventually abolished, and the Yahweh-alone group became the majority. For the first time, worship of Yahweh became the nation's religion.[90] Several of the scholars we studied noted that Jewish monotheism may have been influenced by the Persian belief in the one god, Ahura Mazda. Lang mentions other Zoroastrian teachings adopted by the Jews, such as the doctrine of creation, the uniqueness of God, and the emphasis on dietary and purity laws.[91]

Throughout the fifth century, Yehud/Judah existed as a newly constructed society subject to a number of tensions. As Davies describes it, "We can posit with some probability a conflict between immigrants and indigenous populations, the establishment of a city and temple center in Jerusalem, the institution of a religious law and bond of allegiance to a deity (covenant) and the promotion of an ethical consciousness as features which constitute the emergence of a governing caste or class. These measures constitute a massive exercise in self-definition, in which I take the creation of the biblical literature to be a further enterprise."[92] So Yehud/Judah, an old Babylonian province and now a Persian one, receives a new and transported population and is given funds to build a temple and rebuild Jerusalem. The ruling class may have been under pressure from the Persians to do so, as the Persians wanted the area permanently resettled. And so, Davies postulates, the literate elite (comprising about 5% of the population) generated an identity through literature and chose the name Israel to represent the people designated by Yahweh to inhabit the area, bind it to a covenant, and distinguish it from other peoples. Since those who generated the history were immigrants, the biblical Israel originates as a nation of immigrants.[93] Davies believes this time period provides the "earliest plausible context" for the creation of the biblical Israel and the Old Testament literature.[94]

The Old Testament Writings

Biblical historian Richard Friedman observes that for a long time it was believed that the first five books of the Bible (the Pentateuch) were written by Moses. No doubt this was based on the fact that each of these books is identified as a book of Moses, for example, "The First Book of Moses, called Genesis" and "The Second Book of Moses, called Exodus," and so on. Deuteronomy (the fifth book) begins by saying, "These are the words which Moses spoke to all of Israel." So at first glance it certainly seems that Moses wrote the Pentateuch. However, Friedman observes that by the eleventh century CE, both Jewish and Christian commentators were noticing that parts of these books could not have been written by Moses for various reasons, especially those sections that claim to have been written after his death. All of these scholars were condemned by their peers, some had their books banned, and some were arrested by church authorities.[95] In the seventeenth century, scholars again pointed out that some, or even most, parts of the Pentateuch were not written by Moses. These scholars saw their books burned and some were forced to recant.[96]

However, Friedman observes that since the nineteenth century, the majority of biblical scholars have come to agree that the Pentateuch is constructed from two bodies of material they have named J and E. The J material is distinguishable by the use of Yahweh as the name of God, and E by the use of El or Elohim as the name of God. Deuteronomy is considered its own source and is referred to as D, and another large body of material that deals mostly with laws and priestly practices has been named P. Together these four sources comprise the books of the Old Testament.[97]

Many mainstream scholars believe that the author of J came from Judah (the southern kingdom) and could possibly have been a woman, and the author of E came from Israel (the northern kingdom), may have been a displaced Levite priest, and was almost certainly a man.[98] These scholars date the J material to approximately 848–722 BCE and the E material to 922–722 BCE, based on dating given in the Old Testament itself, in both cases before the northern kingdom was destroyed by Assyria.[99] It is then postulated that an editor combined the two versions into one, known as JE, by 722 BCE at the latest.

The book of Deuteronomy is presented as Moses's farewell speech, in which he reviews forty years of wandering in the desert, gives a code of laws, and then appoints his successor. The language of Deuteronomy and the next six books of the Bible are very similar and are considered to be a carefully constructed work that tells a continuous story. These seven books comprise the work of the "Deuteronomists" discussed earlier. Friedman believes that all seven books are the work of one person who created a history going from Moses to the destruction of Judah in 586 BCE.[100]

In keeping with the mainstream position of dating the writing of works to the time period mentioned in them, scholars believe the core or center section of Deuteronomy, chapters 12 to 26, was written during the lifetime of Josiah and presented to him as the newly found scroll discussed earlier. Then an editor added the beginning and ending of the work during the exile in 586 BCE. Since the time from Josiah to the exile spans only twenty-two years, Friedman theorizes that one person could have done all the D writing, though other scholars think it was written by a school of scribes.[101]

The P source is the largest body of material in the Old Testament, and it is believed to have been completed by at least 609 BCE, the date of Josiah's death. The P material includes the creation story in the first chapter of Genesis, one version of the flood story, stories of Abraham, Jacob, and the Exodus, a large body of law covering thirty chapters of Exodus and Numbers and all of Leviticus. P appears to follow the format of the combined JE material. Conventional scholars believe that P was written not long after JE and that the writer may have had a copy of JE at hand as it was written.[102] P approaches the subject of worship in a structured, codified manner that explains how to make the proper sacrifices. P routinely rejects stories that contain angels, dreams, talking animals, or other anthropomorphisms.[103]

Friedman dates Chronicles, part of Kings, Micah, Hosea, and Proverbs to approximately 722 BCE. He believes very little literature was produced after 586 BCE, although he dates Psalm 137, Lamentations, Ezekiel, Deutero-Isaiah (chapters 40–55), and the last part of Jeremiah to just after the exile.[104] Finally, the majority of mainstream scholars in the historical school believe that the final edition of the Pentateuch was produced by an editor they call the Redactor, just after the rebuilding of the temple in 516 BCE. As Friedman puts it, the Redactor was "not merely combining [J, E, D, and P] side by side, as stories. He or she was cutting and intersecting them intricately."[105] The Redactor likely added chapter 15 of Numbers, the Feast of Booths, and verse 39 of Leviticus 23, which is the creation of the sabbath.[106]

In contrast, Smith, although a scholar in the historical camp, places the bulk of the Old Testament writings during the 500s BCE, during and following the exile, rather than during the time of Josiah (600s BCE) or before the fall of the northern kingdom (700s BCE). He believes the Old Testament literature was continually edited from the 500s through 100 BCE, after which time the scribes stopped making deliberate alterations or new editions. He agrees that every book in the Old Testament was heavily altered in this four-hundred-year period.[107]

Albright also assigns later dates for some of the writing. He places Chronicles in 400 BCE, Ecclesiastes in the 200s, and a number of books between 600 and 200 BCE, such as Proverbs, Isaiah, Ezekiel, Habakkuk, Song of Songs, Ecclesiastes, Jubilees, and parts of Daniel. He is also of the opinion that many of the psalms were adaptations of Canaanite hymns.[108] Concerning Moses, he agrees that a variety of stories circulated for several hundred years, and that the entire epic was probably added to the Old Testament in one piece.[109]

Davies, being the most skeptical and tending toward a non-historical view, believes that the Old Testament literature was all composed or compiled after the exile (538 BCE and later). The social situation addressed by the Deuteronomists is more suited to the post-exile period, in which the society was being governed by a code of law and not a monarch. He says that "an impressive case can be made for the fifth century BCE as the time and Yehud as the place" for the writing of the Old Testament literature.[110] He notes that the process by which books were copied in the ancient world results in every copy being "a newly-created scribal artifact," which could be "as faithful or as deviant as the scribe or his patron determines."[111] He notes that "a conscientious or hardworking scribe in a lifetime of copying could very easily create a 'Deuteronomistic' version of everything that passed through his hands," and that "the Dead Sea Scrolls show that quite complex literary developments can occur over an apparently short period of time."[112] Therefore Davies rejects the view that the Old Testament literature developed slowly and over a long period. He suggests the reader think of the Old Testament literature as simultaneous, although it certainly wasn't homogenous; that is, different writings reflect diverging opinions or debate over certain areas of belief.[113] He agrees with the majority of scholars that the *content* of the Old Testament did not necessarily come only from this period, but was likely based on accumulated stories, fragments, and collections of cultic and legal practices. From this the scribes "constructed a history of the society in which the cult, laws, and ethos of the ruling caste would be authorized," a task he does not think "needs to have taken more than two or three generations."[114]

Although Smith disagrees with Davies that the writing occurred so late, he does characterize it as a cult collection concerned "with the cult of the god Yahweh."[115] Its purpose is to tell "the worshipers of Yahweh what they should do and to persuade them that they had better do it."[116] In the same vein, Dever notes that the Deuteronomist writings are "largely 'propaganda,' designed to give theological legitimacy to a party of nationalist ultra-orthodox reformers" known as the "Yahweh-alone party."[117]

From an archaeological perspective, Dever is of the opinion that most of the Pentateuch is non-historical. He notes that "all responsible archaeologists have given up hope of recovering any context that would make Abraham, Isaac, or Jacob credible 'historical figures,'" and the same can be said of Moses and the Exodus.[118] While the Exodus is not literally or historically true, he thinks the story should be viewed as a "metaphor of liberation."[119] Other non-historical books Dever identifies include Leviticus, Numbers, Joshua, Ruth, Esther, Job, Daniel, Proverbs, Ecclesiastes, Song of Songs, Psalms, and Chronicles.[120]

Dever describes himself as occupying the middle of the road when it comes to the historicity of the Old Testament, with scholars who believe it is entirely historical on one side and those who believe it to be a complete fabrication on the other. He summarizes the middle view as follows: "The biblical writers and editors had some genuine sources, but they did not hesitate to manipulate them. They did this not only with exaggerations and embellishments, but also with additions and even outright inventions, in order to make the stories serve their own ideological agenda. In this regard, they were like most ancient historians. . . . This may be called 'historicized myth,' and that is how much of modern, liberal, critical scholarship regards the Hebrew Bible. . . ."[121]

The process of establishing the Old Testament canon was probably a gradual one. Davies notes that by the third century BCE a rather substantial archive of scrolls had been built up, and by the first century CE there was some tendency toward consensus on the canon, but no consensus yet. Davies observes that while "there is more or less a corpus of literature which defines Judaism," at this time, there remains "a range of attitudes regarding its exact significance."[122] As the process of editing and writing revisions began to come to a halt, which Smith places at approximately 100 BCE,[123] the body of material may have become increasingly venerated. As Davies skeptically puts it, "The ideological triumph of the biblical story is to convince that what is new is actually old," and "What is old contains truth, and the older the truer."[124] Some groups began to read the literature for devotional purposes, and Davies notes that for some of them between 200 BCE and 70 CE, the literature was scripture, while for others it was not. However, after this time and the rededication of the temple by the Maccabees, the writings were fixed and became treated as a canon of scripture.[125]

Lang notes that as the Old Testament canon was being set, monotheism became the yardstick of belief. The biblical canon "could adopt only what was compatible with the Yahweh-alone idea," and "everything else was transformed in the process of revision or thrown out."[126] Much of the prior polytheistic literature was lost. Smith observes that "of course the collectors did not include material in praise of competing deities and their patrons and personnel."[127] He reminds us that this Yahweh-alone bias can be misleading since "although the cult of Yahweh is the principal concern of the Old Testament, it may not have been the principal religious concern of the Israelites."[128] Dever echoes these sentiments when he says that the Old Testament does not show "a picture of what Israelite religion really was, but of what it should have been," and it "almost totally ignores private and family religion, women's cults and 'folk religion,' and indeed the religious practices of the *majority* in ancient Israel and Judah."[129] He further states that the religious ideal espoused in the Old Testament is one thing, while actual practice was another, "reflecting a popular religion that we would scarcely have known about apart from the accidents of archaeological preservation and discovery."[130]

My Journal

What were you raised to believe about monotheism? What do you believe about it today? In what ways does monotheism influence or inform your spirituality currently? What is the divine to you, and how do you describe its nature? Do concepts of oneness or plurality relate in any way to your concept of the divine?

Do you agree or disagree with the findings of scholars and archaeologists about the writing of the Old Testament and the development of the concept of monotheism? What do you find most interesting about their findings? What do you find most unsettling? Do these findings have anything to add to interspiritual discussions?

If these findings were to become the accepted view among practicing Jews and Christians today concerning the development of monotheism, what impact do you think they would have on religion, if any? Would they have any impact on you and your religious beliefs? If so, what?

If you were going to explain monotheism in Western religion to someone, how would you describe it and its origins? How would you explain its impact on Christianity? Do you think Christianity is dependent on a monotheistic view of the divine? Why or why not? In what ways would Christianity change if it were not dependent on a monotheistic point of view?

Monotheism and Interspirituality

Although this has been only a brief overview of a large body of scholarship and research concerning Old Testament writings, the Yahweh-alone party, and monotheism, we think it illustrates some of the issues and findings in this area of the landscape of belief. Rather than having sprung up fully formed, biblical scholarship tells us that monotheism was a religious belief structure that developed over time. In an earlier chapter we defined beliefs as ideas that a person holds to be true. Beliefs often group together into systems or structures that support each other and form a complementary picture of some piece of the world. These systems and structures work to explain reality, why things are the way they are, sometimes so thoroughly that it can be easy to forget the structure is there.

It seems to us that monotheism is an example of such a deeply embedded structure. Most people assume it has simply always been and therefore cannot be approached in the same way as other beliefs and structures. Most people are unaware that monotheism within Judaism developed as a minority movement and remained a minority for hundreds of years, becoming a majority only in the fifth century BCE or perhaps even later. Many people do not realize that throughout most of this time temples, shrines, priests, and ordinary people were routinely polytheistic in their practices and observances and were generally not interested in monotheism. All archaeological findings to date, and they are numerous, support the existence of routine polytheistic practices in the region, both in the temples and among the populace.

Many people assume that Moses wrote the first five books of the Bible and may not know that mainstream biblical scholars have long rejected this, instead placing the writing of the Pentateuch somewhere between 500 and 700 years after Moses supposedly lived. Nor are many people aware that the story of Moses is considered, even by mainstream scholars, to be non-historical, arising from stories that grew over the years and may have begun with Akhenaten.

Many people assume that the other books in the Old Testament were written by the prophets and priests who claim authorship of them, not realizing that scholars have placed their origins much later in time, within two hundred years of the exile, either before or after. The scribes who wrote these books, especially the Deuteronomists, were members of the Yahweh-alone party, and they wrote literature that supported their view. The books they wrote were arranged to present an unbroken history of "Israel," whose existence as a separate nation is still disputed by scholars, and to present an unbroken history of monotheism.

Unless one disagrees completely with these scholars and discounts the archaeological findings on which their positions are based, it seems clear that monotheism must also be seen as an idea, one that came to be adopted as true and around which a belief system was eventually built. Why does it matter whether monotheism can be viewed in such a way? For one thing, acknowledging it as a belief system allows it to be approached as one would any other belief system, and it makes dialogue about it more possible than if it is off-limits to examination. For another, beliefs and belief structures have power in lived reality. They not only group themselves together in mental structures but also stimulate the creation of physical structures in the world. Institutions, buildings, court systems, corporations—all these reflect the underlying beliefs and values of the culture.

While looking at deeply embedded beliefs and structures can be a challenge, it is actually not an unfamiliar activity in our current society, and probably is not for you. Many people are expected to innovate, improve, and invent; find new cures; explore scientific limits; go smaller, faster, and further in computer technology; try out new systems in business; or apply different theories in medicine or education. Each of these activities challenges the status quo and what is believed to be possible. Each new advance or invention destroys what was previously believed to be a boundary and creates a new outer limit. This takes a lot of mental flexibility and ease with the construction and destruction of beliefs. It requires a certain fearlessness in regard to questions and the capacity to process whatever answers or further questions are raised. It also requires the ability to stand outside of the idea just a bit and appreciate that while ideas and beliefs may describe some piece of reality, reality is still something beyond the idea. The belief about it does not *capture* reality, *contain* reality, or *reduce* reality to itself.

Most Pagans approach ideas about God in the same manner. They tend to believe that every belief, every idea, can be examined respectfully and thoughtfully. Where did it come from? How and why was it constructed? Is it beneficial? What does it tell us about reality, and what does it tell us about the people who articulated it? Looking at deeply embedded beliefs is okay, even those on which an entire belief structure is built. Pagans feel this way because they accept that beliefs are ideas, and while ideas hopefully give information about reality, they are not the reality they describe. Looking at ideas about God doesn't threaten the divine in any way, because the divine is not the idea. Put another way, all the concepts of monotheism added together do not amount to the *reality* of God. It is possible that all the concepts of monotheism added together tell us more about the people who formulated them than about God. What monotheism does offer is a collection of beliefs about the divine, not the divine itself. What polytheism offers is a collection of beliefs about the divine, not the divine itself. Perhaps the greatest stumbling block facing interspirituality is this tendency to confuse ideas *about* the divine *with* the divine. This tendency puts these ideas beyond the reach of discussion since the ideas become venerated as the divine itself.

If people would resist the urge to turn their *ideas of God* into God, they would then be left with the ideas, whose merits would be more readily visible. This is a challenging prospect, and it requires soul-searching work from everyone. In our opinion, however, it is an effort that cannot be avoided in today's world if one hopes for a sustainable and peaceful future. Destructive beliefs don't hurt the divine, but they can hurt you and the world. They *already* have hurt the world desperately, and if they haven't hurt you or someone you love personally yet, the unpleasant truth is that they might someday. You have the right and the responsibility to insist that the beliefs you adopt—including those about the divine, whether polytheistic or monotheistic—be healthy and beneficial. We devote ourselves to a discussion of what this means in Part II.

This chapter marks the end of our discussion of the outer landscape of belief, the "what's out there" that comprises the belief systems that go into blended spiritualities. Paganism and Christianity both should look more complex now. History has been a surprise, or maybe a disappointment. The judgment that springs up so readily that Pagansim and Christianity have no common ground and could never share a belief or a practice with each other may not come to mind so quickly now. But remember that this is still the "outer landscape" of what makes up religion. Yet ahead is the "inner landscape," the interior worldview and practice that brings meaning to you and vitality to the world. Even though we now begin to shift attention to "what's inside" of you, remember that the "inside" and the "outside" of the spiritual landscape are equally important, which is why both must be addressed.

Recall Brother Teasdale's statement that interspirituality expresses the fundamental truth that the universe is interconnected and interdependent. He believes that all of the cosmos is one system and that all religions share in it, since the one system underlies all of being, life, and reality. Humanity is connected in its shared experience of physical life and also in its deeper relations to the multidimensional, nonphysical levels of being. While this has always been true, many people are just now expanding into a place where they can see it to be true, and they are looking for ways to express this truth in their spirituality and relationships with others.

The constructed nature of many systems and structures becomes more clear to people as their spiritual capacity expands. This often frees them to observe several points of view at once and appreciate their differences, while still sensing the unity or interdependency that underlies the whole. This ability can lead to a genuine practice of interspirituality, but without it, interspiritual development may not be possible. Since a true interspirituality may depend on a person's developmental unfolding, we now turn our attention to patterns of personal and spiritual development as part of the "what's inside" that makes interspirituality work for many people.

PART II
THE INNER LANDSCAPE

Chapter 6

PERSONAL DEVELOPMENT

In Part I we explored the nature of interspiritual or blended paths and the important role of beliefs. We saw that beliefs tend to group together to form systems, which act as templates for behavior and external structures such as institutions. We examined the outer landscape of Paganism and Christianity to better understand their origins, forms, and practices. In this second part of the book we shift our attention away from the structure and beliefs of the two religions and look instead at what is internal to their *practitioners*.

Beginning with this chapter, we consider what is required internally in order to see the religious landscape with interspiritual eyes. Where do interspiritual eyes come from? Why do some people seem to have them and others do not? One answer is found in research relating to personal and faith development. In this research, social scientists study hundreds of people from different age groups in order to understand the skills and values they exhibit and in order to map the sequence in which they exhibit them. Researchers have discovered a variety of developmental patterns covering areas as diverse as motor skills to cognitive reasoning to moral span to value clusters to types of faith relationships. These developmental patterns appear to emerge in an order that is repeated over and over again. Each developmental capacity brings with it a way of seeing the world and a set of beliefs or values that support this new way of seeing. We believe that understanding this developmental process will help you recognize the where and the why of interspiritual eyes and under what circumstances they may exhibit themselves. So we begin by examining the sequences of development observed in human beings according to two models of personal development, and in the following chapter add the perspective of faith development. In the third and last chapter of this section we explore how concepts themselves expand and contract so that they are capable of supporting various worldviews and an interspiritual perspective.

Growth as Expansion in Capacity

When we speak of personal growth and development, we mean the process of the expansion of human capacities on both the physical and cognitive levels. As motor development unfolds, an individual can be more and do more, beginning with the wiggling of fingers and toes in a crib, to crawling, standing, walking, and running. Each of these motor skills requires the expansion into greater capabilities, which broadens the horizon of what the person can experience. In like manner, as cognitive development unfolds, the individual moves from undifferentiated sense perception to symbols and then language, begins to separate fantasy from reality, and starts to manipulate ideas, first concretely and then abstractly. Look back at your own childhood, and you will recognize that each developmental space you occupied was perfectly adequate for you while you were in it. But as you grew and advanced, the prior skill that had been whole and complete in itself became only a part of a new set of skills. Crawling was adequate at one time, but walking was even more adequate later. When you shifted from crawling to walking, you embraced a greater capacity.

Growth as an expansion of capacity is not limited to human experience but is found throughout the natural world. First there are particles, then atoms, then molecules, then cells, then organs, then organisms. The order of the expansion seems to be important, since cells, for example, do not have to become parts of organs, but no organ can exist that is not comprised of cells. Growth or development is an expansion in which *wholes* expand to become *parts* of greater wholes, whose capacities exceed that of the prior whole. Scientist Arthur Koestler used the word "holon" to describe these nested wholes.[1] Each level of development contains those that came before it and adds its own capacity to it, like layers of an onion. Each layer of the holonic onion tends to "preserve and assert its individuality, such as it is, but at the same time to function as an integrated part of an existing whole, or an evolving whole."[2] If we were to map the holon "onion" of cells to organisms, for example, it would look something like figure 6.1.

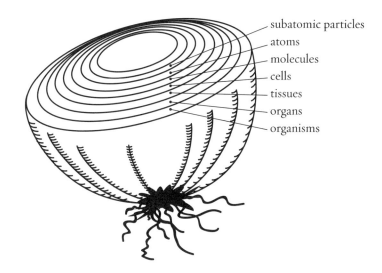

Figure 6.1. Cells to organisms holon onion

Even conceptual or "man-made" creations, such as language and other systems, can be holonic in nature. This book, for example, is an artificial creation of humankind and is built upon a series of nested realities from the human culture of shared meanings and symbols. Although a conceptual creation, its holon can also be mapped. The basic unit of a book, for example, is the individual letter. While whole and complete in themselves, on their own letters can only convey so much meaning. However, when letters are combined, they form words whose meanings far outstrip that of individual letters. Letters are the foundational unit, or center of the onion, and words are the next layer. Individual words, although whole and complete in themselves, can also only convey so much information, but when combined together into phrases and sentences are able to convey blocks of ideas that single words can not. Nor is this the end of the holon, as sentences can be combined into paragraphs, and paragraphs into sections and chapters. Put a dozen or more chapters together, and you are holding this book (fig. 6.2).

This book conveys far more information than, say, the letter *B* alone, and yet each part of this book is comprised of letters. Take the letters away and the book disappears. The basic, foundational unit of the individual letter is still there, never to be lost, but it is now embedded in a wholeness that embraces far more meaning than its parts contain individually. While a book is a physical object, it is also a conceptual creation. Concepts

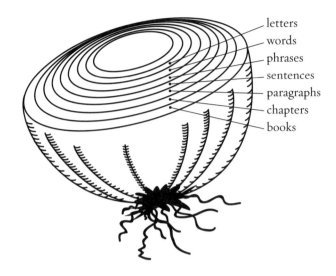

letters
words
phrases
sentences
paragraphs
chapters
books

Figure 6.2. Book holon onion

are also holonic in nature, building from foundational ideas that can expand to hold more and more information or perspectives as the holon grows. This aspect of concepts is very important to understanding how spiritual ideas come to embrace blended paths or interspirituality. We examine the holonic nature of concepts in chapter 8.

Many social scientists believe that human development and faith development also express themselves holonically. In this chapter we outline the sequences of personal development found in two developmental models. We discuss these models and the developmental process in some detail in our book *Pagan Spirituality* (2006), but since we are assuming no prior knowledge in this book, we will cover them again now in an abbreviated fashion. The first model discussed is by Don Beck and Christopher Cowan, based on the work of their mentor, sociologist Clare Graves, which they call Spiral Dynamics. This model identifies a patterned structure of values that emerge sequentially in both people and cultures. They use the term "value memes" to describe these clusters of values.[3] Each turn of the Spiral is associated with a meme or collection of values that evolves through levels of increasing complexity, to which they assign both names and colors.

As we proceed through the value clusters of Spiral Dynamics, we include descriptions of the developmental model created by philosopher Ken Wilber. Wilber's model is based on his research of developmental psychologists and spiritual writers of both East and West. You can see his correlations of the various models of development in a series of charts at the back of his book *Integral Psychology*. If this topic is of interest to you, we recommend these charts as a place to begin a comparative study. Since we wrote *Pagan Spirituality* in 2006, Wilber has changed his developmental sequence in some respects, and we note these changes as we go along.

Spiral Dynamics and Developmental Spaces

The Spiral is a descriptive metaphor for the ways in which people's values grow, change, and expand in a generally predictable order. According to Beck and Cowan, each turn of the Spiral marks the awakening of greater capacities within the individual which are then expressed as values and worldviews. "Values" and "worldviews" are other ways of saying "beliefs," or ideas that are deemed to be important and worthy of support and protection. Change from one group of values or beliefs to the next occurs when pressures build within an existing worldview to the extent that a person is carried to the next set of values, almost as though on a wave. These pressures often build because problems arise that the individual's current value level cannot adequately address; its ability to respond is limited by the beliefs of its worldview, or the individuals in this value cluster may not even be able to "see" the problem adequately because of their worldview. Meeting the problem successfully often means expanding one's values, beliefs, and worldview, so that the problem can be adequately seen and then adequately addressed.

Beck and Cowan see the Spiral of development as fluid, with people and cultures traveling either up or down it in response to life events and conditions. At any time within a given society, different people are at different places on the Spiral, meaning that they subscribe to different clusters of values. However, a culture generally centers around one group of values at a time—perhaps the level occupied by the majority of its members—and so a society can be identified as expressing one set of values more predominantly than another.

This is true for individuals as well, whose selves are composed of many facets such as cognitive abilities, social skills, ethics, aesthetics, altruism, emotions, and sexuality, to name a few. Wilber calls these facets "developmental streams" or "lines of development," and he notes that each of them develops at its own rate, with some expanding faster for some individuals than others. A person may be very highly cognitive but lack a sense of aesthetics or social skills. However, the streams follow the same developmental sequence that he identifies in his spaces of development, discussed in the following paragraphs. Even though an individual has different streams operating at different levels at any one time, Wilber states that the self tends to identify predominantly with one level of development at a time.[4] He also notes that these "lines" or "streams" are essentially equivalent to the model of "multiple intelligences" found in the work of Howard Gardner.[5]

Beck and Cowan assign colors to the turns of the Spiral and divide them into two groups they call First and Second Tier. First Tier levels have to do with "subsistence"—growth of the organism, survival, and cognitive and social development. Without exception, each level of First Tier thinking believes that its way is the only way, and tends to condemn societies and individuals that occupy other levels. Second Tier levels have to do with "being," as subsistence needs have been met and the individual and the culture are free to explore wider frameworks of values. The move from First to Second Tier, which they place at Yellow (explained on page 131), marks a radical shift in thinking, where for the first time the individual is able to see all the levels of the Spiral at once and to travel them at will.

BEIGE. The first value meme Beck and Cowan identify is *Beige*, which they call SurvivalSense. At this level the self is barely aware of itself and its environment, and it is driven by urges to meet its physiological needs. Beige is seen mostly in infants and the elderly, although a person can be arrested here due to illness, accident, disease, or poor nutrition, or regress to this level during emergencies. However, 100,000 years ago, Beige represented cutting-edge thinking that separated humans from animals.[6] At the time of Beige's emergence, the predominant social structure was the band or tribe, and the technology was hunting and gathering. As the sense of self develops, Beige becomes aware of its dangerous and uncontrollable environment and discovers there is strength in numbers. Once it reaches this realization, Beige is ready to transition to the next level.

Wilber identifies a similar stage of development he calls the *sensorimotor* or *archaic*, one of several terms he borrows from social scientist Jean Gebser, and this is a stage normally experienced up to age three. Wilber notes that at this age the self is "fed" primarily by material sustenance such as food, shelter, and clothing.[7]

PURPLE. The second value cluster on the Spiral is *Purple*, also called KinSpirits. Individuals band together to increase their chances of survival. Blood relationships are the connections that are really trusted, while outsiders are viewed with suspicion and hostility. In an attempt to understand the mysterious and uncontrollable world, supernatural explanations are given to events. Myths and legends grow, social and religious events are ritualized, and customs are deeply valued. For the survival of the group or tribe, it is very important to recognize the mystical meanings of signs and obey the desires of spirit beings. Beck and Cowan put the emergence of this level at 50,000 years ago.[8] Purple is in evidence today wherever there are sacred objects, ceremonies, rituals, heirlooms, secret handshakes, and private clubs.

When Purple first emerged, the predominant social structure was the village, and the technology was horticultural. Learning to bond to a group is an essential part of this aspect of development. When Purple begins to see its beliefs as superstitious, it will begin to want less ceremony and move toward a greater sense of self separate from the group. Once Purple reaches this point, it begins to transition to the next level of the Spiral. Beck and Cowan put the current number of the world population in Purple at 10% and the amount of power Purple groups exercise at 1%.[9] Please note that due to the nature of the existence of multiple colors existing or overlapping in any given society, the percentages Beck and Cowan give do not add up to 100%.

Wilber calls this level of development *magical*. Here and in our book *Pagan Spirituality* (2006), we rename this level *egocentric*, since "magick" means specific spiritual practices in Paganism, which is not the meaning given to the word by social scientists. To avoid any confusion due to these different meanings, we have taken the liberty to pick one of the descriptors of this level—egocentrism—as the name for the level itself. This space becomes evident between ages three and six. People at this level may believe that nature and spirit beings obey their wishes, and they have difficulty in seeing or taking the perspective of others. Children at this age, for example, believe that if they hide their heads the rest of their bodies cannot be seen, since after all, *they* can't see anything! In addition to the self's need for material food, Wilber notes that the egocentric self now adds the need for emotional food, which includes bonding, power, and security. The moral span of the self—that is, what the self believes is worthy of respect, protection, or ethical consideration—extends no further than itself and immediate group. If an action benefits the self's immediate circle, then it is considered morally acceptable.[10]

RED. The next turn on the Spiral is *Red*, which Beck and Cowan also call PowerGods. Ego and self-confidence develop and express themselves with a wild impulsiveness. Red eras generally feature imperialism, frontiers, dictators, and warlords. The tribe gives way to strong individuals who take control through the use of both charisma and force. Reds don't plan well for the future and must learn how to govern their use of power. If they do not, they can become exploitative. Healthy Red, however, is creative, adventurous, lusty, and imaginative. Red is seen most often in the "terrible twos" and again in puberty. Beck and Cowan note that most video games are built around Red themes, as they tend to involve warriors, conquerors, and superheroes.[11] Beck and Cowan put the emergence of Red at 10,000 years ago.[12] At the time of Red emergence, the predominant social structure was the empire, and the technology was agrarian.[13] When concerns about its unbridled behavior creep into Red, then it is ready to transition to the next level, which focuses on law and authority. Beck and Cowan put the current number of the world population at Red at 20% and the amount of power Red groups exercise at 5%.[14]

BLUE. The next value meme is the *Blue*, which Beck and Cowan also call TruthForce. Blue gives life meaning through rules and roles and absolute principles contained in a political or religious belief system. Blue societies contain some of the happiest and most contented people, because everyone has a place and stays in it. The society is orderly and punctual and greatly values words and books. Beck and Cowan identify the emergence of the Blue mindset at 5,000 years ago,[15] which corresponds to the period when most of the world's religions were formed. Unfortunately, Blue sees the world in black-and-white terms with no room for gray. Tolerance is low and dogma is at a high. Once Blue stabilizes its world, however, doubts begin to creep in about all this order and conformity. Different versions of The Truth appear and authorities begin to conflict with each other. When this happens, people start disengaging from the opinions of external authorities and begin to rely more on their own opinions. Beck and Cowan put the world population at Blue at 40% and the amount of power Blue groups exercise at 30%.[16]

Wilber calls this developmental space the *mythic*, or *rules-roles*, and notes that it is the first of the "mental" levels.[17] The self moves beyond being nourished solely by material or emotional food and now needs mental food as well. One of the major developments for this level is the awareness of the roles that people play. These roles are seen to be larger than life and may become universal models. The grandiose view the self had of

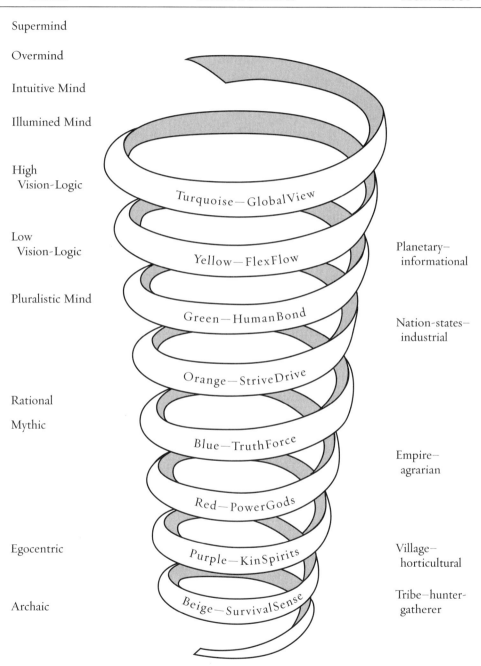

| WILBER'S DEVELOPMENTAL STATES | SPIRAL DYNAMICS | TYPE OF SOCIETY—TECHNOLOGY |

Supermind

Overmind

Intuitive Mind

Illumined Mind

High Vision-Logic

Turquoise—GlobalView

Low Vision-Logic

Yellow—FlexFlow

Planetary–informational

Pluralistic Mind

Green—HumanBond

Nation-states–industrial

Orange—StriveDrive

Rational

Mythic

Blue—TruthForce

Empire–agrarian

Red—PowerGods

Egocentric

Purple—KinSpirits

Village–horticultural

Archaic

Beige—SurvivalSense

Tribe–hunter-gatherer

Figure 6.3. The Spiral with Wilber's developmental states and types of society/technology

itself at the egocentric level is now transferred to the mythic "gods" of this level, which become the self's source of authority. These authorities may include parents, teachers, deities, or the church. The self is conventional at this stage, because it wholeheartedly adopts the beliefs and conventions of its society. The moral span of the self extends to those groups and entities that share its mythology.[18]

ORANGE. The next turn on the Spiral is *Orange*, also called StriveDrive. This turn of the Spiral is noted for its "possibility thinking"—it is entrepreneurial and competitive, and it is often set into motion by a market economy and rising middle class. Beck and Cowan place the emergence of Orange in the West at 1,000 years ago.[19] Orange is accompanied by a rise in nation-states and the beginning of industrialization. The society becomes more literate and wants to read and absorb information. Orange wants opportunities to excel and express itself. Oranges are masterful and self-reliant, but on the downside generally do not think about long-term consequences. Because of their competitiveness they may struggle with interpersonal relationships. Once Orange begins to find its rugged individualism a bit lonely and becomes more interested in the needs of others, it is ready to transition to the next level. Beck and Cowan put the world population in Orange at 30% and the amount of power Orange groups exercise at 50%.[20]

Sometime during late Blue, the individual will transition into the developmental space Wilber calls the *rational*, a space often reached in young adulthood.[21] The rational self begins to develop its logical skills and encounter universal abstractions such as "gravity" and "equality." It discovers that all people experience these abstractions, even those who do not share its mythos. This realization begins to shake the self loose from its dependence on the prevailing myth as its sole source of authority. This shift frequently brings with it a lot of conflict and turmoil. The new rational self will begin to critique the rules of society and rationalize the beliefs of its religion and culture. If the beliefs cannot stand up to rational scrutiny, they may be abandoned. The self's moral span increases to include all the citizens of its country, regardless of their mythic affiliation.

GREEN. The sixth value cluster is *Green*, also called HumanBond. Green is community-oriented and interested in fairness and the proper use of resources. It is concerned with people's feelings and with revitalizing spirituality in a nondogmatic way. Ecological issues and longer-term consequences become important. Gender roles are relaxed, and many other cultural distinctions such as race, ethnicity, and sexual preference diminish in importance. Tolerance is at a high and dogmatism is at a low. Beck and Cowan place the emergence of Green at 150 years ago.[22] The social structure becomes increasingly planetary in scope, and the technology informational. On the downside, Green enforces its own version of "political correctness" and is particularly harsh toward Blue. Because Green is still in First Tier thinking, it believes its point of view is the only correct one no less than the earlier stages on the Spiral. Greens also favor giving entitlements or reparations to groups who have been damaged or overlooked in the past. Eventually the expense of these entitlements stresses the society and Green begins to question the cost of all this togetherness. Global problems may be pressing urgently for a response, and consensus decision-making may be unable to cope with them. At this point a person may transition to the next turn of the Spiral, which also marks the beginning of the Second Tier. Beck and Cowan put the world population at Green at 10% and the amount of power Green exercises at 15%.[23]

Wilber introduces a new developmental space at this level which he calls the *pluralistic mind*.[24] At this level the self can operate within "meta-systems thinking" and be at ease with a variety of perspectives. The self is fully capable of abstract thought and is able to see multiple perspectives at once. Its moral span becomes planetary in scope, encompassing all humans on the planet.

YELLOW. The turn from Green to Yellow on the Spiral marks a significant shift, as *Yellow*, also called FlexFlow, is the first of the levels in the Second Tier. According to Beck and Cowan, the Second Tier brings with it a complexity in thinking that surpasses even the best of the First Tier.[25] Now all the turns of the Spiral can be seen simultaneously and recognized as being legitimate and necessary. Yellow can balance contradictions and is at ease with paradox. It is inner-directed with a strong ethical sense developed from within the self, often created from many sources. Its need for success and acceptance fades and usually favors minimal consumption. Yellow moves freely among all levels of the First Tier of the Spiral and can interact effectively with persons at any level. Beck and Cowan place the emergence of Yellow at fifty years ago, its presence in the world population at 1%, and the power it holds at 5%.[26]

Wilber has divided his previous developmental space he called vision-logic into two levels, which he now identifies as *low vision-logic* and *high vision-logic*, with low vision-logic corresponding to Yellow. Here the view of the self expands to embrace paradigms and is able to see the system as a whole. This space is at home with Yellow's strengths, since it is also capable of holding multiple perspectives, is comfortable with paradox, and has a high level of tolerance for differing beliefs.[27]

TURQUOISE. The final turn on the Spiral is *Turquoise*, which Beck and Cowan call GlobalView. Turquoise digs deeper into the self and discovers that its subconscious aspects can be used and tapped as readily as its conscious aspects. This opens up even more possibilities for ideas and solutions. Turquoise values instinct and intuition equally with the intellect. It senses an underlying order and interconnectedness in the scheme of things. Its interest lies with dynamics that affect the earth as a whole and with macro-level decisions and actions. Turquoise believes that no one can ever know and understand everything, and that reality can only be experienced, not known. Beck and Cowan believe that the Turquoise space is still emerging and so do not yet know all of its characteristics. They put the percentage of Turquoise in the world population at 0.1% and the power it holds at 1%.[28]

Wilber calls this level *high vision-logic* or higher mind, and states that it operates from a global perspective.[29] This is beyond a planetary perspective in that it includes in its moral span a concern for all beings and life on the globe, not just human life. The individual is not only able to sense and operate within paradigms as a whole, but can now function cross-paradigmatically, balancing seeming opposites and paradox with ease.

At this point the Spiral ends, though Beck and Cowan note that the nature of the Spiral is such that new capacities continue to open as humans grow into them. They have reserved a space for the next level of the Spiral, which they call Coral, but they do not know what this level will become once it emerges. Wilber also assigns colors to his developmental spaces, some of which align with the Spiral and some of which do not. For purposes of consistency we have used the Spiral's colors to this point, but since the Spiral ends and Wilber's spaces continue, we now shift to Wilber's colors.

TRANSPERSONAL STAGES. Above Turquoise, Wilber's spaces expand into a region he calls the transpersonal.[30] The levels we have examined so far, from archaic to high vision-logic, he calls *personal* spaces because they are centered in the individual and his or her sense of self. The spaces he calls *transpersonal*, however, shift to a focus on the self as part of a nonphysical or spiritual world. Wilber previously called these spaces the psychic, subtle, causal, and nondual, but now believes these four are *states* of consciousness, not *stages* of consciousness, which we will discuss in a moment.[31]

His new transpersonal stages are called Illumined Mind, Intuitive Mind, Overmind, and Supermind. In these stages, the self moves away from nourishment for the mind and toward nourishment for the soul, which includes such things as meditation, contemplation, visions, and union with the divine. He assigns the color indigo to the level of the Illumined Mind, whose moral span is trans-global.[32] He assigns the color violet to the level of the Intuitive Mind. The third transpersonal level is the Overmind, to which he assigns the color ultraviolet, and finally the Supermind, to which he assigns clear light.[33] Unfortunately we could not locate more in-depth descriptions of these stages by Wilber, although in previous writing he equates the highest levels of development with the self coming to the realization that nothing exists that is not spirit. The self begins to let go of all forms it has adopted for spirit, from nature to deity to archetype, and becomes more formless. The self sees that it is directly connected to spirit and has access to all of consciousness all the time. It also realizes it always had this direct connection, and so comes to an appreciation that every point in development is perfectly adequate for embracing spirit. Not finding anything to the contrary, we have assumed for now that his view of higher development for the transpersonal stages remains in effect.

STATES OF CONSCIOUSNESS. Wilber's prior categories of psychic, subtle, causal, and nondual continue, but as *states*, not stages of development. States describe a certain type of experience within a given stage, like a peak experience, that opens the self to a particular encounter with the universe. These experiences are transient, not permanent. Wilber associates the psychic state with experiences in which the self feels at one with all of nature or the physical world. The subtle state is related to dream states, which a person might enter while daydreaming or doing meditations that require visualization. Wilber compares the causal or formless state to dreamless sleep and spiritual experiences involving vastness and emptiness. He also adds a witnessing state, in which the self is able to observe itself in other states and to dream lucidly. The nondual state is one in which the self is present to the source and ground of all states.[34] People may have such experiences no matter what stage of development or turn on the Spiral they occupy, although they will interpret their experiences according to the value system they hold. In other words, a person in a Red space and a person in a Green one can both have psychic experiences, but they will interpret them differently because of their developmental capacities.

My Journal

Which colors of the Spiral or which of Wilber's developmental spaces do you believe you have occupied? Where are you now? Identify significant events that happened to you while in each space. Look at the beliefs you identified in your journaling for chapter 2. Do you associate any of them with particular capacities of development? When you transitioned from one to the next, what happened to bring on the transition? Was it easy or difficult?

Which value clusters or developmental spaces do you feel comfortable with and why? Which make you uncomfortable and why?

Make a list of several people you are close to or interact with regularly. What value clusters do they tend to act from? Do they shift depending on what they are doing, such as being with family, playing sports, going to work, to church, etc.? Do you tend to navigate or balance more than one level of the Spiral in your life? How does this make you feel?

What does healthy development mean to you? What things might help people to grow healthily? Pick a level of the Spiral and brainstorm on what the healthy expression of it would look like. How might society aid in encouraging healthy development and transitions? How might religion?

The Developmental Picture

Sometimes people wonder why we spend time discussing development when it's not a topic encountered in spiritual or interfaith discussions. We disagree, as we believe that developmental issues are present at *every* discussion of spirituality, whether or not they are openly acknowledged. Why? Because those in the discussion bring their developmental perspective with them and speak directly from it. Developmental perspective shapes spiritual worldview. Whether the connection between a person's development and worldview is obvious or not does not make the connection less real. You need look no further than current world events to know how real the effects of spiritual worldviews can be. Since spiritual worldviews do arise out of developmental capacity, how can those interested in interspirituality afford *not* to educate themselves on these issues? Ignorance is not a viable option.

For these reasons we believe that understanding development is important. Models of development such as Spiral Dynamics and Wilber's spaces explain how people's beliefs and values come together to create an interior capacity that holds a certain way of being in the world. Some of these ways tend to support interspirituality and mutual cooperation while others do not. We are giving you as complete a picture of this subject as we can, first because we think you are entitled to all the knowledge you care to gain, and second because if we skip over what the interior landscape is built upon, the foundation for understanding the rest of this topic will be missing.

We understand that developmental models can feel artificial and unconnected to real life. Social scientists look at growth and development from the *outside*, while you experience it from the *inside*, and the insides don't necessarily feel like the outsides look. These are very different perspectives, but observing growth from a vantage point outside your personal experience offers you a view of the entire inner landscape, regardless of whether you have yet traveled there yourself.

We also understand that some people are uncomfortable with models because they present growth as a progression from one "level" to another in a ladderlike fashion (despite images of spirals), when again, growth doesn't necessarily feel that way when experienced. Due to the holonic nature of development, however, it is legitimate to describe growth in a progressive manner—that is, with new layers building on those that came before. This is not the only way to describe growth, of course, but it is a legitimate way. It can also be difficult to describe a holon without setting up "levels" that move from one to the next. If you doubt this, try describing a holon from its outside and see how your description looks on paper.

However you prefer to imagine the nature of growth and development, the studies of social scientists can help you understand the process and the sequence in which capacities evolve. With this knowledge you can begin to identify value systems at work in certain groups and individuals as you encounter them. You might recognize Red's emphasis on the "strong person" and his or her power in foreign dictatorial governments, local urban gangs, video games, or even your own boss. You might notice Blue's emphasis on orderliness and black-and-white "truth" at work in politics or economics, train schedules, children arguing over the correct rules of a game, or in religions all around the world, including Christianity, Judiasm, Islam, Buddhism, Hinduism, and Paganism.

The values of a given developmental capacity are the same regardless of the context in which they are expressed.

Understanding developmental capacities as *containers of values* can help you appreciate the worldview of a given person or group, and how they might behave in a given circumstance. It can also help you understand the developmental *how* and *why* of those who are attracted to interfaith work, and the *how* and *why* of those who are vehemently opposed to it. With this in mind, we now turn to James Fowler's model of faith development and look more closely at growth in the context of spirituality.

Chapter 7

Faith Development

If growth is an expansion into ever larger capacities and perspectives, what does this mean in terms of faith and spirituality? James Fowler, a noted social scientist, provides an answer. In his studies he interviewed several hundred Christians, and from those interviews he came to observe a pattern of faith development that led him to identify several stages of faith. We examine these stages as follows and compare them to the levels of the Spiral and Wilber's developmental spaces.

Stages of Faith

STAGE 0. The first stage Fowler identifies is the *undifferentiated* or *primal* stage, which is experienced in infancy. Here the self experiences faith as a trust relationship between itself and its caregivers, upon whom it is completely dependent. This stage is essentially equivalent to Wilber's archaic or sensorimotor space and Beige on the Spiral. Once thought and language develop, the self transitions to the next stage.[1]

STAGE 1. The next faith stage is the *intuitive-projective*, which emerges around age two and lasts until age six or seven. The self's principal ways of knowing the world are through perceptions, feelings, and imagination. Deep and long-lasting images are formed here, which are enriched by symbols and stories. Children are beginning to awaken to the world around them and to the mystery of death. They will combine pieces of stories to create an image of God.[2] Since the self cannot separate fact and fantasy, frightening images can overwhelm it. Fowler notes that adults should be very careful with the images they offer to children at this time. As an example, he relates the following story in which a child tells him, "My friend told me that the devil will come up out of a hole in the ground and get me if I'm not careful, so now I won't play in the backyard anymore."[3] This stage seems to correlate to the egocentric space and to Purple and early Red on the Spiral. With the development of certain rational skills, the self begins to transition to the next stage.

STAGE 2. Fowler calls the next stage of faith the *mythic-literal*, which usually emerges around age six or seven and continues to adolescence.[4] The self is less dependent on feelings and fantasies, and it can begin to reverse its thought processes. Reasoning begins to develop, and the self demands empirical proofs to separate fact from fantasy. By now the self is able to see the perspectives of others and becomes focused on right/wrong thinking. Both the world and the self's understanding of it become more orderly, and if the self follows this order it is "good" and will be rewarded; but if it does not, it is "bad" and deserves its punishment. Faith relationships are based on reciprocity, that the self will do what it is supposed to do and God will do what He/She has agreed to do. Faith is also reliant on stories, particularly those of its family and tradition. Knowing the stories of one's people is an important part of the self-identification of this period. God images are fully anthropomorphic (that is, they have human or animal characteristics) and always take the form promoted by the self's family, culture, and religion. The self's thinking is literal and concrete. People are defined by their roles and affiliations, not on their individual personalities.[5] You should recognize the Blue level of the Spiral and Wilber's mythic phase in this description.

STAGE 3. The self can enter the next stage, which Fowler calls the *synthetic-conventional*, as soon as it is able to reflect on its own thinking, an ability that usually emerges in adolescence. The self observes that moral reciprocity does not always occur and so its concept of reciprocal faith from the prior stage begins to break down. In the earlier stages, the divine was rather impersonal—a keeper of order who rewards and punishes. But now the divine becomes deeply personal and knows the self intimately. Fowler remarks that God at this stage resembles a "divine significant other."[6]

Authority still originates from outside the self and the self relies on others to define its faith relationships. Fowler calls this stage conventional because the self derives its sense of identity and faith from the values of others. He calls it synthetic because the self is now capable of pulling together differing elements to create its own stories and sense of identity. Yet this synthesis is largely tacit, or unexamined. While it can pull stories together into a system, the self is not able to reflect critically on the stories themselves. For this reason, the edges of the self's beliefs are surrounded by mystery. Asking too many questions is uncomfortable—there are things the self can't explain and doesn't particularly want to.[7]

The self, then, is still embedded in its story—the stories of its faith, the stories it creates for itself. Symbols of the sacred are confused with the sacred, and any attempt to separate the two is seen as an attack on the divine itself. Many people are currently in this stage, and many will never leave it. Fowler notes that if an individual stops his or her faith development here, he or she will move through life "with a set of tacitly held, strongly felt but largely unexamined beliefs and values."[8] The transition to the next stage can be triggered by the individual leaving home, by finding the self at odds with authority, or observing conflicts between authorities.

STAGE 4. This faith stage, which Fowler calls *individuative-reflective*, can emerge when the self's reliance on external authority is disrupted, and if the self is willing to take responsibility for its own choices. What was previously tacit and unexamined now becomes explicit. The self is able to choose its own values, beliefs, and commitments. The best time for this emergence is during a person's twenties. If it happens later, Fowler notes that the transition will likely take longer and cause more disruption to the self's network of roles and relations.[9]

The process of individuation is not easy. The self is busy questioning and reflecting critically, and begins to detach itself from symbols. That is, it begins to realize that symbols, representations, and stories about something are not the thing they represent. This is the same concept discussed in chapter 5, about not turning *ideas about God* into God. The self is able to make this separation now and deal with beliefs more objectively. Fowler calls this process *demythologizing*, and he notes that it brings both gains and losses.[10] On the side of losses, the self's reliance upon and trust in the truth is forever interrupted. As Fowler puts it, "for those who have enjoyed an unquestioning relation to the transcendent and to their fellow worshipers through a set of religious symbols," demythologization can bring on "dislocation, grief and even guilt."[11] On the side of gains, however, what was accepted tacitly and responded to without reflection can now be identified and conceptualized. Symbols are "broken open" such that their inner meaning can be removed and communicated with directly. Weighing and comparing a variety of meanings is now possible. The inner capacity of the individual has expanded. You may recognize Wilber's rational space and the beginnings of Orange in this description.

STAGE 5. This stage, which Fowler calls the *conjunctive*, is usually experienced in midlife if it is reached.[12] In this stage, the self goes beyond the rational constructs it created in the prior stage and begins to let reality speak with its own voice, regardless of the impact this voice has on the self's worldview or sense of security. The self can see both sides of an issue simultaneously and accepts that truth "is more multidimensional and organically interdependent than most theories or accounts of truth can grasp. Religiously, it knows that the symbols, stories, doctrines, and liturgies offered by its own or other traditions are inevitably partial, limited to a particular people's experience of God and incomplete."[13] The self appreciates its own and others' symbols because it understands the greater wisdom they reflect, and it is ready to have encounters with other belief systems. In the prior stage, the self identified itself with its conscious awareness. Now the self incorporates the subconscious and unconscious as well. Fowler notes that its commitment to justice "is freed from the confines of tribe, class, religious community or nation."[14]

This stage seems to correlate with Wilber's vision-logic spaces and their skills in appreciating multiple perspectives. The Green level of the Spiral also seems related to conjunctive faith, with its concerns for justice across all lines of creed or ethnicity, its global view, its nondogmatic interest in spirituality, and its ability to be at ease with multiple perspectives.

STAGE 6. The last stage Fowler identifies is *universalizing*. At this stage the self makes the divine real in its person. As Fowler describes it, the person becomes "a disciplined, activist *incarnation*—a making real and tangible—of the imperatives of absolute love and justice."[15] Individuals in this stage usually detach from their local communities and come to identify with a community that is universal in scope. They challenge unjust social, political, and religious structures, and they do so without regard for their own safety. They may indeed be considered subversive by the general culture. This does not mean that these people are perfect or always easy to get along with, and Fowler notes that some do tend to become overly detached and isolated. However, they are generally comfortable with people at any developmental space and from any religion. Examples

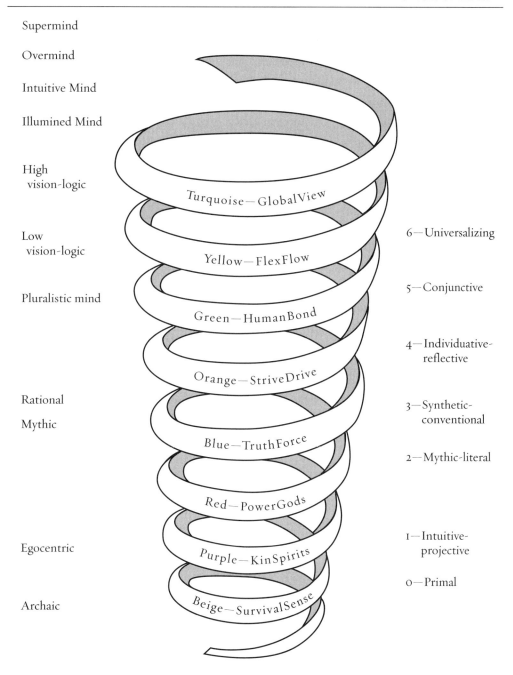

WILBER'S DEVELOPMENTAL STATES	SPIRAL DYNAMICS	FOWLER'S STAGES OF FAITH
Supermind		
Overmind		
Intuitive Mind		
Illumined Mind		
High vision-logic	Turquoise—GlobalView	
Low vision-logic	Yellow—FlexFlow	6—Universalizing
Pluralistic mind	Green—HumanBond	5—Conjunctive
	Orange—StriveDrive	4—Individuative-reflective
Rational		3—Synthetic-conventional
Mythic	Blue—TruthForce	2—Mythic-literal
	Red—PowerGods	
Egocentric	Purple—KinSpirits	1—Intuitive-projective
		0—Primal
Archaic	Beige—SurvivalSense	

Figure 7.1. The Spiral with faith development correlated

he gives of people who have reached this stage include Gandhi, Martin Luther King, Jr., and Mother Teresa, among others.[16]

Sociologist Nicola Slee, who studies faith development in women, generally agrees with Fowler's model but believes he overemphasizes the development of analytical thinking and detachment in the higher levels of spiritual development. She notes that women at more advanced levels of faith development continue to emphasize intuitive knowledge, imagination, concrete forms of thinking, and metaphor, for which Fowler scores them lower.[17] Also, women emphasize relational forms of faith over those that are more abstract and impersonal. She notes that Fowler, on the other hand, tends to equate growth with separation from the demands of relationship. Slee observes that the women she interviewed stayed conscious of relational faith throughout every stage. As they advanced, women moved toward a consciously owned faith, not by distancing themselves from relationship and commitments, "but precisely in and through these relational ties."[18]

Perhaps there is a correlation between the universalizing stage and Second Tier thinking on the Spiral. In the Second Tier, the self breaks free of its attachment to any of the lower levels of the Spiral and can see them all simultaneously. With that perspective, the self can readily see the issues and blind spots, as well as the strengths, of the various levels. It also has an unusual ability, at least according to First Tier's perspective, to travel the levels of the Spiral at will and be able to interact with the levels in ways they can understand. The Second Tier self is concerned with the overall health of the Spiral, not just that of one level, one group, one country, or one set of political, corporate, or religious concerns. If Fowler's universalizers represent Second Tier thinking within a religious context, such people will be rare and misunderstood, as the edge of their horizon is significantly larger than that of their contemporaries.

My Journal

Do you recognize any of the stages of faith as places you have visited in your spiritual journey? If so, which ones? What was your spirituality like in those stages? What stage do you believe you are in now?

Which stage would you like to be in and why? Would your life change if you were in that stage? If so, how? Would any of your beliefs change? If so, which ones and how would they change?

Have you ever had a symbol, practice, or belief lose its meaning for you? What happened? How did you feel while going through this experience? How do you feel about it now? How did your spirituality change because of it?

Relationships with Myth

In our years of teaching, we have noticed that the relationship our students have with myth or story often changes over time. You will recall that Fowler describes myth as a "narrative structure of meaning."[19] This structure of meaning can be personal to an individual or shared among members of a group, but the self will give meaning to its experiences through the use of a story about itself and its world. In regard to spirituality, the issue is not *whether* the self has a story concerning its spiritual identity, despite the exercise we gave you in chapter 3, but what the *nature* of its relationship to the story is. Myth is a tool humans have created for their use, but it is also a tool that, in turn, helps create the self and its culture. In other words, the self uses myth both to give meaning to its world, and also to explain the meaning it is already giving to the world.

If the self's moral span expands from caring only about itself to caring about all creatures, then how does this process impact the story it adopts about how the world works? How does the self interact with or adapt its story about what is worthy of its moral regard? We could ask many such questions. What happens to the self's myth when it moves from unexamined belief to rational scrutiny? How does the self relate to story when its source of authority is external to itself, and how does it relate to story when the source becomes internal? How does the self approach myth when it is comfortable holding multiple perspectives, as opposed to only one? Based on our observations of our students and others in teaching situations, we have come to identify the following six *relationships* to myth:

MYTHIC TANGIBLE. We call the first relationship with myth the *mythic tangible*. Here the self is learning all sorts of things about its own identity, its family, and its immediate surroundings. Story tells the self who it is—the oldest child, the youngest child, a member of a family, a certain country, a particular church. It learns about the world through its senses and is told what is safe and what is not. Myth explains why things happen in the world and the powerful forces that are behind those events. If the story contains powerful beings, the self will also be instructed on how to relate to them, bringing it a sense of safety, security, and reassurance. If the self does certain things, all will be well; if it doesn't, the self and possibly the group could perish.

Since the self in this mythic relationship tends to deal with the world immediately and concretely, this concreteness is evident in its spiritual mythos. A certain spot of ground is holy; the divine enters a physical object, such as a bush, dove, or volcano; blood is protective; amulets carry power; certain objects have healing powers; natural phenomena carry messages from spirit; certain animals are holy or taboo; menstruation or pregnancy is holy or taboo; illness is divine punishment; one can be cursed by an evil eye; rituals must be performed correctly with appropriate clothing and tools at the right time of the moon; and so on. In other words, the physical world is the embodiment or carrier of spirit, which makes the divine tangible and *real* to the self in an extremely powerful way that no other mythic relationship will ever match.

MYTHIC LITERAL. If the self's rational abilities develop, then its relationship to myth will change. The self begins to notice that behind or beyond the sacred tangible *things* it had been focused on previously lies the *story* that tells it these things are sacred. Now the story takes center stage and gains tremendous power. It is beautiful, it is pure, it is magnificent, and it is true. The divine has opened itself and touched the intelligence of humankind with this story. The self feels it can study the particulars of this myth its entire life and never plumb its depths. The self orders its life around the letter and law of the story, and believes that doing so makes it right with the divine, since the divine gave this myth to be followed. The self does not question the story, as it is immersed in it entirely and finds it to be so beautiful and powerful that it is dismayed if others do not embrace it. The existence of others who reject the myth, or have their own story to which they ascribe similar power, is in fact threatening to the self. Borrowing one of Fowler's terms, we call this relationship to myth the *mythic literal*.

This relationship with myth brings its own sense of safety, found in the cohesion, order, and predictability of many people following the expectations of the same story. As this relationship matures, the story will be extensively written about through exposition, theology, instruction, and learned discourse. This relationship with myth brings with it great power, not only through the governmental support that often accompanies it, but also through the security of knowing the truth with certainty.

MYTHIC RATIONAL. As reason keeps discoursing on the myth, it will eventually ask whether the myth itself is rational. Previously, whatever supported the myth's point of view was considered to be rational, or supported by reason, as the myth was the final measure of what is correct. But as reason progresses it will relentlessly hold everything up to examination, including its own measuring standard. The self comes to realize that behind or beyond the story lies a rationale or purpose for it, and also a mind or minds that created it. The self shifts from being focused on the details of the story to being focused on the *purposes* the story serves. Borrowing a term from Wilber, we call this relationship to story the *mythic rational*.

As the self subjects its mythic narrative to rational examination, it comes to realize that certain universals apply to everyone. All of humanity is born and dies and experiences the ebb and flow of life currents and seasons. The joys and griefs of Jewish people appear to be the same joys and griefs as of Christian people, and of socialist people and capitalist people, and of conservative people and liberal people. The self notices that the avowed purposes of many systems are often similar despite differences in belief and structure. This awareness of universality is new, and can sometimes burst upon the self suddenly and unexpectedly; or it can creep up gradually until the self realizes one day that it feels differently.

MYTHIC GLOBAL. When the self comes to an awareness of universality, it often moves into a relationship with story we call *mythic global*. Here is where the skills of holding multiple perspectives and standing in the midst of paradox combine into an appreciation of story in its numerous forms. Like a flash of lightning that illuminates the entire landscape for an instant, the mythic global self sees the entire range of myth at once. As with Second Tier thinking and the ability to see all levels of the Spiral simultaneously, the self gains a new appreciation for story as a whole, whether it is political story, economic story, or religious story. Just as the Second Tier flexibly navigates through the Spiral at will, so the mythic global self comfortably visits and engages with any myth as a narrative structure. The world of myth and story, both past and present, offers itself up as a banquet that the self can sample or devour at will. The self may become quite a student of world religions, mythologies, or the developmental process. It may be astonished it did not see these interrelationships before.

For a time, the self can be very absorbed by this global realization, busy exploring the contours, messages, and uses of myth by people over the centuries. One day, however, it may suddenly sense that behind the stories lies a deeper pattern, that myth wraps universal creative patterns around a story. The story's function or purpose becomes less important and the underlying *patterns* are what gain the self's attention. The self begins a relationship with these patterns, which may be visualized in a number of ways. The

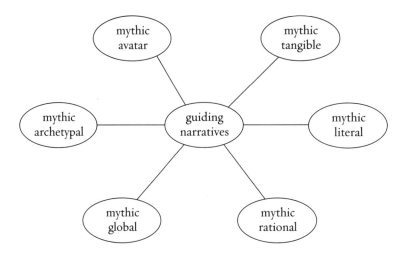

Figure 7.2. Mythic relationships

self may anthropomorphize them into human or other forms or it may not; it may deify them or it may not. We call this relationship with myth the *mythic archetypal*.

MYTHIC ARCHETYPAL. In wrestling with the question of patterns and what they are, the self may identify spiritual realms where beings or elements of consciousness exist. It may form relationships with these spiritual realms or beings. At earlier points the self interacted with spirit beings; indeed, its myth of origin likely contains angels, jinnis, spirits, saints, or demons, and how they are to be approached or avoided. The experience now, however, is different. The self goes outside the mythic structure that previously defined such beings for it and approaches the energetic patterns directly. It is experiencing *something*, but what is it? The self may be very hesitant to apply labels. Is creative patterning a collection of deities and spirits, or is it the underlying structure of the physical world (such as the quantum realm), or is it something else altogether? It may call this realm of mysteriousness the realm of spirit, or it may not. As it encounters, struggles with, and navigates through this realm, it begins to have moments where it not only feels like a *part* of the creative patterning, but *becomes* the creative patterning. It gets sucked into the multidimensionality of the universe, if you will, and becomes one with it. These experiences are very difficult to verbalize. This vastness of perspective can hardly be put into words, and if the self were to describe it, how should it do so? The often fleeting nature of these experiences and the difficulty in describing them, plus the attempt to find people with whom to share them, can make this relationship with myth challenging.

MYTHIC AVATAR. A final relationship with myth that we have observed occurs when the self gives up speaking in terms of archetypal forms or other concepts it has relied on, including images and constructs it had for God. When we have talked to such people about their inner process, they tend to speak in terms of surrendering to what is, without necessarily needing to label or define it, or even understand it. Here the self realizes that myth is a vehicle whose purpose is not to describe something *external* to people (such as God, angels, ethical rules, and so on), but to stimulate internal *transformation* by directing people's attention to some truth about themselves or reality. We call a person in this relationship to myth a *mythic avatar*.

The avatar may set about to create opportunities for people to experience directly the transformative potential that they have sensed within story. They may do this by means of classes and retreats, or more indirectly by how they live their daily lives. They offer the opportunities, and from there leave the powers of transformation to do their work in their own way. In our experience the avatar tends to take people at face value—whatever their beliefs, problems, or skills—and allows them to discover whatever insights they are led to at the moment. The avatar seems to have a great deal of trust that the universe, the divine, or spirit—however they envision deep layers of being—will guide the transformational process in the way it needs to go. They do not seem attached to the outcome of this process or to any particular myth or its interpretation. While they often use story in their transformational work, they find a dozen or more ways to interpret aspects of it, some of which can be quite unique. We have never seen avatars use myth to sanction a particular religious viewpoint or dogma, although they may focus on one body of myth rather than another, depending on the needs of the situation or group.

The avatar may also offer opportunities for people to live their transformations more consciously day to day. This may happen through the creation of organizations, churches, retreat centers, magazines, intentional communities, or service opportunities such as relief work or activism. These opportunities will likely be open to people of all faiths and ideologies, with no requirement to join a particular religion or denomination. All of the avatars we have met are actively engaged in some fashion with the people and needs around them, even if only quietly and privately, often serving as catalysts of change for others just by being who they are.

We are not social scientists and so do not claim that the relationships to myth we have observed are scientifically verifiable, are the only relationships possible, or that they must progress in a set manner. We know people who have experienced more than one of these relationships over time, and have done so in the general order described. It does seem that some relationships might need a certain degree of life experience or maturity to arise. For example, we have never met a six-year-old mythic globalist. We do not claim it is impossible, only that we have never met one. The time spent in a given relationship does not seem to be of a set period either. We know people who spend the bulk of their lives in one mythic relationship, and others who touch on a relationship so briefly that it is almost as though they were not there at all before moving on. It also seems to us that people are able go back and forth between more than one relationship as circumstances require, or operate out of two simultaneously, particularly if they are consciously working with ways of understanding story. In any event, we have found an awareness of the different mythic relationships to be helpful to us in planning effective classes and rituals.

Trading Places

Here is an exercise to stimulate your imagination. Imagine that Paganism and Christianity have traded places in history. If Neo-Paganism as we know it now had arisen centuries ago, instead of Christianity, what might it look like today? If you wish, write a story about what might have happened, or a newspaper article as though you were a journalist covering this topic.

Now imagine that Christianity did not begin until the 1950s in the United States. It is a new religion, arising in a postindustrialized society and has only existed fifty or sixty years. What might it look like today? What issues is it addressing in a modern world? What do its worship forms and organizational structure look like? How many members does it have after two generations? Does it have scriptures or not? Again, write a story or article about it if you wish.

Developmental Expectation

Fowler believes that the goal of faith development is "not whether we and our companions on this globe become Muslims, Jews, Buddhists, Taoists, Confucianists or Christians," but rather "will there be *faith* on earth and will it be *good* faith—faith sufficiently inclusive so as to counter and transcend the destructive henotheistic idolatries of national, ethnic, racial and religious identification and to bind us as a human community in conventional trust and loyalty to each other and to the Ground of our Being?"[20] He believes that religions need to be accountable for their contributions, or lack thereof, to *good* faith on the planet. It is their role to nurture persons "who are fit to be partners in a global covenant" of faith relations.[21]

To accomplish this, he states that religion must first take faith development seriously, and it can do this by acknowledging that development happens and learning about the sequence in which it happens. Religious groups should also be aware, Fowler advises, of the tendency to center around one stage of development to the exclusion of other ones. That is, a given community will have conscious and unconscious images of what adult faith looks like and will aim its classes, services, and political governance toward that level. These patterns will prepare children and adults to grow *up to* the expected level of development but not beyond it, and persons joining from outside will be attracted to the group because of the particular level of development it expresses. These factors together set an effective limit on the growth of faith in that community. Based on his research, he believes the majority of faith communities in the United States operate at the synthetic-conventional (or Blue) level, with a slight push to the next.[22]

Fowler also believes that religions need to re-envision the nature of truth, which from the Blue synthetic-conventional perspective is identical to *belief*. This is the tendency, discussed earlier, to make the *idea of a thing* into the thing itself. From this perspective, propositional or doctrinal statements "are supposed to 'contain' truth."[23] Fowler, however, sees faith as relational, not propositional, as a "pledging of trust and fidelity to another" and a way of "moving into the force field of life trusting in dynamic centers of value and power."[24] These centers of value and power change as faith development occurs. Faith communities that encourage growth need to be prepared to support people who are struggling with doubt and issues of belief, and, we would add, whose views of spirituality are changing because they are moving through various relationships to myth.

Communities that succeed in creating a nurturing space for growth in their members create what Fowler calls a *climate of developmental expectation*. This climate takes the full development of faith seriously and provides rites of passage and opportunities for service that are faith-stage appropriate.[25] We believe such a climate is in essential harmony with the goal of keeping all the levels of the Spiral healthy. It encourages healthy expression of faith at each stage and keeps an open-ended attitude so that individuals can grow as far as they are capable. It also seems to us that such a climate supports Wilber's four quadrants and integral development. A healthy and integrated climate of developmental expectation will obviously not neglect inner development nor encourage it at the expense of the external world, the sciences, or the environment. No quadrant can discount or hold the others captive for faith development to be truly nurtured. Wilber muses that "clearly, the interior quadrants have some catching up to do. What good is it to continue to focus on the exterior technological wonders before us . . . if all we carry with us is an egocentric or ethnocentric consciousness?"[26]

Rationality in Religion

If Beck and Cowan are correct and Blue is fading while Orange is peaking in the United States, then a mythic rational approach should have been building for a while. Indeed, the transition to mythic rational has been underway since the nineteenth century. Religious historian Karen Armstrong notes that the evangelical Christianity of the mid-1800s in the United States was heavily influenced by rationalism. She observes that it was based on a literal reading of the Bible by lay church members, not clergy, and on a personal conversion in Christ and a rejection of all forms of mediation between the individual and God.[27] Historian Richard Tarnas believes this change arose from the Reformation generally, as Luther taught that religious authority existed in each individual, who must read and interpret the Bible for himself or herself according to his or her own conscience and personal relationship to God.[28] The Reformation stressed discovering the truth for oneself and the importance of subjecting all beliefs to rational testing. Entrenched doctrines were to be confronted, and reality was to be determined without the interference of authorities or tradition. This change gained steam from the sixteenth to the eighteenth centuries.

This is a very self-reliant and rational version of fundamentalism. It left the Red-Blue of the Crusades and the Blue of the Middle Ages behind and became the Blue-Orange of the Enlightenment. By the nineteenth century, reason's interest in fairness and the application of universal principles was also evident in that era's focus on social reform, including feminism, abolition, women's suffrage, penal reform, and educational reform. Armstrong notes that what we know as fundamentalism in the United States is a modern and rationalist development, since the way in which its members read the

Bible was unheard of in earlier societies. She observes that fundamentalists treat their doctrines as "facts" in the same way that scientists treat their data as "facts," which demonstrates a "way of being religious in an age that values the logos of science above all else."[29]

As the mythic rational approach has grown, there has been a proliferation of Christian writing explaining its theology and practices, demonstrating its logic, its reasonableness, its relevance to today. Scholars intricately trace the history and origins of the scriptures, as we have seen over the last several chapters. Theologians and scholars debate whether archaeology does or does not support its claims. Where the evidence does not match the insistence of tradition, it is tradition that is giving ground. The myth's stories are explained, explored, taken apart, and reassembled in innumerable ways in order to make them more meaningful and to plumb them for more and deeper nuggets of understanding. This is the work of the mythic rational relationship.

This is not the Red-Blue Christianity that used the might of armies to impose its structures by force as it built its empire throughout the Western world. It is not the settled Blue of the Middle Ages, which concerned itself with maintaining order by purifying its members of error, as with the Inquisition. Today's Christianity, at least in the West, is most definitely Blue-Orange. It has combined literalism with rationality in a way that focuses on the "facts" of religion, as Armstrong notes. As Christianity continues to move toward full Orange in the West, literalism for its own sake will no longer be as attractive. Already beliefs are being subjected to the light of reason and asked if they are supported by findings in science, history, and archaeology. Beliefs will have to pass muster with concepts of fairness and equality and will be expected to do their part in creating a just world. Meanwhile, Orange-Green Christianity is also developing.

As we watch this unusual mixture of mythic literal and mythic rational Christianity progress, we are interested to see what develops. Millions of mythic literal Christians keep pushing the envelope of the mythic for more ideas and more interpretations, and find their literalism increasingly challenged. While the mythic rational hungers for information and facts and mental food, what happens when the facts thus discovered challenge the literal and historical truth of the myth? Much of the research set out in chapters 3 through 5 concerning early church formation, the creation of the gospels, the Old and New Testaments, and the relationship of Christianity to ancient Mystery religions, is a product of mythic rational investigation. What will be the impact of such research on Blue and Blue-Orange Christianity?

One response, of course, is to ignore this research or explain away what cannot be ignored. Doing so eliminates the discomfort raised by the findings of these scholars and scientists and keeps the self's belief filter intact. Beck and Cowan, you will remember, state that people transition to the next level of the Spiral when problems or issues arise that the self's current capacities cannot solve. These problems and issues create a tension and internal pressure that propel the self into finding a solution, which on the Spiral means that the person may transition up a turn and adopt a new cluster of values that are able to address the problems and issues at hand. Eventually, new issues will arise that again create discomfort, and so the individual continues to grow and expand to the extent he or she is able or willing. Since it is the discomfort of inadequate solutions, values, and worldviews that often triggers growth, this means growth can be an uncomfortable proposition. One way to avoid the discomfort is simply to stop moving on the Spiral. Beck and Cowan note that individuals might do this by either arresting at a given level, which involves a clinging to the status quo, or by completely closing.[30] In the latter case, the permanently closed self will not be able to "see" the problems and issues that could cause it discomfort, and this also makes the problems go away.

Some people in all religions will choose this response to avoid the challenges that the mythic rational and mythic global worldviews will otherwise demand of them. But not all will, and probably not even most. According to Beck and Cowan, Wilber, and Fowler, it is natural for people to move on and keep growing. Where will the millions of Christians in the United States currently at the mythic literal to mythic rational levels go next in their faith development? What is unprecedented is not the probability of their transition, but the *numbers* of them who are poised to do so or are already doing so in the West. In the history of humankind, a world religion has never grown a population of millions up to the edges of the mythic rational before.

Wilber identifies a problem that only complicates matters. He asserts that science has claimed Orange for itself, and in reaction religion has claimed Blue for itself. A line has been drawn across which religion refuses to pass and science will not let it pass, and that line is the division between Blue and Orange. Modern religion is pushing against this boundary, but meets with resistance from both within and without, and so has not crossed it. As millions of people keep pushing against it, pressure builds. Wilber calls this the Orange pressure cooker. As he puts it, the lid of the pressure cooker sits on the point where "ethnocentric fundamentalist beliefs run into worldcentric reason and postconventional morals."[31]

At the heart of the pressure cooker is a confusion—religion has been confused with being pre-rational, mythic literal, and Blue, and science is confused with being all there is to Orange. According to Wilber, this happens when one *level* of development gets confused with an entire *line* of development. Then if a particular level is despised, the entire line is despised. If a particular level is revered, the entire line is revered. In both cases development is frozen, because people do not feel that it is possible to move on.[32] If being religious is equivalent to being mythic literal, for example, how does one be religious *and* mythic global, or religious *and* mythic archetypal, when both the scientist in the laboratory and the preacher in the pulpit say it is not possible? Wilber notes that the pressure cooker is especially agonizing for college-age youth, as they have reached the age of transition from Fowler's Stage 3 to Stage 4 (Blue to Orange) and do not know how to go forward. As Wilber puts it, these college students "cannot discuss their faith with their professors, who are mostly orange to green, and who ridicule it," and yet "they are no longer really comfortable with the mythic and ethnocentric version" of their religious beliefs.[33] This leads many students to believe that their only choice is either to remain forever at Blue or renounce their faith. The Orange pressure cooker does not suggest other options and so these students "have no avenues where they can explore the orange or higher levels in the development of spiritual intelligence."[34]

How did religion become confused with being pre-rational, mythic literal, and Blue? Well, for one thing, most world religions were created at moments in history when society was pre-rational but moving into the mythic literal and Blue worldviews. Most scriptures were also written during these periods and affirm the mythic literal perspective as *the way* to be religious, since at that time it was. According to Wilber, the underlying myths of all religions, Christian and Pagan both, arose in mostly Beige, Purple, and Red societies and probably could not be recreated in a world of cameras and film. Wilber is convinced that we will never get a new supply of myths—just try videotaping Moses parting the Red Sea, for example.

Now the only ones to routinely experience Beige, Purple, and Red are children. Wilber says that "the 5-year-old child today [produces] all of the major contours of the world's great myths" in their magical, pre-rational view of the world.[35] Spiritual philosopher Richard Potter puts it slightly differently when he says, "Wisdom regarding ways to live a meaningful life is saved within the myths and stories of a culture and can be deciphered, layer-by-layer, as consciousness awakens and develops in the individual."[36] Orange and Green need to be careful to remember that myths and stories are very precious legacies.

They are irreplaceable, for a number of reasons, and it is not a matter of derision that they originated from early levels of development. Recall our discussion of how people experience different relationships with myth—for the mythic tangible self, story holds identity and a sense of safety; for the mythic global self, it becomes a banquet that brings both appreciation and a struggle with paradox; for the mythic archetypal, it brings a universal creative pattern to be explored. We believe this is part of the "layer-by-layer" deciphering of myth that Potter refers to. When the self grows developmentally it does not abandon myth, but instead sees new worlds within myth because it has eyes it never had before.

Wilber says that the solution to the Orange pressure cooker is to be found in allowing religion to move on so that it can embrace Orange and later forms of spirituality (even those that include atheism and agnosticism). For this to be successful, religion must be willing to relax its fixation on the mythic literal and open itself to worldcentric, mythic global views. By the same token, science must relax its fixation upon Orange, as it does not own the Orange level.[37] But since religions control the pre-rational body of myth and the legitimacy that is given to beliefs about it, Wilber is convinced that only religious institutions can give permission for religion to move on into Orange and higher levels.[38] So far it seems that most religious authorities are not relaxing their official stance on mythic literalism, and the Orange pressure cooker continues. Perhaps some authorities would like to prevent a full transition to the mythic rational and the mythic global and beyond. But can they really stop the momentum of millions of people pushing against the Blue-Orange boundary? We think the transition is impossible to stop. Ultimately, no institution can keep all of the people from transitioning all of the time, and certainly not millions of people. We believe the days of the Orange pressure cooker are numbered.

You may be tempted to think that this is only the opinion of scientists or secularists who don't really understand what's going on inside Christianity. If so, you may be interested in the findings recently published by the Barna Group, a Christian research and survey organization that has tracked demographics and beliefs within Christianity for decades. This chapter was finished and ready to go to the publisher when the president of the Barna Group, David Kinnaman, released findings concerning trends among young people in a book called *unChristian: What a New Generation Really Thinks about Christianity . . . and Why It Matters*.[39] He identifies several trends that are relevant here.

One of the items the Barna Group tracks is the percentage of people in various age groups who consider themselves "outsiders" to Christianity. These people may be members of other faiths or members of none; some are former Christians. Kinnaman notes that the percentage of "outsiders" among older generations, such as the Boomers and the generation older than the Boomers, is generally steady at around 25%. However, the next two younger generations, which he calls Busters and Mosaics, have increased this percentage to about 33%, and if we look only at the youngest segment (sixteen- to twenty-nine-year-olds), it climbs to 40%. This is a significant increase by generation. Extrapolated out to the U.S. population at large, this means that 34 million people between the ages of eighteen and forty-one consider themselves "outsiders" to Christianity.[40]

The "outsiders" give a number of reasons why they remain outside Christianity, but Kinnaman notes several responses as being typical of the answers received. One person, for example, said, "Most people I meet assume that *Christian* means very conservative, entrenched in their thinking, antigay, antichoice, angry, violent, illogical, empire builders; they want to convert everyone and they generally cannot live peacefully with anyone who doesn't believe what they believe."[41] If you were to categorize this response by worldview, color on the Spiral, or relationship to myth, how would you classify it? Some of the descriptions could be found in a number of developmental spaces (such as angry), but many or even most of them are clearly mythic literal Blue. If this response is typical, as Kinnaman tells us, then it appears that the younger generations are increasingly repelled by Blue faith, which would be consistent with Beck and Cowan's position that Blue is fading in the United States, Orange is peaking, and Green is significantly gaining ground. Even those surveyed who identified themselves as active Christians shared many of the same criticisms of the faith as "outsiders," and even one-third of active Christians say that the way Christians act and the things that they say make them embarrassed to be a Christian.[42]

The single most common positive statement about Christianity selected by "outsiders," at 82%, is that it "teaches the same basic idea as other religions."[43] This is a mythic global statement if we ever heard one! How interesting. Additional findings about this group further support a shift to a mythic global mindset; indeed, Kinnaman's description of the sixteen-to-forty-one age group could be taken straight from Beck and Cowan's list of Green-level values. For example, Kinnaman says that these young people's lives "consist of an eclectic patchwork of diversity, perspectives, friendship, and passions," that they are exposed to more philosophies and ideas about life than any other generation,[44] that they "resist simplistic answers" and "relish mystery, uncertainty, and ambiguity," that they are not "bothered by contradictions," and that they are comfortable with "nuance and subtlety, expressing awareness of context in complicated and intricate issues."[45] In regard to intercultural and interfaith attitudes, Kinnaman says that these young folks enjoy being around people whose views differ from theirs in order to "push and expand their opinions."[46] A spirituality that focuses on dos and don'ts "rings hollow" to them.[47]

Kinnaman notes that the majority of "outsiders" are not strangers to Christianity; in fact, 65% of eighteen- to forty-one-year-olds say they have been Christian at one time and made a commitment to Jesus earlier in their life.[48] Kinnaman believes that if they could make such a commitment and then leave, they probably didn't have a deep faith to begin with. That could be a true, or perhaps the kind of faith they became interested in over time does not match the faith being offered in church. As Fowler has shown, faith looks very different from one stage to another. However, Kinnaman tells us exactly what he means by "deep faith" so there need be no confusion. While he acknowledges that there are different ways to measure the depth of faith, he makes no mention of Fowler or other developmental models, so perhaps he is not familiar with them. He believes instead that the correct way to assess the depth of faith is by measuring the extent to which a person adopts a "biblical worldview." He then proceeds to outline what a biblical worldview is, and what he identifies would make an excellent checklist for mythic literalism—a literal view of Jesus as a historical personage, Satan as a real and literal being, the mythos as a historical document rather than metaphor, truth as fixed and unchanging, and so on. Interestingly, he notes that the Barna research indicates that only 3% of the sixteen-to-forty-one age group have this worldview.[49] That leaves 97% in this age group for whom a mythic literal worldview is not attractive. Nationwide, that's a lot of young people.

Kinnaman's personal reaction to the findings is worth noting. He says, "The new generations are increasingly resistant to simplistic, black-and-white views of the world. We do not have to like this element of their generational coding, but it is a feature of the way they process life—nothing is simple."[50] We give no argument here. Dealing with subtlety and multiple perspectives is not simple or easy; it demands a lot from people. We find it interesting, though, that he perceives this lack of simplistic black-and-white thinking to be an unfortunate thing. But fortunate or not, the data supports that a shift in religious thinking to Orange and beyond is well underway. Those who believe that religion is only valid when limited to Blue mythic literalism are going to be increasingly disappointed in the years ahead. We no longer have to decide whether to believe social scientists telling us this change is happening; it is now being confirmed by data gathered by Christian organizations such as the Barna Group.

As the future unfolds, Wilber wonders if religion will choose to be a "conveyor belt" that takes people safely from developmental levels that are pre-rational to rational and beyond, or if it will ignore the challenges of the Orange pressure cooker and remain "the repository of humanity's childhood."[51] He says that

> if religion chooses the latter, then all around it, the other disciplines (law, medicine, science, education) will continue to move into the things that adults do, and religion will remain the things that children (and adult children) do—like blow things up. But if religion lives up to its promise as being that endeavor in humanity that allows Spirit to speak through it, and Spirit is indeed evolving in its own manifestation, then religion becomes a conveyor belt for humanity, carrying it from the childhood productions of Spirit to the adult productions of Spirit . . . and beyond that into the great tomorrow of Spirit's continuing display.[52]

Mythic Global Communities

Churches and communities of any faith who wish to act as the conveyor belt Wilber describes can begin by avoiding the problems of the Orange pressure cooker. They can find ways to open to rational and global worldviews in a manner that remains authentic to their own traditions. Those who do so will be in a position to minister to people who no longer find either the mythic literal or the mythic rational particularly meaningful to their spirituality. If established churches are not able to make the needed changes, then new churches and new communities will spring up to meet this need. Those of you who are interested in interspirituality and blended paths should be aware that your outlook may be in increasing demand. There is a need to be filled here, a growing need to speak to mythic global and even mythic archetypal spiritual seekers. Blended spiritualities may be in a unique position to fill this need, because blended spiritualities are inherently mythic global. This is one reason why understanding paths such as ChristoPaganism is important.

There are already a variety of institutes and communities in existence that approach personal and spiritual growth from mythic global or mythic archetypal perspectives. If you are interested in the work of Ken Wilber, as discussed in this book and our other books, you may wish to explore his Integral Institute. The Alban Institute can be a good place to start for congregational resources, books, and teaching materials suitable for many faith traditions. A number of interfaith communities or alliances can be located on-line, and most larger cities have interfaith associations, councils, and activities. Relief programs and activist groups often encourage interfaith cooperation. We are familiar with several Pagan organizations that offer mythic global teachings and rituals, with online and on-site intentional communities that are open to people from a variety of belief systems. These include Circle Sanctuary in Wisconsin, and Ozark Avalon and Diana's Grove in Missouri.

We believe that organizations and communities such as these embody the very spirit of interspiritual relations and mythic globalism. They and others may serve as models and provide resources for those looking for ways to give form to their new relationship with myth, and the more universal perspective it brings.

My Journal

How would you envision religion providing a climate of developmental expectation? How would it address the needs and health of each level of growth?

Toward what level of faith development is your faith community aimed? What type of faith relationship does it prepare its people to grow into? When people leave, what reasons do they tend to give?

In what ways would you like your faith community to provide a climate of developmental expectation for its members? In what ways is it doing that now, and in what ways might it improve? Write down your goals for your faith community. To meet these goals, would anything need to change? What would stay the same? Identify several ways you can help your faith community reach these goals. How will you know when the goals have been reached?

Identify a time when someone provided developmental support to you and helped you through a transition, or challenged you with a developmental expectation. What happened? What did that person do? What did you do? What changes happened in your life?

Have you ever provided developmental support or a challenge of developmental expectation to anyone else? What happened?

Chapter 8

CONCEPT DEVELOPMENT

In the prior two chapters we examined personal and spiritual development as a holonic expansion of capacities and worldviews. Familiarity
with this process can help you understand how the self evolves to become more comfortable with multiple spiritual perspectives during its development. But this raises some
questions. Even if the self enters a worldview where it is comfortable with interspirituality, how does it make the religious *ideas* fit its new perspective? Aren't we talking about
the same old literal doctrinal statements here? Surely it is one thing to believe the self
capable of expansion but another to believe it of religious ideas.

Here is where the holonic nature of concepts becomes important. It is not just the
physical world that builds itself in a nested fashion—the mental world does as well.
Ideas also expand and contract, and hold either more perspective or less. In this chapter we focus on the holonic nature of concepts and the process by which ideas move
from the more limited to the more expansive, from the particular to the universal and
back again.

Concepts as Holons

You will recall from chapter 6 that a holon is a way to describe how the world builds
itself in a nested fashion. Foundational skills or units, whole and complete in themselves, become parts of greater wholes as growth and expansion occurs. We looked at

two examples of holons in that chapter, one from the natural world dealing with cells and organisms and the other from the "man-made" world that generates this book. We mapped these on a holon "onion" which demonstrates how one layer builds upon another. The idea of holons as an expansion of capacities was then applied to patterns of personal and faith development, described in the developmental models presented.

Because the world of ideas is invisible until acted upon, its holonic nature is not necessarily outwardly obvious. Yet concepts have layers that build upon themselves, too, beginning with very basic or foundational assumptions and moving toward broad purposes and goals. The holonic nature of concepts is what makes the creation of belief systems and structures possible, as one idea builds upon another until it is capable of supporting an overarching structure.

Many people move through multiple layers of idea holons every day that range from the narrow and particular to the very expansive, and think nothing of it. Most can focus on whatever level of a concept serves the needs of the moment, and then move to another level as required. If your manager at work asks your department to focus on "the big picture," for example, you know what this means. The manager is asking you and your co-workers to let go of the details and particulars of a project and draw back to a wider, more general, or universal view. The "bigness" of the picture is not determined by how much more minutiae is stuffed into it but the extent to which the minutiae gives way to larger goals and principles. The process of mentally moving away from the minutiae to the larger picture is the process that underlies the concept holon. As with any holon, this process can be mapped on a holon onion.

Mapping a concept is simply an exercise that allows you to visualize a process that otherwise occurs automatically and invisibly. It is a way to diagram what is happening mentally. As you can see in figure 8.1, the concept onion begins with a foundational unit that is placed at the center. From there the foundational unit expands into larger and related concepts, ideas, goals, or purposes. The further out into the onion you go, the bigger the picture gets and the further removed from particulars. Each layer of the onion is a valid perspective in and of itself and contains its own focus and goals. In a corporation, entire departments might be devoted to working on the goals of one layer. The work of one department might then support the efforts of other departments, who build on the work according to their goals and focus, and so on.

We do concept mapping exercises at our workshops in order to illustrate this process of idea expansion. As a part of these exercises we ask those attending to help us develop

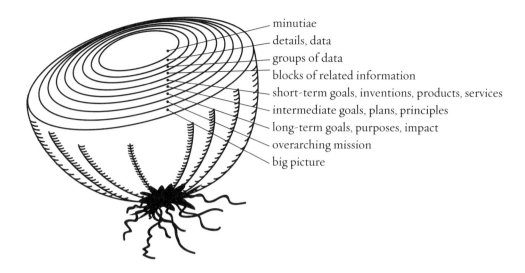

minutiae
details, data
groups of data
blocks of related information
short-term goals, inventions, products, services
intermediate goals, plans, principles
long-term goals, purposes, impact
overarching mission
big picture

Figure 8.1. Big picture holon onion

different concepts in order to see what happens. We begin with ordinary, everyday concepts and move on to religious and ethical ones. In the examples that follow, we walk you through some of the concept mapping we have done at our workshops, and then encourage you to practice it yourself with ideas that are of interest to you.

We like to begin with examples that are simple and familiar as well as emotionally neutral. A concept we have frequently chosen for practice is the traffic law of "no right turns on red." Since a concept holon onion is begun by putting some foundational idea, rule, or piece of data in the center, we start this onion by placing the law itself—no right turns on red—in the center. By doing so, we are making it the foundational, or most basic, unit on which this particular holon onion will be built. This is the "detail" level, if you will. But how do you get from the details to the "big picture"? In some instances it is easy enough to proceed intuitively, while in others this doesn't work as readily. We have found it helpful to use a series of questions that we ask of each layer of the onion. The answers to these questions help to elicit one or more goals or purposes that relate to this layer or toward which it could expand. The answers to the questions are put on the onion, becoming its next layer, and so the process continues until the onion is expanded as far as desired.

Keep in mind that you may come up with multiple answers for each question, all of which you feel are correct. You may put all the answers on the next layer if they are closely related, but if they identify very different aspects of the issue then choose only one to focus on for the remainder of the onion. You can always come back and develop the onion again using answers that take you in a different direction. While we provide answers to the questions in each of our examples, we do not claim that these are the only answers possible. You may think of others. You can experiment with the onions again with different answers if you like, but remember to stay with one focus for the entire onion.

The questions are:

- Why?

- What is its purpose, or what is its greater meaning?

- What values or goals does it support? What's to be gained?

With "no right turns on red" sitting at the center of the onion, you can now apply these questions and see what happens. We will map it with you. The answers we provide are a composite of responses given at several of our workshops and classes. So let's get started. We begin by addressing the center of the onion and ask it, "Why the law of 'no right turns on red'? What is its purpose?" A typical response from a workshop group is that its purpose is "To control traffic behavior." That seems clear enough, and so it becomes the next layer of the onion. Questioning this layer we ask, "Why control traffic behavior? What is the purpose of that?" The group might answer, "To avoid chaos in driving, or to increase predictability and safety on the road." That makes sense, and onto the onion goes the answer. So then we ask of this layer, "Why is it important to avoid chaos and promote predictability and safety?" The group answers, "So people can get to their destinations smoothly." Onto the onion goes this answer. Looking at this layer we ask, "Why care whether people get to their destinations smoothly? What purpose is served here?" Several possibilities may be given, which we will combine together in one answer, which typically looks like "So people can go places, have fun, take care of their families, and contribute to society and the economy (as in getting to their jobs and the store)." This answer is added to the next layer of the onion.

Then we ask, "What's the purpose of people being able to do these things? What values and goals does it support for people to get to work, travel around with their families,

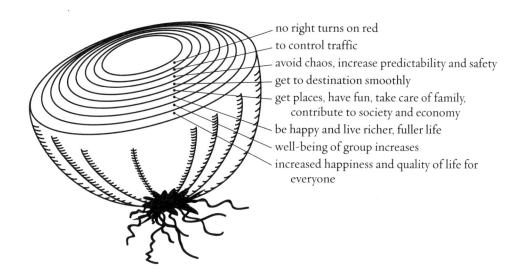

- no right turns on red
- to control traffic
- avoid chaos, increase predictability and safety
- get to destination smoothly
- get places, have fun, take care of family, contribute to society and economy
- be happy and live richer, fuller life
- well-being of group increases
- increased happiness and quality of life for everyone

Figure 8.2. "No right turns on red" holon onion

and have fun?" Now we're getting into broader concepts that are harder to pin down, but the group comes to an agreement that it is "So they can be happy and live richer and fuller lives." We write this onto the onion. Then we ask, "What is gained if people live richer and fuller lives?" This is a tough one, but the group consensus frequently is that "If everyone is living more richly and fully, then the overall well-being of the group will increase." This answer is added onto the onion. Taking this one step further we ask, "Why do we care if the well-being of the group increases?" The group might struggle with this one, but they decide to answer that "Increased well-being raises the overall happiness and quality of life for everyone, perhaps for everyone on the planet." Onto the onion goes this answer, and that ends the exercise. Let's see what the onion looks like now (fig. 8.2).

As you look over this concept holon, identify which levels seem to deal more with particulars and which with universals. At what level do the concepts shift from the particular to the universal? At what point would you say you are looking at the "big picture"? Which levels do you think might appeal more to Blue thinking? To Orange? To Green? Which levels might appeal to those who are mythic tangible? Or mythic rational? Or mythic global?

Now we're going to take this example and give it a twist. Imagine that a neighboring town passes a different law permitting right turns on red. This law is directly opposite to the law in our first example. What happens if we put the conflicting law into the center of its own onion and develop it? Will we discover that the second town does not care about safe and orderly traffic or the welfare of its citizens?

When we do this exercise in a workshop, we typically ask for two volunteers. We tell the first volunteer that he or she lives in the town that allows right turns on red, and then we ask this person to leave the group briefly so he or she cannot hear what is discussed. Once the first volunteer is gone we tell the second volunteer that he or she is from the neighboring town that passed the "no right turns on red" law. This volunteer, with input from the rest of the group, creates the onion in figure 8.2. We then hide this onion from view and ask the first volunteer to return. We begin a new onion and in its center write "Right turns on red are okay." We develop this onion as we did the first, asking the same questions of the volunteer concerning the reasons and purposes for each layer of the onion. Let's try this exercise now and see what happens. Again, the following answers are a composite of those given by volunteers from several classes and workshops.

We begin by asking, "Why allow right turns on red? What is the purpose of such a law?" The volunteer might answer, "So people know what to expect at intersections." This becomes the next layer of the onion. We then ask, "Why do we care if people know what to expect at intersections? What goal is served by that?" The volunteer answers, "So they don't get into accidents." Onto the onion this goes. We ask, "Why care whether people get into accidents? What purpose does it serve to avoid them?" The volunteer answers, "Because accidents use up time (by keeping people from their destinations) and money (by fixing the damage) and people get hurt." This is added to the onion and we then ask, "Why care that people don't lose time and money, and that they not get hurt?" The volunteer answers, "So they stay healthy and can get done what they need to get done." This is added to the onion. Then we ask, "What purposes are served by people staying healthy and getting done what they need to do?" The volunteers may give several answers here, the core of which is "So that people can be productive and happy and have the kind of life they want." Onto the onion this goes and then we ask, "Why do we care if people are productive and happy and have the kind of life they want?" The volunteer might answer, "Because that makes life better for everyone." In our final question, we ask, "What goal is served or purposes advanced if life in this

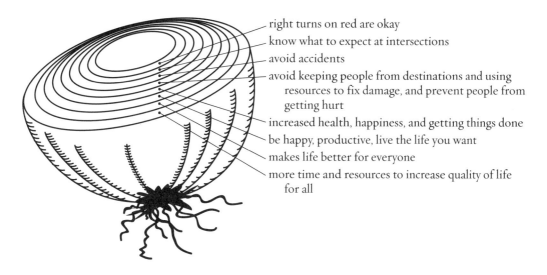

right turns on red are okay
know what to expect at intersections
avoid accidents
avoid keeping people from destinations and using resources to fix damage, and prevent people from getting hurt
increased health, happiness, and getting things done
be happy, productive, live the life you want
makes life better for everyone
more time and resources to increase quality of life for all

Figure 8.3. "Right turns on red are okay" holon onion

society is better for everyone?" Again, several answers may be given whose general core is that "People then have the time and resources to increase the quality of life for everyone everywhere." Let's see how this looks on the onion (fig. 8.3).

Identify at which layers in this onion the particular gives way to the universal. Once attention shifts to more universal principles, do you see what happens? Repeat out loud the last three layers of both onions, first one, then the other. Do it a second time. What do you observe about the principles identified in each? While they are somewhat different in the direction they take and the language they use, both onions end up in a similar place. We have done this exercise many times, and it has never failed to end in this manner. The onions always expand until they identify the same or very similar principles, much to the amazement of the class.

How is this possible when the laws put in the center of each onion are in direct opposition to each other? How can contradictory beginnings lead to similar results as the holon grows? The answer to this question is an important key to understanding interspirituality and how it works.

My Journal

Identify a couple of concept holons from experiences in your daily life. Use the preceding questions to help you identify the next more-expansive concept. Examples of concepts you might choose from are political or military structures, corporate cultures, criminal justice systems, approaches to education, artistic techniques, and so on.

On your concept onion, mark several of the categories mentioned previously, such as where the particular gives way to the universal, where different colors of the Spiral might be comfortable, where Second Tier thinking might begin, and which relationship to myth might be operating.

Pick one of your concept holons and write a conversation between a mythic literalist and a mythic globalist about their differing (or similar) perspectives concerning what they find important.

How would you identify where your spiritual focus is generally? Is it in a different place now than ten years ago? Twenty years ago? Where are you most comfortable in concept holons regarding spiritual matters? Where are you most uncomfortable? If you were to explain to someone else why your spiritual focus is where it is and why you keep it there, what would you tell that person?

Religious Concepts

Now that we have warmed up on traffic laws, let's see what happens when we map some religious concepts. In our workshops we do two maps, one each for the most common ethical guidelines in Paganism and Christianity. For Paganism we choose the Wiccan Rede, which states, "If it harm none, do what you will." For Christianity, workshop groups cannot always decide between the Ten Commandments (see Exod. 20:3–17) or the Golden Rule ("Do unto others as you would have them do unto you"), so we have tended to include both on the onion. We will do so here as well.

Let us begin with Paganism's onion and in its center put the ethical guideline of the Rede. Religious holons are developed in the same manner as all others—each layer of the onion is asked the same questions set out previously, the answers are added to the next layer of the onion, and so on. We realize there are a number of directions in which answers regarding religious ethics can legitimately be taken. One might be from the individual's perspective, such as securing personal salvation or right relations with deity. Another might be from the perspective of the social impact of ethics in terms of stability, crime, family values, war, and so forth. Another might be from an activist perspective, as in securing justice and access to resources, fair wages, and otherwise using ethical guidelines as a means to effect change. If you decide to experiment with religious concepts on the onions, we encourage you to map them in whatever way you wish, but once you pick a particular focus, stay with it for the duration of the onion. As before, the answers we give to the following questions are a composite of responses given by groups at our workshops.

We begin by putting the foundational unit into the center of the onion, in this case, the Wiccan ethic of the Rede. We then question this layer and ask, "What is the purpose of having this ethical rule?" The group participants might answer, "To give a framework for acceptable behavior." This becomes the next layer of the onion. We then ask, "Why do we care if we have a framework for acceptable behavior?" The group answers, "So we have guidance in how to treat each other." This is added to the onion. We ask, "What do we hope to gain by knowing how to treat each other?" The group answers, "Peace, order, and harmony." This goes onto the onion. Next we ask, "Why do we care about peace, order, and harmony?" The group wrestles with this a bit and then decides it is "So life can be stable, energy is freed up, and resources combined and used wisely." We add this to the onion and then ask, "What goals are served by combining resources, freeing up energy, and living stable lives?" This is a much broader question and the group comes up with several responses, including such things as ensuring survival, increasing longevity, encouraging artistic and cultural achievement, having a positive impact on the world, and exploring spirituality. The core of the responses seems to be "To help individuals and society flourish physically, culturally, and spiritually." This is added to the onion. We then ask, "What's to be gained if individuals and societies flourish?" The group answers, "People are then able to reach for their highest potentials." We take the onion one further step and ask, "Why do we care if people develop their potentials fully?" The group debates this for a while and decides that the answer is "To leave a legacy that helps others in their personal and spiritual growth, and helps society evolve to its ethical best."

Let's put this on the onion and see how it looks (fig. 8.4).

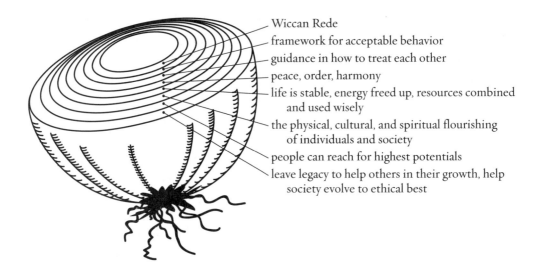

Figure 8.4. Wiccan Rede holon onion

Then we begin another concept onion, and in the center of this one we put the ethical guidelines of the Ten Commandments and the Golden Rule. We ask the group, "What is the purpose of having the Golden Rule and Ten Commandments?" The group answers, "To provide moral guidelines or an ethical yardstick for behavior." This becomes the next layer of the onion. Then we ask, "What's gained by having moral guidelines and an ethical yardstick for behavior?" The group answers, "So we know how to treat each other and to reduce conflicts." This is added to the onion. We ask, "What purpose is served by knowing how to treat each other and reducing conflicts?" The group decides it is "To have predictability, stability, peace, and love." This goes onto the onion. We then ask, "What goals are supported by having predictability, stability, peace, and love?" The group can think of several goals and answers, which can be summarized as "So the society has greater prosperity and continuity without disruptions like war, and people live longer and are more secure." This is added to the onion. Then we ask, "Why do we care if society prospers, is not disrupted, and people live longer and are more secure?" The group debates a variety of answers here and then decides on "Peaceful co-existence leads to greater quality of life, the freeing up of time and resources, and the chance to develop spiritually and personally." Taking this one step further, we ask,

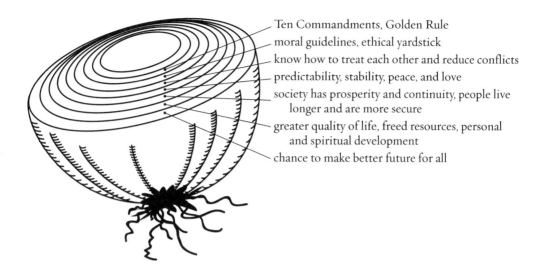

Ten Commandments, Golden Rule
moral guidelines, ethical yardstick
know how to treat each other and reduce conflicts
predictability, stability, peace, and love
society has prosperity and continuity, people live
    longer and are more secure
greater quality of life, freed resources, personal
    and spiritual development
chance to make better future for all

Figure 8.5. Christian ethics holon onion

"What is gained by a greater quality of life, freed resources, and personal development?" The group answers, "The chance to make a better future for everyone."

Let's put these responses on the onion and see how it looks (fig. 8.5).

Take a moment and look over these two holon onions. Do them again if you wish, and come up with your own answers. Then spread all the onions out and study them. Which of the concepts in the holons do you think will appeal most to Blues? To Oranges? To Greens? Which concepts might mark the beginning of Second Tier thinking? At what level does the particular give way to the universal? Once attention shifts to more universal principles, what happens? Are there any layers where an interspiritual outlook would not be welcome? With which layers would an interspiritual person be most comfortable? As before, state out loud the last three layers of the onions, your own included. What do you observe about these outer layers? How do you feel about these Pagan and Christian ethical guidelines now, and how they might relate to each other?

Once you become adept with concept holons, you can see them at work in spiritual and theological writings. Sometimes authors work with holons consciously (though they may not use the term *holon*) and take the reader through their idea development step by step. Other authors navigate holons intuitively and do not show their mental process. Still others state a conclusion and give no hint of how they got there, yet

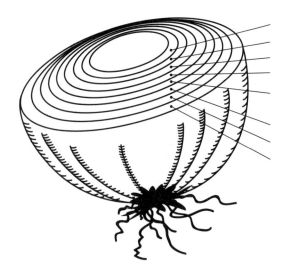

Figure 8.6. Blank holon onion

the feeling of underlying layers is present. Take for example this statement by Catholic priest and theologian Pierre Teilhard de Chardin, who said, "The God of the Bible is not different from the God of Nature."[1] This is a holon talking. Fr. de Chardin may have worked through the holons of these concepts in his mind, perhaps unconsciously, discovered that the outer layers of their onions were similar, and drew his conclusion. Yet he does not leave a road map for later readers to follow his process, at least not overtly. Readers will react to his statement from the values of their own developmental worldview. Regardless of your worldview and whether you ultimately agree or disagree with Fr. de Chardin, you can map his process as a holon and come to a greater appreciation of his vision.

To try this, make several copies of the onion shown in figure 8.6. If you do all three exercises given, you will need at least eight copies. For this first exercise, take two copies and in the center of one onion write *God of Nature* and in the center of the other write *God of the Bible*. Begin by asking the "God of the Bible" onion this question: Why have the idea of a God of the Bible? What purpose does such an idea serve? Write down your answer on the onion and then ask this answer questions for the next layer. Feel free to use the questions provided on page 162, or develop your own. When you finish this onion as far as you decide to take it, repeat the process with the "God of Nature" onion. Then set both onions in front of you and read aloud the last several layers. What similarities and differences do you notice? Why do you think Fr. De Chardin drew a comparison between these two concepts? How would you respond to his comparison?

For the second exercise, here is an example of Brother Teasdale wrestling with the holons relating to reincarnation and life after death. Notice the direction in which he takes the holonic development in this quote: "I don't think these two outcomes of the spiritual journey—reincarnation and life after death in heaven—necessarily exclude each other. They may, in fact, complete each other. In the Catholic tradition, there is an intermediate state of the afterlife called purgatory. This state is designed for those who need further development, who must pass through a purgation of their limiting qualities that obstructed their spiritual lives. Theologically, reincarnation is compatible with purgatory because it serves a similar function: preparing the individual for liberation and the higher life with God in eternal paradise."[2]

To map Brother Teasdale's ideas, take two more copies of the onion and in the center of one write *purgatory* and in the other write *reincarnation*. Beginning with "purgatory," you might ask this question: What is the greater meaning of purgatory, what is its purpose? and write your answer on the onion. Continue as in the first exercise, and when you are finished with the "purgatory" onion, begin the "reincarnation" onion. When this one is also completed, place the two onions side by side and read the last several layers aloud, first one then the other. What similarities and differences do you notice? Why did Brother Teasdale draw the comparisons that he did?

For an example that relates directly to ChristoPaganism, consider these words of religion professor Mark Wallace: "Animism is the belief that the sacred permeates all living things; in Christianity, the belief that God's Spirit imbues all creation roots biblical faith in the Pagan animist soil of its primitive origins. . . ."[3] This tendency is particularly evident in the Trinity, he says, which stresses "both the unity and the plurality of the Godhead," as it "is both 'other' and at the same time pervasively 'present' in all things. . . ."[4] So, he concludes, if God is "both 'up there' and yet still 'everywhere' at the same time, then Christianity is not opposed to Paganism . . . but a rearticulation of the radically earthen sensibility of Paganism in a new biblical idiom. . . . The promise of the Trinity is that God is beyond and in everything and thereby wonderfully present everywhere, infusing all things with the vigor and power of the Spirit. As in Neopaganism, nothing is dead and matter is not inert because all things are charged with the sacred power of the Spirit."[5]

Try to follow his development of these concepts by taking two more copies of the onion, and in the center of one writing *animism* and in the other *the Trinity*. Since Wallace looks at both the "unity" and the "plurality" of divinity in his comments, choose one or the other aspect to be your focus. If you choose unity, for example, ask "animism" about its purposes, meanings, and goals as it relates to presenting a unified, merged, or singular view of the divine. Then do the same for "the Trinity." If you wish, do the exercise a second time, focusing on the "plurality" aspects of both animism and the Trinity.

As before, study your completed onions and observe what happens as you move outward from the center. What similarities and differences do you notice? How would you respond to Mark Wallace concerning his comparison of animism and the Trinity after doing this exercise?

Concept Holons and Interspirituality

The preceding examples illustrate that every spiritual idea contains within it a range of viewpoints that extends from the most detailed to the most universal. Every concept, whether religious in content or not, shares this characteristic. No idea or belief is exempt, and by extension, no belief system is exempt. The viewpoint, or level of the onion, on which the self concentrates can vary with the needs of the moment, but it generally does not go further than the horizon marked by the self's aptitude, interest level, and developmental capacity.

One way to understand this horizon is to appreciate what it is that the self sees as a *means* to an end versus what it sees to be the *end* itself. Take as an example the physical needs of the infant archaic self. Getting its needs met is the primary *end* of the self beyond which it cannot see and is not particularly interested in seeing. As the edge of its horizon expands and opens to others, the meeting of its needs becomes only one *means* by which it is now available to relate in larger contexts. For the mythic tangible self, honoring and preserving the group's sacred objects might be an *end* in itself. Later, for the mythic literal self, the preserving of sacred objects is only a *means* of bringing the self to an appreciation of the saving power of the mythos, which becomes the new *end*. This in turn may become a *means* to serving other ends for the mythic rational self, such as in providing opportunities for rational inquiry and individual success (the Protestant work ethic being an example), which in turn may become a *means* to achieve communal support and diversity in Green and mythic globalism.

Is not the holon a primary example of the process of ends becoming means to greater ends? What was once whole and complete in itself—an end in itself—becomes absorbed into a larger whole. This is the nature of holonic or nested growth. People don't seem to mind this when it relates to their motor skills or the structure of the physical world, but when it comes to their ideas and value systems, it can be threatening. It can provoke strong reactions in people who sense that the end point of their horizon is but a means to someone else who has a different horizon. Even the act of pointing out another level of the onion for their ideas can be threatening.

This reminds us of an experience we had at a Catholic high school when we were invited to be guest speakers on earth religions. River and I had both been invited, but as he was unavailable that day, I went alone. During my talk one of the students asked about Pagan views of God, and to answer him I outlined and discussed a concept we call the God Map.[6] This map lays out a grid of two lines, one horizontal and one vertical, with the horizontal line measuring the extent to which a God idea is either concrete or abstract, and the vertical line the extent to which the idea is either transcendent (God is wholly other and "out there") or immanent (God is wholly permeating or present in creation). A student said he did not understand what was meant by immanence, and even after I defined it further he was still confused. So I cast about in my mind for an example in Catholicism in which the divine is believed to permeate the physical, or to pervade creation, or otherwise to be actually and physically present in the world. Those of you who are Catholic or familiar with Catholicism can probably guess what idea came immediately to my mind—communion.

So I said, "You know that during Mass the priest consecrates the host?" "Yes," said the student. "When it is consecrated," I asked, "Jesus is really and truly present in the host—that is, his presence permeates the host in some divine fashion, right?" "Yes," said the student. "Well," I said, "to some people this is an example of immanence. A Pagan, for example, would see this as an instance of the divine being present in something that is physically tangible to us (in this case the host), and making itself known to us in that way." "Okay," said the student. I asked, "Does the word *immanent* make more sense to you now?" The student said, "Yes, it does," and others in the room nodded their heads. The discussion moved on.

"Just a minute here," said the teacher, interrupting, "I am really quite offended by your example. You dare to compare something in the Mass to a Pagan idea such as immanence?" *Oh no*, I thought, *I better not mention that immanence is not just a "Pagan" idea*. Instead

I said, "If my example was offensive to you, I am truly sorry. It was the first example of the divine permeating the physical world that I thought of in your tradition." A couple more minutes of discussion on other topics occurred, and then the teacher interrupted again. "You know, I'm really, *really* offended by what you said earlier about communion, and the more I think about it, the more offended I get." I wasn't sure what to do. Had I really been insulting? I frantically reviewed everything I had said.

I said, "I am very sorry if my example offended you. That was not my intention at all. I intended to illustrate the general concept of immanence with some example familiar to the students." This only enflamed the teacher further. "I cannot believe you are being so insulting!" His voice rose to a shout. Some of the students, who were all older teenagers, began trying to calm him down. I stood still, not sure what to do or how to proceed. Finally, the teacher declared, "I will not tolerate such disrespect from a guest. You are no longer welcome in this class." Pointing to a student he said, "Escort her out of the building," I packed up my materials, thanked the class and the teacher for having me, and left. As the door closed behind me I could hear the class erupt. This teacher later called the bookstore that referred us and asked that they never recommend us as speakers again, because we "spread lies about the Catholic Church."

I am no stranger to Catholicism, having lived in a convent for a year, sung in a Gregorian chant choir for a decade, and studied theology and church history. I admit I'm no expert on the theological intricacies of transubstantiation, but I don't believe I committed any error in relating the Catholic view of consecration (if so, perhaps a reader will inform us) and I know I didn't concerning many Pagan views of what comprises immanence. Looking back on this incident now, which I still consider to be one of my most spectacular failures in teaching, I believe that the high-school teacher was threatened because I expanded the concept onion of the Mass and consecration one ring too far for him. It was not the accuracy or inaccuracy of my statements that were at issue, but the fact that I made the comparison at all. For this teacher, the consecration at the Mass is the end of all spiritual ends. It cannot be used as an illustration for other ideas or taken in a different context, because that implies there *are* other contexts, which is clearly impossible. Even the suggestion that consecration could have other meanings to people in earth religions, or worse, might link the teacher's spiritual beliefs with the spiritual beliefs of others (in earth religions, no less), was too threatening. I unknowingly crashed headlong into the boundary of his spiritual horizon.

This horizon marks the outer edge of a person's spiritual onion and the end of the self's region of comfort. Horizon edges or boundaries vary from onion to onion, based on the self's level of growth within a given developmental stream. Recall that Wilber identifies a number of developmental streams that exist simultaneously within the individual such as altruism, social skills, cognitive reasoning, spiritual perspectives, and so on, all of which can be developed to different layers. If the spiritual stream is focused on inner layers at or near the center of the onion, then the self's spirituality will be more interested, focused, or comfortable with details and foundational units. As you have seen in the holon onions set out earlier in the chapter or that you created yourself, foundational units include things such as rules, roles, a body of scripture, a particular practice, specific beliefs, and so on. Since the foundational units and details of the world's various mythologies differ markedly from each other, one could say that *a spiritual horizon drawn at inner layers anchors the self in a spiritual place where difference and contradiction tend to live.*

For those whose capacities, aptitudes, or choices permit a horizon drawn at outer layers of the onion, the self is able to access concepts that are closer in nature to the "big picture." As you will recall, one of the features of the "big picture" is that the person holding it has let go of a focus on details. This is not a denial that details exist, nor is it a criticism of the details. But it is a different focus. These individuals recognize that while there are indeed differences among mythologies, the differences often expand into concepts that are increasingly universal and even tend to support similar goals. One could say that *a spiritual horizon drawn at outer layers anchors the self in a spiritual place where universals tend to live.*

By the time a person reaches late Orange or early Green, or Wilber's vision-logic level, or Fowler's conjunctive faith stage, the inner layers of the onion will not be as satisfactory as they once were because the self needs a bigger horizon. The mythic global self is not satisfied with anything less than a global horizon, which at the very least means including those onion layers where the particular gives way to the universal. It may surprise the self that it is no longer as caught up or engrossed in the details as it once was. It may be surprised by how at ease it feels with the centers of several spiritual onions, and discover it can engage in a variety of spiritual experiences because it is no longer attached to the details of one system.

When the self shifts its focus to the outer layers of the onion, "big picture" concepts take the foreground while the details found in the inner layers fade into the background. This shift often brings with it an emotional nonattachment to contradictory details and gives the self freedom to approach onion centers in creative ways that would have been impossible for it earlier. It may work with them in a parallel fashion or combine them and feel no discomfort in doing so. We call this working with "multiple centers" or "multiple cores." In so doing, the self is able to balance or hold any contradictions found in the centers respectfully and lightly without having to resolve them, because ultimately the self sees that they are absorbed into the universal, outer layers of the onion, similar to the way sugar dissolves in water.

It is here, finally, that interspirituality becomes genuinely possible. Both the capacity and the choice to stay focused on outer layers need to be present for a blended spirituality to become a reality. If they are, interspirituality will make sense to the self in a way it did not when its horizon was focused differently. The self may feel attracted to interspiritual studies and experiences since such studies and experiences meet its growing need for a global relationship with myth. Such individuals may agree with theologian Arthur Bellinzoni when he says that "the challenge now is to find the timeless message within those ancient books, the 'truths' that are not conditioned and limited by time and place, the insights that are not dictated by culture and bias, but rather to look for those ideas, those truths, that reach more deeply into the universal spirit of all of humankind . . ."[7] This does not mean that such individuals *will* create a blended spiritual path such as ChristoPaganism for themselves, but they have the capacity to do so if they wish.

Every layer of the onion offers a valid spiritual focus. We do not believe that one layer is more valuable or legitimate than the next. All are needed for the holon to be complete and grow in a healthy and balanced fashion. The question is not which layer is correct or approved or popular, but which one reflects your values at this point in your development. Where do you want your spiritual focus to be? What do you want your relationship to the *details* of your mythos to be? What do you want your relationship to the *universals* of your mythos to be? What do you value spiritually in your life? What vision of spirituality are you willing to spend your time and resources to create? These are the sorts of questions and issues that present themselves whenever you holonically examine the concepts you currently value. Perhaps you can take a few minutes now and think about how you would answer these questions.

This brings us to the end of the second section of this book. It is time for us to shift our focus now, away from the philosophy and history of Christianity and Paganism, away from the mechanisms of growth and the inner space occupied by interspirituality, and toward the lived experience of ChristoPagans. In the third and final section we bring you the stories of real people who have chosen a blended path for themselves, and listen as they share their spiritual journey, their thoughts, beliefs, doubts, and experiences of what it is like to live the path they have chosen.

My Journal

Fowler says the development of abstract thinking is like stepping "outside the flow of life's stream. From a vantage point on the river bank, as it were, one can take a look at the flow of the stream as a whole."[8] We think this description beautifully captures what happens whenever the self steps beyond a perspective in which it found itself immersed, and discovers yet another perspective awaiting it. In terms of faith development, at one point the self is immersed in its faith's mythology to the point that it cannot see either the mythology or the fact that it is immersed in it. In a sense, the self is the story and the story is the self. Then something happens that enables the self to step back from some aspect of the myth, or some part of the story, and see it from a different vantage point. At that moment it is as though the self is catapulted out of the river and onto the bank, and says, "Hey, I was in that river and I didn't know it."

Have you ever had an experience like this, when you suddenly found yourself on a riverbank and realized you had been immersed in something you are now detached from enough to observe? If so, what happened?

Find a time when you have about thirty minutes when you can be undisturbed. Close your eyes and let your mind relax for several minutes. Watch yourself breathe in and out while you become more relaxed. Then begin to imagine that you are floating in a river. It is carrying you along with no effort on your part. This is the river of your current spiritual and religious beliefs. Maybe you've been in this river a long time, or perhaps you are new to it. As you float along, what do you see around you? Who is there with you? What are they doing or saying? How does it feel to be in this river? After a few minutes, find a place along the bank that looks inviting where you can step out. Turn and observe the river you just left, the river of your religious myth and belief at this moment. What do you see? How do you feel? What are the most distinctive features of this river? As other people in the river swim or float by, you can hear their conversations. What are they saying?

Ahead a short way you notice a bridge that crosses over your river. A set of steps leads up to the bridge and you climb them. At the top you begin to walk along the bridge. As you look around you notice that this bridge spans a number of rivers, a dozen or more, flowing next to each other and stretching out into the distance. Each of these rivers represents a religious faith or spiritual perspective. As you walk across the bridge, observe these rivers as they flow by. What do you see? How does it feel to be on this bridge and have this perspective? Does being here feel different from being in or next to your river?

You notice that between each river is a set of stairs like the one you came up. Each set of stairs leads to the bank of another river. Choose one that looks interesting to you and go down its stairs. As you stand on the bank of this river, take a look at it, observe it. This is the river of a religious or spiritual perspective that is different from yours. What perspective is it? Does it look or feel different here at the bank than it did from the bridge? Notice the people floating and swimming in it. Are they aware of you? You can hear their conversations. What are they saying? How does it feel to be able to see and hear them but be outside of their perspective? At the point the stairs join the riverbank, you notice that the water eddies and is calm. You can step into the river and experience it but not be carried along with it while you are in this eddy. Step from the riverbank into the river and float in the calm eddy. How does the river look now? How do the people in it look now? Do their conversations change? Pay attention to what you are seeing and hearing. How does it feel to be immersed in this faith? Does your perspective change by immersing yourself in it?

When you are ready, step out of the river and back onto the bank. Send a sense of gratitude to the river, the tradition it represents, and the people in it. Is there anything from this river you would like to take with you? Identify one positive impression you have had of this river.

Climb the stairs and move along the bridge until you are above the river of a spiritual perspective or tradition that makes you uncomfortable or that you dislike. Study this river for a moment, and ask yourself why it makes you feel as you do. What does this tradition look like from the bridge? What do you see? What do you think you will experience if you go down the stairs and climb in this river briefly? (If this exercise makes you too uncomfortable or you are in professional counseling for some event that happened in connection with this river, do not go further with this part of the exercise without the approval and supervision of your counselor.)

Go down the stairs to the riverbank. How does it feel to be here? What are you feeling and why? What do you think you will see if you take on the perspective of those who occupy this river? You see the calm eddy of the water at the base of the stairs. You know you can enter the river here and not be caught up in its current, and that you can leave it at any time. You enter the river slowly and sit down in it. The water comes to the top of your chest. If you want to swim around, you can, knowing you can easily return to the stairs. As you float in this river, notice what you see. What are the people in the river saying and how are they behaving? Do they notice you? If so, what do they say? How does the river itself feel to you? How does it feel to be in it? What would need to shift for you to feel more comfortable with this river, or dislike it less? Now that you're immersed in the river, is this perspective different than you thought it would be? Does your perspective of this river change in any way by immersing yourself in it? Sit up straight and see if you can see your own river from where you are. If so, how does it look from here?

When you are ready, leave the river and stand on its bank. Does it look or feel any different to you now? Identify one positive thought or impression about this river that you can take with you. Send gratitude to the river and its inhabitants for sharing itself with you. Express gratitude to yourself for doing something that was uncomfortable. If it seems appropriate, send a healing blessing to yourself and to the tradition and the people this river represents. Then walk up the stairs and back onto the bridge.

Take a moment on the bridge to observe all the rivers flowing beneath you. What impressions come to your mind? How does the bridge's perspective feel to you now compared to when you first stepped onto it? What do you want to remember from this experience?

Walk along the bridge back to your own river and observe it and the people in it again. Does anything look or feel different about it now? If so, what? Walk down your set of stairs to the riverbank. You may get back into your river if you like, and end the exercise.

Journal about your experience.

PART III
THE LIVING LANDSCAPE

Chapter 9

FINDING CHRISTOPAGANS

In this third section of the book we talk to real ChristoPagans about their spirituality and journey in faith. It is here, in lived experience, that the inner and outer landscapes of Christianity and Paganism come together to create the living landscape of interspirituality. In the chapters that follow, a group of ChristoPagans share their spiritual journey from childhood to adulthood and describe their spiritual life and practices. They share their viewpoints on the nature of God, sin, raising children, holidays, and liturgy, among many other topics. They describe experiences they have had with their families, friends, and other Christians and Pagans concerning their spiritual path.

To create this section, we went looking for ChristoPagans who would be willing to share their stories with you. Over the course of two years, as we traveled around the country to festivals, Pagan Pride Days, and other appearances, we announced that we were looking for ChristoPagans interested in being a part of this project. Wherever we went, we offered workshops on ChristoPaganism and interspirituality. These workshops included talks and discussion groups and a sung morning devotion we call Pagan Gregorian Chant, which consists of interfaith texts set to chant tones. After the workshops, many people confided in us about their spiritual practices and how they blend them, thinking perhaps that there was something odd about themselves. They wondered if they were the only ones doing such things. Letting folks know they aren't alone in combining spiritual practices came to be an important part of these workshops, and it helped us decide to go forward with this book.

Pagans not only came to tell us about how they were weaving aspects of Christianity into their spiritualities, they also came to tell us how their Christian families and relatives were incorporating earth-centered practices into their Christianity. Sometimes they did so knowingly, and other times not, acting instead out of instinct and what "felt right." Many of these families did not know their practices are considered Pagan or earth-centered and did not use such words to describe them. Examples of these practices include attending solstice ceremonies at a sacred site, going to drum circles, attending handfastings, gardening by moon and star cycles, addressing God as "my heavenly Father and Mother" or "Mother-Father God," holding services in circles, hailing God or Jesus in the four directions, and so on.

Even Pagans who are not ChristoPagan came to tell us about their involvement in interfaith work and how important to them interfaith sharing, tolerance, and understanding are. Many of these folks enjoyed our interfaith Pagan Gregorian Chant workshop and wanted more of the same for their daily practice. Such requests have led us to consider creating an interfaith Book of Hours in the near future. Oddly, not a single Pagan came to us with negative comments about blended spiritualities or interfaith efforts.

Since our appearances in that two-year period took us through the Midwest and the South, these areas represent the regions most of our project volunteers are from. We did not attempt to gather volunteers in a scientific fashion to insure randomness and the representation of every part of the country. We took those who came to us, and we realize there are many more who could have been included. In the end, fifteen people participated in this project. These folks graciously gave their time and energy in a process that spanned several years from start to finish. Of these, seven are from Missouri, two are from Texas, two are from Indiana, one is from Illinois, one is from Kentucky, one is from Ohio, and one is from Vermont.

We asked the volunteers to give us several pieces of demographic data about themselves, including their age, occupation, and educational level. In terms of age, the youngest volunteer is thirty-one and the oldest is sixty-five, with one choosing not to answer. Of those who provided their age, two are in their thirties, six are in their forties, four are in their fifties, and two are in their sixties. In terms of education, nine have bachelor's degrees in subjects such as religious studies, philosophy, business administration, home economics, physiology, and biology. One is a certified gemologist, one graduated from broadcast school and is an active radio announcer, one has a PhD in counseling and also a law degree. Three have master's degrees in the fields of counseling, nursing, and divinity. Three did not answer this question. In terms of occupation, the volunteers cover a variety of fields, including law enforcement, retail management, acupuncture and herbology, chaplaincy, Christian ministry, professorship in psychology, nursing, and computer technology. There is a college student, a stay-at-home mom, a school lunchroom supervisor, and a part-time religious educator. Two are accountants, one is retired, another is about to retire, and one did not answer this question.

Each volunteer was sent a questionnaire, which they completed and returned to us. As part of this questionnaire, they were asked to pick a name to be used in the book, which might or might not be their real name. The names they are called in the following chapters are the names they chose for themselves. We also created a private e-list for the purpose of discussing topics and sharing ideas. Discussions on this e-list continued for more than a year and touched on any topic the volunteers wanted to raise. It was interesting to read the wide range of ideas and opinions that were expressed on this list. In addition, several of the volunteers were able to meet in person at various events and festivals, and they enjoyed having the chance to meet each other.

We also gave each volunteer the opportunity to read the chapters that follow and offer suggestions and corrections. If a volunteer wanted to clarify or expand on a comment made in one of the chapters, he or she was free to do so, and we incorporated these changes whenever possible. No material was retained that a volunteer objected to or said did not reflect their true opinions. We sought the input of our volunteers because we wanted to be sure we captured the true meaning and intent of the information they shared with us. The stories and points of view that follow, therefore, are as accurate and thorough as both we and our volunteers could make them.

We divide this final section into a number of chapters devoted to particular subjects or time periods in the lives of the volunteers. We begin with their childhoods and faiths of origin, and follow them as they grow into adulthood and wrestle with questions of belief and spirituality. Thereafter, the group has discussions on specific topics such as ethics, sin, the nature of God, how they worship and observe the holidays, relationships with friends and family, and so on. We end with their thoughts on the future of Christianity and Paganism, and what they most want you to remember about them as you reflect on their journey to ChristoPaganism.

We are very grateful for the time our volunteers took to make this part of the project possible, and for being willing to open themselves to you so candidly. We believe you will find these chapters enlightening and perhaps a bit surprising. You might even catch a glimpse of yourself and your own spiritual journey in the stories that they share.

Chapter 10

GETTING ACQUAINTED

"Welcome everyone," River says to the volunteers as they assemble. "We're glad you are here and willing to share your spiritual journeys with us. Our readers are interested to know more about you—who you are and how your journey began."

"Let's start by getting acquainted," Joyce suggests. "We would like to know your names and a bit about you. How old are you? What do you do for a living? Do you have children? What are your interests? Are you active in any organizations, and what faith were you raised in?" She laughs. "I know that's a lot to begin with! Anyone feel like jumping right in?"

"Sure, I will," says a volunteer. "My name is Michael, and I am forty-three years old. I currently work as a detention officer, specifically as a supervisory deputy jailer, and am also the department chaplain. Before that I worked eleven years in patrol at a small agency for the Commonwealth of Kentucky. Prior to that I was a petty officer in the Naval Reserves, where I served as a chaplain's aide for seven years. At the moment I'm working on a dual bachelor's degree in religion and philosophy, and my interests include ceremonial magick, kabbalah, and history. I am a founding member of international orders of ceremonial Christian magicians known as the Order of the Astral Star and the Order of the Star of Bethlehem. I currently am the Chief Adept and President of these groups."

"So were you raised as a ceremonial Christian magician?" asks River.

"Oh no," Michael answers, "I was raised Southern Baptist, although my parents were very open-minded. My grandmother referred to herself as a psychic, for example, and was interested in the paranormal and supernatural, so I was exposed to those ideas also. Perhaps the formative experience of my childhood was the near-death experience I had on Easter Sunday when I was eight years old. I feel that my life was never the same after it. My family was considering going fishing after church that Sunday. There had been a lot of rain and the creek was high with rushing water. On the edge of the dam I slipped on some moss and went into the water before I could even catch my breath. I remember seeing a fish hovering about two feet over my head, looking at me; it was then I realized I was underwater. I didn't know how to swim. The current was pulling me toward the dam; I tried to swim and resist it, but couldn't. I felt water enter my lungs, I remember coughing, and then I lost consciousness.

"The next thing I remember," recalls Michael, "is floating down a tunnel. I could see a bright light ahead in the distance. The walls of the tunnel were blue-gray, and every now and then I would pass a ring or band of dull, white light as I moved forward. Then I entered a very bright light, which blinded me, and when I could see again, I saw that I was in a glade or meadow. The colors were bright and vivid—the grass was very green, and there were flowers and bushes of many colors. I asked, 'Where am I?' and heard a voice that said, 'Don't be afraid.' Well, it hadn't occurred to me to be afraid until the voice said that, then I was afraid. I perceived a presence and tensed up. This presence told me that I had come too early, that I had things to do in my life. I was told I would be sent back and not to worry, that I was loved and had a purpose. I would be guided. Then I was told to breathe and relax. I breathed and felt like I was falling, then I jumped sharply and felt myself back in my body. I was on the bank of the creek about thirty-five yards from the dam with my head on a rock. I was throwing up water when my parents found me and I said, 'I fell in.'

"The next Easter Sunday, when the pastor made the altar call, I heard the voice from the same presence calling me by name," continues Michael. "I stood up and began to move toward the altar. My mom stopped me because you had to be thirteen before you could come forward on your own unless you got permission from the Board. At this time I was only nine. So I met with the Board and told them of my near-death experience the previous year and then how I heard the voice again, calling me by name. They believed me and felt it was a genuine call, so they allowed me to be baptized. Because of that experience, I have always believed that Yeshua (Jesus) is the Christ, the Son of God and is divine. I have never changed that view."

"Thanks, Michael, for sharing that amazing experience," Joyce says. "Has anyone else had a near-death experience?" No hands go up. "Okay then, Michael, you are our only one. However, like Michael, I imagine several of you were raised Protestant. How many of you come from Protestant families?" Six additional hands go up. "Okay, that's seven total. How many of you were raised Catholic?" Five hands go up. "Since more of you were raised Protestant, let's begin with you. Any other Baptists?" No one answers.

"I was raised Lutheran," offers one volunteer.

"Okay," says River, "tell us about yourself."

"My name is Eleanor, and I'm thirty-one years old. I'm currently unmarried and have no children. I work as a financial analyst for an IT department and have a bachelor's degree in business administration. I've always felt strongly attracted to the ministry and have recently decided to take the plunge and enroll in a divinity school. With my blend of Christianity and earth religions, however, I'm not quite sure which divinity school will be a good fit . . . so I'm still considering my options.

"I'm a member of the Lutheran Campus Ministries 'grad group' for grad students and young professionals," Eleanor continues. "I'm also a member of Diana's Grove Mystery School, which is an earth-based program for personal and spiritual growth that uses myth as a catalyst for growth. They are open to people of all faiths, so I feel comfortable there and being both earth-centered and Christian."

"Does this differ from your childhood upbringing?" asks River.

"Yes," Eleanor replies. "I was raised Missouri Synod Lutheran, which I consider the second-most conservative Lutheran denomination after the Wisconsin Synod. This is a very strict form of Lutheranism. Even today, women cannot be ordained and the Bible is viewed as literally true and the inerrant Word of God. Considering how contradictory the Bible is and how inconsistently the churches I attended interpreted it, I had to suspend my disbelief throughout my youth in order to believe that the Bible is 100% literal truth, and 100% God's word.

"I grew up in a family," notes Eleanor, "that was very active in church. We attended every week without fail, as well as special services. My parents volunteered for many roles at church, such as treasurer, president, vacation Bible school coordinator, and so on. My grandfather was a Missouri Synod minister. I attended the Lutheran school and in high school became president of the youth group at church. Despite all of this, home was a chaotic place where my brother and I suffered abuse—physical and sexual as well as mental. I won't go into the details, but as with most abused children, I blamed myself and somehow combined my shame and guilt with the idea of Original Sin. This left me with feelings of hate for myself and my body, which I still struggle with today."

"My goodness," Joyce says, "thank you for sharing this. I imagine there are many readers who will be able to relate to your story—unfortunately."

"Despite all of this," says Eleanor, "church was a force that brought our family together, and was a stable place for me to be. God and church were central to my life as a child. Good things came of it too. I learned how to pray and develop a relationship with God. I was a member of a caring community that gave me a sense of belonging and helped me survive the situation at home."

"Later we will focus on your experiences after childhood that bring you to where you are today, and we look forward to hearing more," notes Joyce.

"That's fine," Eleanor agrees.

"I was also a Lutheran in my youth," speaks up another volunteer, "although I didn't have the home life struggles that Eleanor did."

"Tell us about yourself," encourages River.

"My name is Blaine, and I am forty-seven years old. I am married and have two children. I have a bachelor's degree and currently work in the IT department of a large state university, but also have a strong background in theater. My interests include silversmithing, woodworking, cooking, and camping.

"My parents were easy-going about attending church," notes Blaine, "although my brother and I were encouraged to go if we wished. I often went to church with my grandmother, who I believe was Methodist. I eventually decided to be baptized into the Lutheran church. Like Michael, I had an experience when I was eight that affected me profoundly."

"What happened?" asks River.

"Shortly after my baptism my grandfather died. A couple of weeks after his death I was in the choir loft practicing for an upcoming service when I started thinking about my grandpa. I remembered the things we did together and wondered what I would do without him. At that moment," Blaine says, "I saw him walking toward me on the other side of the railing, which was an accomplishment since I was on the second floor. He hovered there and told me he would always be there for me. If I needed him all I had to do was think of him, ask him a question in my head, and he would answer me. At this point I began to cry and the teacher took me to the pastor. I told him what had just happened."

"How did he react?" Joyce asks.

"Unlike Michael's experience," Blaine says, "this minister was not supportive. He told me it was a trick of the devil, and that the image was not my grandpa but a demon that had come to steal my soul. My experience felt so strongly otherwise to me that I didn't believe him, and I decided I could do without religion. I did not go back to that school the next year. Since I've gotten involved with Paganism, I still tend to stay to myself. I don't belong to any Pagan or ChristoPagan organizations at the moment, and consider myself to be a Solitary practitioner."

"Since Solitaries make up about half of all Pagans, you're in good company," observes River.

"I also am a Solitary who comes from a Protestant background," speaks up another volunteer.

"Okay, tell us about yourself," says River.

"My name is T.J. and I am forty-eight years old. I currently work in payroll and accounting, but also love making jewelry. I have a jewelers certificate and am working to get my gemologist diploma. I also enjoy music, crafts, and cooking, and I have two children.

"When I was a child," notes T.J., "I went with my parents to a Methodist church. They switched to the United Church of Christ when I was twelve as they were looking for a more open-minded fellowship. I was always allowed to have my own opinions as long as I discussed them in a civil way. My parents never gender-assigned God, and while the Bible was seen as a valuable resource, it was never considered to be an absolute authority. Unlike Blaine's situation, I grew up around people who did not believe in the existence of the devil or Satan."

"That must have been nice," observes Blaine.

"It was," T.J. agrees, "especially since around the age of twelve I became interested in divination, witchcraft, and astrology, and my curiosity on these subjects was not discouraged by my parents. Today I also practice primarily alone, as a Solitary, although I participate in the Christian Witch e-list on Yahoo! and go to one large Pagan gathering every year, called the Pagan Picnic."

"Who else comes from a Protestant background?" asks Joyce.

"I do," speaks up another volunteer, "although it was pretty sporadic."

"That's fine," says Joyce. "Tell us about yourself."

"My name is Hilary, and I am forty-three years old. I am a stay-at-home mom and work part-time as a surgical assistant. I am taking classes to earn a bachelor's degree in biology. I enjoy gardening, cooking, sewing, hiking, fishing, art, music, and literature. I am a member of the Episcopal church, where I sing in the choir, serve on the board of the women's group, and am in the sewing guild.

"My childhood was unusual," Hilary notes, "because my mom was the only divorced woman in town *and* a hippie. Most people didn't associate with us, so I spent a lot of time outdoors and alone. I could hike all day through the woods and I knew each bush and tree. I related to them as entities, not objects, even naming and talking to some of them. I remember once laying on my back in a pasture, looking up at the sky, and having the sensation I was being cradled in the large hands of an omniscient being."

"That's beautiful," comments Joyce.

"Yes," Hilary agrees. "There was an old man, a caretaker, on the property next to us, who taught me how to fish and catch turtles and fry chicken. He also taught me about charms, talked about the devil and evil spirits, and told scary stories about what happens to children who don't mind their parents." She laughs. "That was the first time I got the idea that I could interact with spirits. Sometimes I would go to the Baptist church with one of my friends and their family, but I didn't quite understand it. When I was eleven I began attending a Lutheran school, where I learned a lot more about Christianity. I loved that church and the pastor—he had a big booming voice, was very kind, and we all adored him."

One of the volunteers signals for attention, and says, "I have a question. I'm wondering if anyone here has been ordained in a Christian tradition and is still active as a minister today."

"Great question," says River. "Anyone here an ordained Christian minister?" Five hands go up. "How many of you actively use this ordination or perform ministerial duties because of it?" All five hands stay up. "Okay," asks River, "since we began with the Protestants, how many of you have your ordination through a Protestant denomination?" Two hands remain up. "We'd like to hear about you—who wants to go first?"

"I guess I will," says one of the two. "My name is Brighid, and I am sixty-five years old. I am an ordained minister of a large Christian denomination, though I would rather you not say which one."

"All right, we won't," Joyce says.

"Both of my parents were Christians and active in the church. I went to church regularly all through my childhood. Even so, my parents were generally tolerant of other views. I was expected to be a Christian and to follow Christian precepts, but was never told that Christianity is the only way to find God. I remember deciding to 'come forward' when I was ten and become a full member. There was a series of questions we were asked during our reception. One of them was 'Do you believe in the Holy Scriptures and that therein only is revealed the way of truth?' I told my mother that while I believed the Bible was an important source of truth, it is not the only place where God reveals truth to people. She agreed with me and said I could still answer yes to the question while continuing my own quest for truth. I remember this conversation vividly. I see it now as the beginning of my tension with the church, though not necessarily with Christianity.

"In the 1980s," Brighid continues, "I had the opportunity to take a workshop given by Starhawk, a well-known Pagan writer. I had one of her books and she autographed it to me as 'one who stands in two worlds.' I certainly did then and still do now to some extent. I've come a long way, though, from being merely concerned with inclusive language to working seriously on my theology/thealogy, as well as developing a satisfying spiritual practice."

"I can relate to the feeling of standing in two worlds also," says the other of the two Protestant ministers. "My name is Cern, pronounced 'Kern.' I am forty-seven years old, married, but have no children. I have a Masters of Divinity and currently work as a hospital chaplain. I got my seminary training and ordination through the same denomination as Brighid, believe it or not. I am also a priest of a coven that belongs to the Thalia Clan Wiccan tradition and have been a member of that clan for five years. Standing in both worlds as I do allows me to be more effective in my chaplaincy work. Since I actively blend Paganism and Christianity, I feel comfortable interacting with a variety of people and faith traditions. I see myself as an interfaith chaplain and feel comfortable giving spiritual support to people of all faiths, be it Christianity, Judaism, Islam, Hinduism, or Paganism. I am also active in a local interfaith group."

"It sounds like you enjoy your work as a chaplain," comments River.

"I do, very much," says Cern. "For several years before doing my chaplain residency, I pastored a couple of congregations. While this has its own rewards, I eventually decided to focus my energies in another direction. It's strange, really, but I did not grow up in a particularly religious household. My father was a Baptist and he dropped me off at their Sunday school a few times, but I didn't like it. The teacher spent a lot of time talking about hell. My mother was United Church of Christ, and I don't remember much about them, except that once she was divorced we weren't welcome there.

"My great-grandmother believed in ghosts and spirits and so did the rest of the family," Cern recalls. "Sometimes a family member would report that a deceased relative had come and spoken to them. A belief in fairies was respected but not talked about. My grandfather collected stones and even though he had a scientific interest in geology and lapidary, he could tell me the magical qualities of the different stones.

"Most of my religious training in childhood came from scouting, which also taught us about Native Americans and their spirituality. I felt a strong connection to nature whenever the troop went camping," Cern remembers. "Being a part of that small group was important to me and stuck with me. I've preferred small groups ever since. My mom remarried when I was thirteen and we moved into my stepfather's home, but I never felt welcome. I began going to Bible study and became born-again when I was fourteen. I started out at a Methodist church but then switched to a fundamental, evangelical, and pentecostal church because they seemed more literal and serious about the Bible. At that time in my life I tended to view everything in black and white and was very attracted to the authority and certainty these preachers seemed to have."

"This need for certainty reminds me of the mythic literal or Blue worldview," observes River.

"I can see that now as well," Cern remarks.

"As we continue on with the introductions," says Joyce, "let's hear from the other three ministers. Can you tell us who you are?"

"I am Kirk," says one.

"I am David," says the second.

"And I am Paul," says the third.

"Okay," says River. "You say you are Christian ministers but that you are not Protestant. Does that mean you are Catholic, then?"

"We are ordained in the Independent Sacramental Movement," says Kirk.

"I am not familiar with this movement," notes River. "Can you tell us what it is?"

"I'll be happy to describe it," offers David. "The Independent Sacramental Movement is a movement that has its origins in the apostolic succession of those Christian denominations that value apostolic succession, namely, the Roman Catholic Church, Eastern Orthodox Churches, and the Anglican Church. At various times in history, individuals consecrated as bishops in these churches disassociated with them and founded independent churches (also known as jurisdictions), as in the case of the Old Catholic Church based out of Utrecht in the Netherlands in protest to the First Vatican Council in the 1800s. Apostolic succession is a theological idea that involves the belief in an unbroken succession going back in time to the original Apostles who were believed to have been consecrated by Jesus Christ. This apostolic succession is passed on from bishop to bishop and bishop to priest or deacon in the sacrament of Holy Orders. Many ISM jurisdictions ordain and consecrate women and openly gay and lesbian members. Theologically, ISM jurisdictions and individual clergy are very diverse. There are independent jurisdictions that are theologically conservative (sometimes more conservative than the Vatican), and there are also those jurisdictions that are extremely liberal. Another phenomenon of the ISM movement is the esoteric and Gnostic element. There are many small ISM jurisdictions who claim to be Gnostic and esoteric (occult) in nature, yet still subscribe to the concept of apostolic succession and the sacraments. For those readers who are interested, I recommend the book *The Many Paths of the Independent Sacramental Movement* by John Plummer as a good place to start."

"You asked initially if we were Catholic," says Paul, "and I do think of myself as a catholic, but a catholic with a small *c*. The word *catholic* really means 'universal,' and the form of Christianity I find meaningful is the one with a universal message. I also look for the universal messages in my Pagan and Buddhist spiritualities. There are several branches of Christianity that claim universality, including the Roman Catholic, the Oriental and Eastern Orthodoxies, the Anglican, and even high-church Lutherans. All of them are far more liturgically oriented than the evangelical churches, although the Anglicans and Lutherans do try to bridge the connection to Protestant thinking and practice. The importance of the sacraments in spiritual life is a key feature of the ISM movement," continues Paul. "Ritual acts such as the Eucharist, baptism, confirmation, marriage, and Holy Orders are seen as important vehicles that link the human spirit with the divine. Most of those for whom the sacramental life is a major part of their spirituality are drawn to the independent churches because their form of worship is very liturgical in nature, in contrast to the greater emphasis placed on preaching in the more evangelical branches of Christianity."

"Thanks for this thorough explanation. We want to hear about each of you in turn. Who would like to go first?" asks Joyce.

"I will," says Kirk. "My name is Kirk, and I am forty-four years old. I am married and have one child. My family and I live on a fifty-six-acre farm with one cat, two dogs, and a llama. I have a master's degree in counseling and a double bachelor's in psychology and religion. I make my living as a licensed acupuncturist and Chinese herbalist. I enjoy kayaking, hiking, and playing basketball; and I also love to read and meet new people. I am also very involved in local business and governmental organizations. I am the director of our area rotary club, chair of my town's revitalization initiative, chair of the business association, a member of the county Democratic Committee, and chair of the local Democratic Committee. In terms of religious organizations, I served as co-president of the Covenant of the Goddess for one year. And I am the founder and president of Cherry Hill Seminary, a Pagan seminary focused on offering training in ministry skills."

"Oh yes," says River, "we're familiar with your seminary."

"I was not raised in any faith tradition," notes Kirk, "as my parents wanted me to explore religions for myself. They were nominally Methodist, although later in his life my father said that if he were to practice a religion it would be Paganism. I would say my upbringing was secular. My aunt introduced me to New Age books early on, in my teens. Unlike many Pagans, then, I found Paganism early in my life and studied it throughout high school and college. I really had no interest in Christianity until my thirties."

"My upbringing wasn't secular as such, although my father wasn't particularly active in the church, despite being Mormon," says Paul.

"A Mormon, you say," comments Joyce. "I was raised in a branch of Mormonism."

"I grew up in Salt Lake City," Paul replies. "I am fifty-nine years old and a professor of clinical psychology with a PhD in counseling psychology. I also have a law degree, although I do not currently practice. My interests include cooking, taking walks, and studying history and philosophy. In my childhood I was raised as a Mormon in Salt Lake City, which is the capital of the Latter Day Saints church. Which Mormon-based tradition did you come from?" asks Paul.

"The group that has its headquarters in Independence, Missouri," replies Joyce.

"Yes," Paul continues, "I am familiar with them. My family has an ancestral village in central Utah, which my great grandparents settled as the first pioneers in that area. On my father's side we are Mormons for three generations, but even so, my father was not very active in the church. My mother was not raised in a particularly religious household, and she explored a number of religions in her life. She did not ever join one until several years after she married my father. Growing up, I was sent to Sunday school and youth activities, but around age nineteen I left the church. I was ordained an independent bishop by this guy right here." He gestures to David.

"Really? That's interesting. Tell us about yourself, David," River says.

"I am thirty-seven years old and have one child," begins David. "I work part-time in religious education while I finish a double major in religious studies and philosophy. I enjoy reading, watching movies, and participating in multiplayer games online. I am also involved in several organizations. I am a member of a local Unitarian Universalist church, where I serve as the director of religious education, focused primarily on adult education and the Coming of Age program. This is a paid position. I am a Freemason and belong to several Masonic groups. I am a third-degree Druid Adept as well as Chief Druid of a local grove of the Ancient Order of Druids in America. I am an ordained bishop in the esoteric gnostic Christian church called Nova Roma, where I serve on the board and as secretary, and have been a past president. I also participate in a networking group for esoteric Christian bishops called Sophia Circle."

"That's quite a variety of organizations," observes River.

"Yes," David agrees, "but my spiritual path has taken me in a variety of directions. I wasn't raised in any particular religious tradition, and as a child I felt a connection to all faiths. By that I mean I didn't know which was right, so I accepted that they could all be right. My father was Lutheran and my mother Methodist, but they didn't push either faith onto me. I felt free to develop my own path. I identified with Wicca early on, but after I left the Navy I became a Catholic and entered a Benedictine monastery for a time. It was some years later that I became involved in the Independent Sacramental Movement."

"Interestingly, there is another volunteer on this project who has lived in a monastery, as a cloistered Carmelite nun," Joyce observes. Turning to a lady near her, Joyce says, "That would be you! Won't you introduce yourself?"

"Sure! My name is Barb, and I am sixty-two years old. I have never married and I have no children. I am now retired, although I have a bachelor's in biology and worked for many years. I enjoy reading books and studying, and also giving tarot card readings.

"I did live in a cloistered community for a time," Barb continues, "after my conversion to Catholicism in the 1980s. I was raised, however, as a sort of combined Baptist and Presbyterian in a very fundamental and evangelical home. I was only allowed to have Christian friends and was expected to attend church several times a week. My father was very strict and judgmental. My conversion to Catholicism was part of my journey in moving away from my fundamentalist upbringing. But I could not stay in the convent for several reasons, some of which were physical, since about that time I began to develop disabilities, which are with me still. Other reasons included my broadening view of religion in which I became less interested in dogma as I got older. Part of what attracted me initially to Wicca and Paganism was its relative lack of dogma."

"I was raised in a Presbyterian family also," observes River, "although it was the branch of Presbyterianism that was more liberal, not evangelical. It is quite a change to go from your evangelical background to Catholicism and a Carmelite monastery, and we look forward to hearing more. I see that we have four other Catholics among our volunteers. Is that right? Who would like to begin?"

"I'll be happy to start," says one of the remaining volunteers. "My name is Victoria, and I am fifty-seven. I have a master's in nursing and have worked as a nurse for thirty years. I will soon be retiring and am looking forward to doing work as a healing touch practitioner and reflexologist. I enjoy writing poetry, knitting, and creating altars.

"Every week I meet with a small Catholic community that gathers at a local university," Victoria continues. "I am a member of a labyrinth committee at an Order of Dominican Sisters. I am the convenor of a local labyrinth group, a member of an international labyrinth organization, and a trained labyrinth facilitator. I am a member of the World Community for Christian Meditation and a member of Tejas Web, a group in the Reclaiming tradition of witchcraft. I am also a student of the Anderson Feri tradition, which I have been studying for the past four years. My mother was an Irish Catholic," Victoria says, "and my father was the great-grandson of a Methodist circuit preacher. I grew up in England in the 1950s."

"You are the only one of our volunteers to grow up outside of the United States," observes Joyce.

"Am I?" Victoria wonders. "Well, my mother saw that I was raised Catholic, baptized and confirmed. I attended a state school, however, which was run by the Church of England, so as a Catholic I was in the minority. When I was eleven I decided I wanted to participate in their services and my mother did not object. My father proclaimed himself to be an atheist and never came to church with us. I went to Mass on Sunday with my mother, but church was not discussed at home. We never prayed at home either. When I was fifteen I began going to a Baptist youth group and soon after I converted. My mother was very opposed to this and we became estranged. When I was eighteen I began attending a charismatic church and loved the ecstatic experience of speaking in tongues and so on. It would be several years before I found my way back to Catholic spirituality, and thereafter I encountered Paganism."

"I also came from a family where my mother was Catholic and my father was Protestant," speaks up another volunteer.

"Please introduce yourself, if you will," says River.

"My name is Raven and my mother was a Catholic, and I was baptized a Catholic. My father was Protestant, although it was rumored that he had a Native American background. I did sense that he had a connection to the earth. We weren't particularly active in church, although it seems that religious knowledge came naturally to me, maybe because I went to Sunday school with my cousins, or my grandmother told me stories. I'm not sure. But I remember that I had opinions about religion and didn't hesitate to voice them. I sometimes had debates or arguments with my mom about religion.

"I believed in spirits and an afterlife," Raven notes. "In fact, I took those beliefs for granted. Ghosts, angels and spirits were everywhere for me. I had a strong feeling that I was being watched over and protected by a benevolent force in my youth, which at that time I saw as a male force. It would be true to say that I love religion. I love the stories and the music and the feelings I have that bring on a sense of awe—including awe at the history and creativity of the human spirit. I see my life in the cycles of nature but I could as easily see it in the cycle of the life of Jesus. It is natural to me to see the divine in nature."

"I see it there too," says another volunteer.

"Tell us about that," suggests Joyce.

"My name is Charlene. I am fifty-three years old, married, and have children. I have a bachelor's degree in home economics and am certified to teach kindergarten. My interests include folk music, needle arts and crafts, cooking, and reading. I am not currently affiliated with any group and practice as a Solitary.

"Like Raven and Victoria, I was raised a Catholic and attended Mass on the holy days at least, but not every week," continues Charlene. "My father had the responsibility of driving us to Mass, because my mother never learned to drive. Come Sunday morning, we would take our cue from Dad as to which Mass we were attending. If he had his suit on, we were going to Catholic Mass. If he had his boots on, we were going to Nature Mass, which included hiking, fishing, or camping. Sometimes Mom went with us.

"Our trips to the outdoors may not seem spiritual to others," Charlene observes, "but they were to us and to Dad. He taught us an appreciation of the earth, the moon, and nature. We learned about the seasons and phases of the moon, the stars, and constellations. He also taught us about the value of self and working toward common goals. My mother was a gardener, and she planted organically and by phases of the moon. At the same time, we burned candles and incense and prayed to the saints for specific purposes. Due to this upbringing, I feel that I was raised a sort of Pagan, but we didn't call it that."

"There are probably many families that have adopted a Pagan outlook in some aspects of their lives but don't call it that," muses River. "Looks like we are to our last volunteer. But last is not least! What can you tell us about yourself?"

"My name is Francis, and I am fifty-four, currently unmarried, and have two children. I attended broadcast school and have worked as an announcer for NPR since 2001. I am also a manager at an organic grocery store. I enjoy science fiction and have collected comic books all my life. I also like to perform music, often with rock bands, although recently I have switched to doing more acoustic music.

"I am active in several organizations," Francis notes. "I am a member of the local Zen center, where I participate in weekly Soto zazen services. I am also affiliated with the Shining Heart Sufi community and attend their gatherings several times a year. Locally, I founded a group that hosts the Dances of Universal Peace, which were created by an important Sufi teacher. I also participate in the Dervish healing ritual on occasion. In addition to this, I am a priest of Yarrow Coven, a local group that practices North American Eclectic Wicca. In this role, I assist in planning gatherings, considering new members, and preparing for our Sabbat observances. Yarrow also puts on and sponsors a large free public gathering each year called the Pagan Picnic. This is the same event that T.J. mentioned earlier, which she attends every year. The Picnic occurs in a public park, is open to the public, and draws close to three thousand people. I have been the entertainment coordinator for this event in past years.

"I was raised in a large Catholic family," Francis continues, "which was very devout. Several members of my mother's family were priests and nuns. I grew up with the Catholicism of the 1950s. We went to Mass every week and sometimes daily, at a time when it was still said in Latin. I had First Communion when I was five and was confirmed at age six. I practiced Catholicism until my twenties, at which point I began to drift away. I then encountered other spiritualities and explored a number of different paths. Yet I began that exploration as a Catholic who had discovered the mysticism of his native religion. You might say that through the sacrifice of the Mass I discovered magick."

"That is a very interesting thing to say," observes Joyce, "and I'm sure that Paul, David, and Kirk will be discussing magick in the context of esoteric, gnostic Christianity later on. Perhaps you'll join in that conversation and give us some of your perspective."

"I'll look forward to it," says Francis.

"Thank you, everyone, for introducing yourselves and telling us a bit about your childhood and spiritual upbringing," comments River. "Next we would like to ask you to share your spiritual journey from childhood up to the present. For some of you it sounds like it was quite a journey, with a number of profound changes and decisions along the way. We look forward to hearing more."

Chapter 11

THE JOURNEY CONTINUES

"**P**reviously, you told us about yourself and your origins," says Joyce, "but we know your life has involved much growth and change. Many things must have happened for you to find yourself today in a group discussion on ChristoPaganism."

"We want to hear about your journey as you left childhood and began to grapple with issues of faith and belief," continues River. "Since we have gotten to know you in a specific order, it might be easier for our readers if we keep to this order for now. In that case, we begin again with you, Michael."

"That's fine," says Michael. "You'll recall that I was raised Southern Baptist and had a near-death experience when I was eight. I think this experience impacted me from that moment on, as I did not feel like a child through my youth. I did not seem to fit in with the other kids, as I was more serious and disciplined—traits my parents encouraged. My grandmother suggested I befriend other kids who, like me, weren't particularly popular, and I took her advice. Some of these folks have remained my good friends to this day. Some of them became founding members of the Order of the Astral Star in 1980.

"Working on this order, which is a high-ritual, ceremonial, and mystical Christian order, received a lot of my focus in high school and college," Michael recalls. "The other founding members and myself developed a basic curriculum of self-exploration and research into the occult arts and psychic sciences. By the time I went to college, which was a Baptist college, things were going well with the order. We only had ten members, but they were dedicated, and we had a number of applicants. Some applicants were accepted and some were not.

"One of the applicants who wasn't accepted," Michael continues, "was the fiancée of one of our members and also the daughter of a local Baptist minister. We did not accept her because we knew she was abusing drugs and alcohol, among other reasons, and eventually her behavior caused her to flunk out of school. Rather than admit to the real cause for flunking, she told her parents that she had been recruited on campus by a Satanic cult, of which I was the leader. You can't imagine the uproar this caused, especially as I was a religion major."

"I bet I can," Joyce comments. "Not to mention that this was in the 1980s, a time when there was a lot of focus on, almost an hysteria about, Satanic cults. There seemed to be a constant parade of stories in the news regarding accusations of cultic brainwashing and 'ritual abuse' due to Satanic rituals. It seems hard to imagine now, but people saw Satanic cults everywhere."

"Yes," agrees Michael, "and we found ourselves right in the middle of it, even though the Astral Star has nothing whatsoever to do with Satanism. I was called before a tribunal to answer questions. The tribunal said the young lady accused me of being the head of a group called the Satanic Order of the Astral Star. Since that was not the name of our order, I could in all honesty say that I was not the head of such a group, nor had I ever heard of a group by that name. I also told them I believed the young lady did not want to admit to her parents that she had a substance abuse problem. I expressed my willingness to take both a drug test and a polygraph test, as long as they administered the same to her. The charges were dismissed.

"This incident, however, brought me to the attention of one of the faculty who believed the order existed," Michael continues. "A couple of weeks later he called me to his office and told me he knew that the order was real. I didn't know how to answer. He asked me if I was a Christian and believed I had a calling to the ministry. I said yes. He then had me swear on a Bible to keep his name and position, as well as the content of our conversation, private. He swore to do the same. We were only to refer to each other by our order mottos, or names, and other information was to be given only generally. He then identified himself as a practicing occultist, an Adept of an organization called the Hermetic Order of the Golden Dawn. This group is a well-known ceremonial magick organization that had its beginning in England in the late nineteenth century.

This faculty member was very influential for our order," Michael notes, "and helped establish us as a high ceremonial magick and mystical Christian group. His advice over the years was very helpful."

"Things certainly got off to a dramatic start for you," observes River, "and I know we will hear more about the order later on. But now, Eleanor, we come to you. I recall that you were raised in a very strict fundamentalist Lutheran home, which was also chaotic and abusive."

"That is true," Eleanor states, "but fortunately things began to shift for me when I won a scholarship to an exclusive girls school in a well-to-do neighborhood. I learned about class differences then, for sure. But I also was exposed to a more liberal and feminist worldview. In my teen years I began questioning my family dynamic and the church's teachings. *Why couldn't women be ordained?* I wondered. I began to argue more in Bible class. It was about this time that I remember sitting outside one day while in Bible class and thinking 'God is in the grass.'

"I really began to think for myself," Eleanor continues, "when I went away to college in 1993. At the university, I found a women's spirituality group that was offered by the chaplain's office. All kinds of women came to this group—Christian, Jewish, Buddhist, agnostic, atheist, and Pagan. We would create a circle by singing chants, which I learned later were often Pagan chants. We were given a word each week and would bring something to share with the group about that word. The word served as a theme or focus. I was participating in co-created ritual, though I didn't have those words at the time. When I went home for summer break, I continued these circles with a group of my friends.

"Eventually I left college for a variety of reasons," Eleanor notes, "but continued to search for a spiritual community. I went to some Goddess Women Gatherings, which were organized by another women's spirituality group, and they told me about Diana's Grove. I went to one of the Grove's events in 1997, and it was life-changing for me. I joined Diana's Grove Mystery School the next year and have been a member ever since. By the way," Eleanor adds, "Raven is also involved with Diana's Grove. I don't believe she mentioned that in her introduction."

"No, she didn't," says River. "We'll be sure to ask her about it this time around. Blaine, I believe you are next. You told us about an experience where your grandfather appeared to you in church and the pastor said it was a demon that had come for your soul. What happened then?"

"As I said," Blaine notes, "I did not return to that school the next year. Although I continued to go to church with my grandmother after that, services were never the same for me again.

"By the time I was in high school," Blaine recalls, "I had friends from several different faiths, particularly Jewish and Buddhist. I was very curious about their faiths and asked them all sorts of questions. As I learned more about them, I realized we shared some basic tenets. It was then, I think, that I began to create my crazy quilt of faith. I began to adopt and merge into my spirituality those portions of others' beliefs that rang true to me.

"My first encounter with Paganism occurred when I was eighteen," continues Blaine, "and I met two Pagan women who talked to me a long time about their spirituality. I also met other Pagans when I was twenty-one and lived in Las Vegas for a time. A woman there helped me develop some of my psychic and divinatory skills. When I moved back to the Midwest, I discovered an active and fairly large Pagan community. I attended a number of gatherings and helped put on the Pagan Picnic that Francis and T.J. mentioned, for a couple of years. Once I had my children, my wife—who is Baptist but open-minded—and I created a ChristoPagan parenting group in our city. Unfortunately, we have moved to another state, and for the moment I am being more solitary. However, I remain comfortable with a variety of images of the divine, regardless of what name it is called."

"Perhaps you'll be able to start another parenting group in your new city," River says. "I know your first one was popular. There isn't much opportunity for ChristoPagan parents and families to meet each other."

"That is true," agrees Blaine.

"Now, T.J., when we last spoke to you, you talked about being twelve, when you were just becoming interested in divination, witchcraft, and astrology," Joyce says. "And your interest was not discouraged?"

"No," says T.J., "it never was. My parents were very open-minded and encouraged me to explore all kinds of spiritual subjects. As I got older, I continued learning about the topics that interested me. I did not know any Pagans or Pagan groups, although I did work in our local amateur theatre for a while, and in theatre you encounter everything! However, it wasn't until much later, when my daughter was a teenager expressing an interest in Paganism, that I looked into it more closely. Actually, I was a bit concerned and wanted to know what she was getting involved with. I went to a bookstore and the first book I read was Scott Cunningham's *The Truth About Witchcraft Today*. To my surprise, I found that this book reflected many of my own beliefs, beliefs I had held most of my life. Later on," T.J. continues, "I put the words *Christian* and *Wicca* into an Internet search engine and discovered that there are many others out there who share my views. It was then that I realized I had always been ChristoPagan."

"We have heard many people say that Paganism simply reflects what they already believe," observes Joyce, "which also seems to have been true for you. When you found other ChristoPagans on the Internet, I'm sure it was nice to know that you were not alone in your spiritual interests."

"That is for sure," T.J. agrees.

"Hilary, would you like to continue your story?" asks Joyce. "As I recall, your mother was the only divorcée and hippie in town, which caused you to feel unwelcome in many of the area churches."

"Yes, although when I was eleven," Hilary says, "I began attending the church that had the pastor I adored. Later, I went to a Catholic high school and Mass on Wednesdays. I found this very confusing—like a secret club I was not a member of. As an adult I tried a number of different churches, but none of them felt like home to me. I also felt I was greeted with some suspicion, since at first I was a single woman and later, a single mom. As the 'moral majority' became more prominent politically, I became more disenchanted with Christianity generally. Ultimately I gave up trying to find a spiritual community.

"One day," Hilary recalls, "I saw the Bill Moyers interview of Joseph Campbell. Boy, did that ring true for me! One spirit, many faces. I could live with that. Then in a local bookstore I discovered Wicca. I read *Spiral Dance* and *Drawing Down the Moon*. Wicca seemed as close as I could come to finding my beliefs reflected in a religion. I began as a Solitary witch, then introduced my mom to Wicca and began to celebrate with her and a friend. Suddenly, witches started coming out of the woodwork in my little town. I began holding Sabbats at my house. Some of my Christian friends would come, out of curiosity or concern, and some of them kept coming back. The ones who did said they felt nothing but positive energy and didn't feel like they were doing anything contrary to Jesus's teachings. Then I got involved with a group in the Reclaiming tradition—which is a form of witchcraft started by Starhawk. I attended classes, workshops, and celebrations with them, and found a love and acceptance there that I hadn't ever experienced in church.

"When the War in Iraq began," continues Hilary, "I felt the need to refocus on the teachings of Jesus. I felt the world needed to walk his path and live his message. I discussed this with my sister, and she invited me to her Episcopal church, which she said was different. They *were* different, and I have continued to attend. The members are loving and accepting of me, and say they appreciate my nontraditional perspective. One church member fondly calls me an 'Episco-Pagan.' I am committed to following Jesus's path, because I believe it is my pathway to truth, peace, and enlightenment."

"Hilary's story brings to mind your journey, Brighid," reflects River, "as an ordained Christian minister who Starhawk described as a person standing in two worlds. How did your journey progress?"

"In the years following my ordination," states Brighid, "I began to be interested in feminism and goddess ideology. I consider Starhawk to be my first real mentor on these topics, and I met her in the 1980s. I have continued to look for ways to build a satisfying spiritual practice that includes images of the divine as both male and female (theology and thealogy). As my path continues to meander between the two traditions, it drifts further from the organized church as time goes on. I still value community, connections, and support for others that the church provides. However, I find the institutionalism and conservative, fundamental tendencies of many churches difficult to tolerate."

"As you know," Cern speaks up, "Brighid and I happen to be ordained by the same denomination."

"Yes, that's right," notes River.

"My story is similar to hers in some respects. After I switched from Methodism to a more fundamental evangelical church, I decided to go to Bible college," Cern says. "I graduated, but I struggled to find a paying position. I worked in factories to get by and was disillusioned by the judgmental attitudes of the church, now that they were focused on me. I began to read the writers of the American Revolution and this spurred me to begin to think for myself. I finally found work as a youth minister in a mainline denomination. They saw potential in me and offered to send me to seminary. At seminary I was exposed to liberal Christian theologies for the first time, and I dove into them headfirst. I received my Masters of Divinity degree and then began to pastor.

"Even when pastoring liberal churches," observes Cern, "I had to watch what I said, because most of the members were actually conservative. The church also demanded large amounts of my time, and I had no personal life. After ten years of this, I was feeling pretty burned out. Then I encountered Wicca on the Internet and began chatting with Wiccans in chatrooms. I was very interested in their beliefs and theology. I came to realize that there were dimensions to the divine I knew nothing of, even though I had been to both Bible college and seminary. I felt the Divine Feminine calling to me. I wanted to learn more about her, and met some local Pagans. Soon I began to observe the full moons, but as a Solitary. Within a year my wife began joining me, as she felt empowered by the feminist Wiccan ideas I was sharing with her. We attended our first Pagan Pride Day in 1999, and that same year I did a self-dedication to the Goddess.

"I was still pastoring when I became a Solitary," Cern continues, "and began to lose interest in preaching, since I could not share my new spirituality openly without getting fired. I decided to explore chaplaincy as an alternative, and eventually decided to leave the pastorate and be a chaplain full-time. My congregation was confused and disappointed, but I felt so much freedom upon leaving. As a chaplain I can focus on helping individuals during a crisis and not have to teach or preach anymore. At about the same time I left pastoring, I joined a local coven and have been their high priest for two years. I admit that some days I feel constrained that I can't be fully open as a Pagan, even in chaplain work," Cern notes, "but other days I see that Spirit is all the same and that we just relate to it in different ways."

"It can be very difficult to stand in two worlds professionally," River says, "to use Starhawk's phrase to Brighid."

"I wonder if the other ministers in our group have had similar experiences. The remaining three Christian ministers were ordained in the gnostic or Independent Sacramental Movement," Joyce notes. "Kirk, you went first before. When we last spoke, you told us that your aunt introduced you to New Age books in your teen years, and that you really had no interest in Christianity until your thirties."

"Yes, that's right," Kirk replies.

"What happened then?" asks Joyce.

"I decided that since I live in a Christian culture I should familiarize myself with the religion of the Abrahamic God and his son," Kirk answers. "So I began studying. In the 1990s, a friend of mine converted to Russian Orthodoxy. Since I had some experience in forming a Pagan church, my friend took me with him to a mission he was starting and asked for my help. While there, I met his bishop. The bishop closed his eyes, listened for a while, and then proclaimed that the Holy Spirit told him I would be a priest. I was quite surprised by this."

"I imagine so," observes River.

"I told him I was a Pagan," Kirk continues, "but he said it didn't matter. So I went on to learn some Orthodox liturgies, including communion. Ultimately, however, I didn't feel comfortable being both Pagan and Orthodox, so I stopped the Orthodox liturgies. However, I started getting calls from other Christian denominations who had heard I had some experience in starting churches. They wanted my help. So I went to help when they requested it. Each of them offered me training and I pursued them all—Seventh Day Adventist, Free Methodist, Church of God. I guest-preached, did communion, baptisms, and healing at each for a couple of years. They all knew I was Pagan, and I asked if being one was a problem. They all said no, as long as I didn't teach anything non-Christian in church. Still, I remained uncomfortable with this, and so I did not continue.

"Eventually I met an independent Catholic bishop," Kirk continues, "who is consecrated and cross-consecrated in several apostolic lines, including Greek Orthodox, Roman Catholic, Liberal Catholic, Gnostic, and Old Catholic (Utrecht Succession). He was very open and appreciative of earth religions and Paganism. I took Holy Orders under this bishop through the Old Templar Church, and I was eventually consecrated a bishop as well. As I became more involved in Paganism, I was also ordained by the Wiccan Church of Vermont and served as a co-president of the Covenant of the Goddess for one year. I also founded a Pagan seminary—Cherry Hill Seminary—in 1997."

"Several of our friends have studied at your seminary," observes River, "and a couple have even taught there. It is a much-needed service to the Pagan community."

"Thank you," says Kirk, "I'm glad it has been helpful to many people."

"The second of the independent sacramental ministers is Paul," continues Joyce, "and the last time we spoke to you, we learned you were raised in a family with a long Mormon history, and that you remained involved in the church until age nineteen."

"Yes," Paul agrees, "after which time I went to the University of Utah, where I encountered other points of view. I became heavily involved in the New Left in Utah, decided I was a pacifist, and asked for conscientious objector status in 1968. I was granted this status by the draft board and served my alternative service at a youth crisis center in Denver. While in Denver, I made my first acquaintance with Paganism, as the cook at the youth center was a witch. I did not study with her or any other group, but later I did make a vision quest in the desert of southern Utah, at an important ceremonial site, which is now part of Canyonlands National Park.

"I made this vision quest the summer I returned to Utah for graduate studies," Paul says, "and did it deliberately to ground my new career in psychology in a Pagan spirituality. During my graduate studies I also became involved with the Transcendental Meditation (TM) movement and began to learn more about Eastern paths. But most importantly for me, I also began to make peace with my background in Western traditions and became an Episcopalian. My need for ritual and ceremony was something that had never been fed by my Mormon background. It was also during this time that I got involved in gay activism, particularly in the local chapter of Integrity, a gay Episcopal group.

"After completing my doctorate, I moved to Ohio and connected with the Episcopal church there," continues Paul, "but I entered a crisis of faith. While congregational prayer moved me, inside my private prayer was sterile. I thought meditation might help, so I began to learn about the Buddhist path of *vipassana*. I went on a number of retreats and eventually became a Buddhist in 1981. I continued with this practice for ten years, during which time I moved to Chicago. I looked for a Buddhist community there and, feeling drawn toward Tibetan culture, became involved with a group practicing the Drikung Kagyu lineage. I practiced with them for several years and rose to leadership positions within the group.

"Throughout the years, I never ceased my interest in Paganism," Paul notes, "even if I only practiced it intermittently. A number of losses occurred in my life between 1999 and 2002, which set me adrift. I returned to the site of my vision quest and did another one. I also attended a gathering called Between the Worlds for gay Pagan men. At that event I learned about Pagan Spirit Gathering (PSG), a Pagan gathering sponsored by Circle Sanctuary, which I began to attend. At PSG I was initiated into the Minoan Brotherhood, which is a witchcraft tradition for gay men. Through these gatherings I also met David, who ordained me a couple of years ago as a gnostic bishop."

"Which brings us to you, David," comments Joyce. "Tell us about your spiritual journey."

"As I mentioned, I wasn't brought up in any particular religious tradition," David begins. "When I entered the Navy in 1988, I identified with Wicca, but after a couple of years I converted to Catholicism. When I left the Navy in the early 1990s, after serving in the Gulf War, I joined a traditionalist Roman Catholic Benedictine community. I stayed for several years, but then I realized I was not meant to stay. When I left the monastery I lived for a time with a priest in the Byzantine Rite, and I learned about this tradition from him. I briefly attended a Russian Orthodox church, and then in 1996 I returned to Paganism. When I went back to Paganism, I felt that I was 'casting off Christianity' and didn't want any more to do with it.

"Since then I have been very active in my local Pagan community," David says. "I became a Wiccan high priest and also got involved with Druid revivalry. I was then approached concerning whether I would accept consecration as a bishop in the Independent Sacramental Movement. I responded that I didn't know if I should, since I had been experiencing an anti-Christian period, and I didn't want to be a hypocrite. A friend of mine said, 'Just admit you were wrong and move on.' I did so, and the act of admitting I was wrong to be anti-Christian, and the humility this took, changed me. In 2004 I was ordained an Independent Bishop with apostolic succession through the Old Catholic and Syrian Orthodox Church."

"Three very different paths you each took, and yet you all came to be ordained in the Independent Sacramental Movement," observes River.

"While incorporating a Pagan spirituality at the same time," says Joyce.

"That's right," agrees David.

"Now, interestingly, Barb, like David, also lived in a monastery," Joyce observes. "What happened in your journey, Barb?"

"You may recall that I grew up in a very strict and fundamentalist Presbyterian home," Barb states. "In high school I rejected all this strictness and declared myself to be an atheist. I continued as such for a number of years, generally avoiding religion. Then in my thirties I became interested in yoga, Hinduism, and other Eastern traditions, in part because they had a more immanent view of the divine. You see, my strict father also had a narrow view that God was quite transcendent and removed from us mortals. In the Eastern traditions I encountered a view of the divine that was flowing and permeating, and this fed a part of me that had been long neglected.

"It was the mysticism of Hinduism that led me to the mysticism of Catholicism," Barb observes. "I became a Catholic in 1985 and embraced my new faith wholeheartedly because I was hungry for union with God. In 1992 I entered a cloistered Carmelite monastery that still followed the original constitutions, and so was quite traditional. I enjoyed observing the vow of obedience, because it freed me of responsibility so that I might give all my attention to God. There were difficulties in the cloistered life too, and personalities and points of view I found hard to accept. Yet I think I had my greatest spiritual experiences in the time I was there, and I believe the monastic environment helped make it possible.

"I suffer from physical disabilities now," Barb continues, "which began to manifest themselves in the cloister. I didn't get enough sleep and had trouble with my knees, and eventually could no longer handle the life. From there I left to become a cook at another monastery, and helped with their missionary work. The rigors of this put a great deal of stress on me, and I gave beyond my limits. My physical problems worsened until I was almost completely disabled. I had to leave there as well.

"By 2001 I got a computer and discovered the Internet," Barb recalls. "I encountered Wicca for the first time and ordered some books on it. I also became a student at witchschool.com. I very much wanted to meet local Pagans, so I got onto e-lists and began to attend some gatherings and local events. I have also, like Francis, Blaine, and T.J., been on the committee that plans and hosts the Pagan Picnic."

"Okay," notes River. "Although it wasn't a monastery, like it was for David and Barb, I believe you lived in a Christian community, Victoria. Tell us what happened after you converted from Catholicism to being a Baptist and became estranged from your mother."

"I was raised in England, as you'll recall," says Victoria, "but came to the United States when I was twenty-four. I came in order to live in a contemporary Christian community sponsored by the Episcopalian church, which followed a radical lifestyle. We lived a communal life, and for eight years I lived there in voluntary poverty. The beliefs there were pretty conservative, and a lot of emphasis was placed on the Word of God. It was a charismatic community also, so there was a lot of music and dancing in worship. After eight years, I found myself struggling to believe what they preached. I came to feel that there were other ways of finding God that were also valid. I decided to leave, but I had no friends outside of the community. I left with two cardboard boxes—the sum total of all my possessions. I was thirty-two and had no money.

"I entered a dark time then," Victoria recalls. "I eventually got a job but didn't know what I believed or where I fit. I went to a Buddhist meditation group and a Unitarian Universalist church. I was introduced to Native American spirituality, and in a pipe ceremony I reclaimed my spirit. After that I found women who worked with the Divine Feminine and discovered a new framework for my spiritual practice. I joined a women's spirituality circle where we did some ritual and supported each other. In this circle I was introduced to the Reclaiming tradition and went to several witch camps.

"Meanwhile, I had always had a devotion to Mary and would occasionally go to the Catholic church and light candles," Victoria says. "Living in Texas, I frequently encountered images of Our Lady of Guadalupe, and so I began a devotion to her as Mother Goddess. She also symbolized my Catholic past brought forward into my love for the Goddess.

"In 1996 I became interested in the labyrinth as a form of walking mediation," Victoria continues. "I took training and felt it was the perfect spiritual place to which I could bring all of myself to the divine without any dogma. In 2000 I was asked by the Dominican Sisters to introduce the labyrinth to their community. Working with them caused me to revisit my Catholic heritage, and I joined a local liturgical group.

"At a witch camp in 2002, I did some work with a woman who was a Feri Witch, and it was the most transformative work I've ever done," observes Victoria. "A year later I entered a two-year training program in the Anderson Feri tradition. As I did the Feri work, it took me deeper into my Catholic roots. No matter how I tried to ignore it, I was drawn to practice my Catholic tradition and my Feri tradition. I now train others in Feri and also go to Mass every Sunday."

"That is quite a combination!" remarks River.

"It is, but I am very comfortable with it," Victoria says.

"Raven, like Victoria, you also grew up Catholic," Joyce says, "but you felt that your father had a connection to the earth because of his Native American background. You enjoyed discussing and debating religion, isn't that right?"

"Yes," confirms Raven. "But while I enjoyed talking about religion as I grew up, I was never willing to commit to a religious affiliation. I met a woman who was investigating Wicca and Paganism. Over the course of our friendship we spent many hours discussing religion and what beliefs held up under scrutiny, and what beliefs didn't.

"Thereafter I had an experience that helped me find my direction," recalls Raven. "My grandmother was dying, and I drove six hours to the hospital to see her. As I parked at the hospital, I looked up and saw a cloud float up from the hospital and into the sky. I thought *there goes grandma*, and indeed when I got to her room I learned that she had died as I arrived. The next evening I went to visit my Wiccan friend and attended a ritual with her. When I returned home I told my husband I planned to pursue Paganism."

"How did he feel about that?" asks Joyce.

"He was fine," Raven says, "but I was still feeling unsure. One night as I was lying in bed thinking about my decision, I felt a presence. I believe I saw Jesus standing at the foot of the bed and heard him say that he would always be there for me, but his path wasn't mine. This may sound weird but it was what I needed."

"Eleanor mentioned that you have also gone to Diana's Grove," says River.

"Yes, I've been a member of their Mystery School program for several years," Raven observes, "and plan to keep going. I consider them my true spiritual community."

"And they are fine with your spiritual beliefs?" asks Joyce.

"Very much so," notes Raven. "The Grove is completely inclusive and has no requirement when it comes to belief. People of all denominations, and atheists too, are welcome there."

"Okay, that's great," Joyce says.

"Charlene, I am recalling that you experienced a strong connection to the earth through your father," observes River, "especially as he would sometimes take you to Nature Mass instead of church."

"Yes, my parents were very conscious of their relationship to nature," notes Charlene. "Our family reused, recycled, and composted long before it was the popular thing to do. We realized we were taking our substance from the earth and tried to do so with respect for its care. Although I was raised Catholic, none of us kids were married in the church, which remains a sore spot for my mom. I was married in the Methodist church and took my children there, as I wanted them to have some starting place for their journey. My husband and I have also tried to instill a respect for nature in them and have practiced an awareness of it in our home.

"My spiritual journey unfolded quietly. I have read and studied a number of books on a wide range of religious topics," observes Charlene. "Over the years I have incorporated Christian, Pagan, and Buddhist prayers and rituals into my own practices. I am very private in my spirituality and really don't share what I think with many people. I also don't belong to any groups."

"Many people don't, including several of the volunteers here," observes River.

"I see we have come to the last of you again. Now, Francis, like Charlene, you have also incorporated several different traditions into your spiritual practice, I believe," Joyce says.

"That is true," confirms Francis. "While I was raised in a large, devout Catholic family I drifted away from Catholicism in my twenties and didn't return to the church until my thirties. When I left, the church had just moved into the new 'modernized' Mass of the 1970s, which, frankly, I found bland. When I returned, I went to Mass in a Gothic church, which held services in a circle. Add great music and an enthusiastic congregation to this, and wow! It was a great experience. The energy and the magick that moved around that circle was a new awakening for me. I could see that people were really involved in the worship. So at the ripe old age of thirty-eight, in the early 1990s, I became a 'born-again' Catholic, went back to Mass, and took on jobs such as server and Eucharistic minister. I continue to go to church there every Sunday, which has been thirteen years now.

"These experiences in Mass raised the level of my spiritual expectations regarding the power of ritual. While I was comfortable with my rediscovery of Catholicism, I found it did not meet all my needs, so I continued to explore other paths. In the late 1990s I was exposed to American Sufism, which has also greatly influenced me. Sufism's come-one-come-all approach to earth traditions has taught me something about true eclecticism. I previously mentioned that I formed a group in my city that performs The Dances of Universal Peace, created by a Sufi teacher."

"Yes, you did," notes Joyce.

"I also encountered Zen Buddhism and its form of meditation. I still attend weekly Soto zazen services at the Zen center, where I am a member."

"You mentioned those before. What do these services involve?" asks River.

"We do three things primarily," Francis explains. "We vow to help bring enlightenment to all beings, we repudiate whatever bad karma—like sin—we have created, and we engage in three periods of silent sitting and walking meditation. At the same time that I discovered Zen," Francis continues, "I also discovered Paganism. To learn about all the deities honored in the Neo-Paganism movement has been an education, to say the least. The ritual format and the wonderful people have really helped me understand the nuances of Western religious experience in the twenty-first century. While Paganism honors and observes the sacred year as completely as any path I've encountered, it is the ethic of the Rede that has been of greatest value to me. Perhaps the freedom to create my own path is the true gift that American Paganism has given to me."

"Thank you, Francis, and everyone," River states. "Thank you for sharing your journey as it has taken you into the present. Next, we want to know what you call your spiritual path, and we also want to hear how you blend or mesh together the spiritualities that comprise it."

Chapter 12

WHAT DO YOU
CALL YOUR PATH?

"Now we would like you to describe your path," says River, "and tell us how you combine the spiritualities that make up your path. Let's continue to stay in order for now," River suggests, "as I think it is helping us get familiar with you. Michael, will you begin?"

"Certainly. I refer to myself as a high-ritual, ceremonial Christian magician, and sometimes as a modern Christian mystic. The Order of the Astral Star has a number of members who describe themselves as ChristoPagans, Christian Wiccans, or Christian Witches, although these are not terms I choose for myself."

"As for me," says Eleanor, "I call myself an earth-based christian, and deliberately use a lowercase *c* on christian. I do this to differentiate my experience from mainstream Christianity, particularly evangelical Christianity. My hope is that by using the lowercase, both Christians and Pagans will pause for a moment and notice that I am using the word differently. I want people to wonder what a lowercase christianity looks like. My actual practices," Eleanor continues, "are almost exclusively earth-based. I do rituals and work with the elements, I engage with many gods and goddesses, which I see as faces or expressions of the divine. When I pray, however, it is always to God—which I see as a vast presence everywhere—including to God the Father, a caring, loving, nurturing, and upholding presence.

"I don't gain much peace from traditional Christian worship," Eleanor remarks, "and I balk at the exclusively male imagery, as well as the militaristic and hierarchical language. I generally feel unsafe at church, since I don't know what upsetting thing might be said next. So why do I even still consider myself Christian? My roots are there, and I believe in the ethic of loving thy neighbor as thyself. God as Father is a metaphor that speaks to me, given my history with my human father, and I need as much nurturing male energy as I can get! I think of God's everlasting arms as holding and cradling me. Other parts of Christianity that I resonate with include Jesus as God in the flesh, which for me is a symbol of the divine in each of us.

"I would also describe my spiritual path as eclectic," adds Eleanor, "drawing on many traditions and mythologies. My approach is integrative and very embodied—I like movement, dance, singing, and drumming. I do shamanic journey work and Authentic Movement, which is a form of dancing for the purpose of expressing your soul. Due to the large influence Diana's Grove has had on my spirituality, I work with myth loosely and creatively, as a powerful way to interact with my subconscious and the collective unconscious. I don't really care about finding external truth in myth, as I favor instead the usefulness of myth (including that of Christianity's) as a tool for growth and healing."

"Thanks for that explanation," Joyce says. "As a reminder, you can each speak up when the person before you is finished. Blaine, I believe it is your turn."

"I call myself either ChristoPagan or nondenominational Christian, depending on the circumstances and the perception of the people I am with," comments Blaine.

"I also refer to myself as ChristoPagan," notes T.J. "As for how I combine the two, I really don't think of it as a combination of different things, since I don't see the two spiritualities as differing that much from each other in essentials."

"I refer to myself," adds Hilary, "as a witch whose pantheon is Christian. I combine some Solitary practices with attending church."

"What do you mean by the word *pantheon*, for those who are unfamiliar with it?" asks River.

"*Pantheon* is the term used in Paganism to refer to the group of deities or beings that make up a given religious mythos," replies Victoria. "So, Zeus and Hera are in the Greco-Roman pantheon, and Satan, Yahweh, Jesus, and Mary are in the Christian pantheon."

"Thanks for clarifying," River says.

"I tend to resist calling myself a Pagan," notes Brighid.

"Why is that?" asks Joyce.

"Because it seems as though I am then defining myself over and against Christianity," explains Brighid, "so I prefer the word *Wiccan*."

"When I am among non-Pagans," notes Cern, "I think of myself as a Christian on the outside with a Pagan heart on the inside. As a chaplain, I use Christian words and concepts when I am with Christian patients, and I pray with them in Jesus's name. If I pray with a Jewish patient, I pray Jewish prayers in Hebrew or in English. With a Hindu patient, I will read from the Gita. That's what a chaplain does, in being available to all who ask for help. Inside I am a polytheist and a believer in many points of view beyond the Judeo-Christian. When I am with Pagans, I am thoroughly Pagan. I bring no Christian elements into our rituals. At home my wife and I both identify ourselves as Pagan.

"I still strongly identify with the historical Jesus," observes Cern, "especially Jesus as a Cynic-type preacher, since I believe it is important to question authority, those in power, and also to question our perception of reality. Jesus models this questioning attitude for me. Also, I believe he genuinely loved people, encouraged them, healed them, and wanted them to express their full potential."

"Kirk, how about you?" asks River.

"I call myself a polytheistic Pagan," Kirk answers, "as I also practice Hinduism, Buddhism, and a few other things. Paganism is my foundation, however, and the others are different perspectives or contexts in which I see the world as sacred. In that regard, I don't 'combine' Paganism and Christianity—I honor each of their holidays separately. I don't know that I would use the word ChristoPagan for myself, then. I see myself as Christian *and* Pagan."

"Since I was raised a Mormon," comments Paul, "I see myself culturally as a Mormon, even though I don't identify strongly with it religiously anymore. So I call myself a Mormo-Episco-Buddho-Pagan. I remain involved with my Buddhist group and attend Mass at a high-church Anglo-Catholic parish, since they are gay friendly. I am comfortable performing Christian services by virtue of my ordination as a bishop, and also do Pagan ritual. At this point in my life," Paul concludes, "I've decided not to cut myself off from any stream of spirituality that has meaning for me, however complicated or contradictory that may be."

"Oftentimes I refer to myself as Pagan," notes David, "although depending on where I am and what seems appropriate, I might refer to myself as Gnostic or Gnostic Christian or ChristoPagan. Sometimes I will say I am a Unitarian-Universalist and leave out the rest, when I don't feel like engaging in a discussion. All of this is easier than saying 'I am a Gnostic-Christo-Pagan-Druid-Romano-Unitarian-Universalist-Syncretist,' you know?" he says, laughing.

"That is quite a mouthful," agrees Joyce, with a laugh. "Barb, tell us what you call yourself."

"Well, I describe myself as an eclectic," Barb says, "since it seems the best word to describe my respect for all religions. And I do respect them all because they are all expressions of the yearning for the divine."

"I found this to be a complex question for me," remarks Victoria, "as I realized I don't describe my spiritual path that often to myself or others. In my labyrinth work, I use spiritually neutral language in order to make the concepts accessible to most people. Like Barb, I am truly open to all the ways of God and do not feel there is only one right way, only whatever way is useful to help a person make connection with the divine. I deeply respect that this way is often influenced by history and culture.

"When I do describe my spiritual path," Victoria continues, "I do so differently to different people. To my witch friends I am a Catholic witch. To my Catholic friends I am a progressive Catholic who appreciates earth wisdom and creation spirituality. I'm not sure if I would describe myself as a Pagan influenced by Catholicism or as a Catholic influenced by Paganism. It depends on where I am in my life, I suppose. Sometimes I seem to embrace more of my Catholic side and other times more of my Pagan side. I've never used the term *ChristoPagan*, however, as I'm not quite sure what it means. The ChristoPagan groups I'm familiar with are essentially Pagans who call Christ into their rituals as one of the gods that are invited. That is not the way I practice.

"However, if I were to define the ChristoPagan path for myself," Victoria states, "I would say that it is two separate paths that come together inside of me. I hold both realities equally and honor both realities equally. Inside, they have begun to overlap and integrate. Privately I stand before an image of Guadalupe and call on the holy mother and the star goddess. Privately I call the gods to me along with the saints. Going to Mass brings together various pieces of my path. Sometimes I view the entire Mass as a Rite of Unbinding—a coming together to restore harmony. When I take the cup of communion, I look deeply into it and scry for a fleeting moment, sometimes catching a glimpse from the other world."

"How about you, Raven?" asks Joyce.

"I would describe my path now as mostly Pagan, although I still celebrate Christian holidays," Raven says. "But when I speak about it to others I am careful not to use inflammatory language. I find it interesting that even my friends who know of my Pagan leanings still insist on calling me a Christian."

"My search continues," notes Charlene, "but I believe I am coming to a place where I would call myself Pagan. I combine aspects of Christianity, Buddhism, and Paganism, so I'm not sure how to describe myself."

"Francis, that brings us to you," says River.

"I call myself a Zen-Sufi-ChristoPagan," notes Francis, "as this description honors my present practices and my Catholic background. For about ten years I was able to practice Catholicism, Buddhism, Sufism, and Paganism together, sometimes all four in the same weekend or even in the same day. Today my practices are more limited and have less of Catholicism in them. This isn't because I reject the beauty of my Catholic heritage, but because I have run out of hours in a day."

"Could I bring up a subject that's been on my mind?" asks Brighid.

"By all means," River says.

"Earlier I mentioned that I am uncomfortable with the word *Pagan*," Brighid begins, "because it seems to be a word that defines a group of principles that sets itself against Christianity. I mean, I was raised to believe that the tenets of Christianity reject the tenets of Paganism—the two are irreconcilable or in direct opposition. 'Pagan' meant something bad, it was deemed so by the church. So the term *ChristoPagan* contains within it a tension that I cannot reconcile. If someone can help me understand the word *Pagan* and can help me reclaim it, I would be delighted. Otherwise, I'll stick with the term *Wiccan Christian* to describe myself."

"Thanks for raising this question, Brighid, because I think it's probably one a lot of our readers have wondered about too," observes Joyce. "I'd like to offer a couple of thoughts and then open it to the group for discussion.

"It is my understanding that the Latin word *pagus* means 'the country,' and that *paganus* means a 'country dweller,'" Joyce remarks. "The new Christian religion spread most rapidly in the cities and rather slowly and reluctantly in the country. We still see that happen today with fads, new technology, or new ideas. Pressures to conform to the new ways were generally less in the country, and so the country folk clung to their ways as Christianity continued to spread. Eventually their reluctance necessitated the church's forcible imposition of the new beliefs in some areas. Those who clung to the old ways were called Pagan derogatorily, in the same way that we use the words 'hick' and 'red-neck' derogatorily. As the church began to demonize unbelievers, the term gathered a more negative and sinister meaning until it eventually came to mean godless and without morals. This was not a correct assessment of the country folk, however, who did indeed have gods and their own codes of morals. They just weren't Christian ones.

"Because of this historical link to people who followed the old ways and lived closer to nature," Joyce continues, "many modern Pagans feel a connection to them and see *Paganism* as a word to reclaim."

"I agree that to many Christians the word *Pagan* still means the unchurched," says Victoria. "I see that assumption as a throwback to the days of colonialism when Christian missionaries were intent upon converting natives, who they judgmentally labeled *pagan* and *heathen*. It is a shame that many Christians have little awareness that Pagans are also deeply spiritual people."

"I also have holdover issues with the word *Pagan* because of my upbringing," observes Eleanor, "since in my church, Pagans were the people going to hell."

"Sometimes I think people hide behind labels as a means of working through their identity when they don't know what it is or when they are going through a crisis," says David. "I have seen people use *Christian* as an identity marker, too. I also see the word *Pagan* being reclaimed by some, though sometimes this is done in a militant way, or it's used to mean 'other,' or non-Christian generally, with no correlation to earth-centered or polytheistic paths. I heard someone say they were Pagan once who used it to mean agnostic."

"I agree that a person's identity and self-labeling can change with a crisis," comments Cern. "I don't consider it hiding as much as a sign of the change. I also think there's a need to belong. If your identity change is drastic and you are now outside your group's defined boundaries, then you may need to find a place to belong. Especially if your group kicks you out for being too different. I think most ChristoPagans fear being kicked out of both sides and then having no place to belong. In regard to the word *Pagan*," Cern notes, "most people I know use it to refer to earth-centered spirituality, and on occasion as an alternative to the Christian worldview."

"Let's remember that while many mainstream Christians think of Pagans with disdain," remarks David, "not all do. Some are not afraid of Pagans. Matthew Fox comes to mind, but then he was ultimately silenced by Rome and later left his religious order, the

Dominicans. I don't think the word *Pagan* is as demonized now as it could be, though it's not universally accepted either.

"As for ChristoPagans fearing to be 'kicked out' of both places, we do walk between the worlds in a sense, and are often scorned by both," reflects David. "I know that I am often misunderstood by both Christians and Pagans and not liked by either. I alienated many of my Pagan friends when I was consecrated as a bishop and began to integrate the two paths. Some people are really focused on labeling, but the older I get the more irrelevant labels become to me, especially in terms of spirituality."

"I know that for me it has been hard to walk two paths, and sometimes I have felt that I don't belong in either one and that I am misunderstood in both," agrees Victoria. "But I cannot leave one for the other. I feel compelled to do both, as though my destiny is to stand in the gap or space between them."

"This captures how I feel as well," remarks Eleanor, "although I still find that I avoid talking to folks who know me as Christian about my earth-based practices, and avoid talking to folks who know me in earth-based circles about Christianity. Why? Because I'm afraid in both directions that they'll 'find me out,' that they'll decide I'm not 'really' Christian or not 'really' Pagan, or both. My fear is about not belonging, not having a context, and not being able to define and claim who I am, and about having that taken away from me. Caring about belonging and having a context is about relationships, and I can't have relationships if there are no others to have relationships with. So, if I am rejected by the Christian community and the Pagan community, then I have lost something valuable, and I fear that. I think it's a valid fear."

"I agree that it's a valid fear," notes Brighid. "My solution was to say little in earth-based communities until I thought I was accepted. In the Christian community I have been even more careful because of my leadership role as an ordained minister. Even in my intimate conversations there I am careful of my language, never mentioning Paganism. Sometimes I mention Wicca, but most often I use the term *earth-based*."

"Years ago I knew a man in our Catholic community," says Francis, "who was gay and discreetly so. However, he and his partner planned a commitment ceremony and invited some members of the parish. The pastor of the church learned of it and sent the man a letter stating he was no longer welcome in the parish. When I heard of this, I thought, *what if the pastor decides he doesn't like what I do?* It was not a comfortable feeling. Years later I stood before this same congregation and told them that I had been accepted into the Sufi community, which is Islamic, and the response was overwhelmingly supportive. I felt that I had overcome my fear and was bringing a new level of ecumenism into the church.

"Concerning the misunderstanding Christians often have of the word *Pagan*," adds Francis, "it is interesting that much of the truth and beauty in my spirituality seems to emanate from the interaction of ancient Roman culture with the mysticism of early Christianity. It's fascinating, and almost beyond comprehension, that two thousand years later these sources are still in opposition. What a planet!"

"While I agree that people do sometimes hide behind labels," observes Michael, "I believe that most people label themselves in order to associate with others of like mind, or they are trying to communicate their ideas to people. I have learned that if you don't define your terms, misunderstandings occur more often than not. Similarly, if you do not label yourself, someone else will do it for you. I think it's better for us to label ourselves with meaningful purpose than to have others do it for us out of ignorance.

"I believe that the solution to many problems in communication about beliefs can be avoided," Michael states, "by taking the time to explain your terms and concepts to others, especially in the beginning of forming relationships. The other part of the solution, and perhaps the more important part, is to allow everyone to define their terms and concepts from their own perspective and try not to be offended by language."

"No doubt the debates around the words *Pagan* and *ChristoPagan* will go on for a good long time," Joyce comments. "Since so many misunderstandings are based on either ignorance or fear, it is important for Pagans and ChristoPagans to be clear to others about what their identity means and does not mean. Perhaps then ignorance can be reduced, and as knowledge increases, the fear will also hopefully disappear.

"Next, we want to hear about what holidays you observe, or how you mark the changing of the seasons and the sacred year," concludes Joyce. "We are curious to know whether you have created ceremonies and liturgies for yourself, and if so, what those are."

Chapter 13

HOLIDAYS AND LITURGIES

"We would like to know which holidays you celebrate and how you celebrate them," remarks River. "Do you create ceremonies and prayers for yourself, and if so, will you share them? Michael, we begin again with you."

"I celebrate a combined liturgical calendar of Christian and Pagan holidays, as established by tradition within the Order of the Astral Star," Michael states. "Our sacred year begins with Advent and proceeds to Christmas. Being Kabbalistic, we generally also acknowledge a number of Jewish holidays as well. We continue through the seasons with Lent, which we consider a penitential season beginning on Ash Wednesday. During this time we focus on mistakes we've made in our relationships with others, negative impacts we've had on nature, and shortcomings in our spiritual walk with deity. Members generally refrain from eating red meat throughout Lent, or at least on Fridays, as their health permits. We proceed to Easter and after that enter into Pentecost, which is the longest season of the year.

"In addition, we also acknowledge the equinoxes and solstices," continues Michael. "We keep a rose on our altar that changes color with each equinox and solstice—white at winter, yellow at spring, red at summer, and yellow again at autumn. The deepening or lightening color of the rose reflects the fullness or absence of light at the particular season. Yellow indicates a balance between the light and the dark.

"The order has a number of rituals and rites it has created for itself," Michael notes, "some of which I have helped write. We also make use of Dion Fortune's *Mystical Meditations on the Collects*. Both our calendar and several of our rituals and ceremonies can be found on the order's website, www.astralstar.org."

"I celebrate the eight Pagan holidays," comments Eleanor, "plus Thanksgiving, Advent, Christmas, Lent, and Easter. Gathering with my family for some of the Christian holidays is also part of my observance. I do not follow set rituals; everything I do is impromptu. I like to create or set up new altars that reflect the intention I am focused on at the time. I also like to do tarot and astrology readings with friends.

"As an example of what I might do to observe a holiday," offers Eleanor, "this past Easter I dyed magickal Ostara eggs as spells with friends. I ate lots of candy eggs, too, and a chocolate Easter bunny! I also hid Peeps among a temporary art display sponsored by a local municipality. In connection with my work at Diana's Grove, I dedicated myself to the element of fire for the coming year. It is their tradition to pick an element each year to which one dedicates oneself.

"I do miss much of the liturgy in church," reflects Eleanor, "unless it's 'Praise' liturgy that uses amplified contemporary music and instrumentation, which I really dislike. Give me an organ and Bach any day. And really, PowerPoint should be banned in church—it gives me the heebie-jeebies. I would love to see an earth-based Eucharistic service. I have wanted to take communion in a circle for a while now. I would love to say the Pagan words 'may you never hunger, may you never thirst' while taking the bread and wine."

"In contrast, I tend to celebrate only the Christian holidays with my family," notes Blaine, "but when telling the stories to my children, I add how the holidays relate to the earth and other religions. I have not written any rituals or prayers myself."

"I observe all eight Pagan holidays along with Christmas, Easter, and Thanksgiving," remarks T.J. "My absolutely favorite holiday is Samhain, or Halloween. Generally my rituals and prayers just come to me, sometimes almost as though dictated, and oddly enough they turn out to be very similar to those of other Pagans. I also add 'in Jesus's name, Amen' at the end of prayers and rituals."

"I celebrate the Sabbats, or eight Pagan holidays, but do so alone and not with other Pagans," observes Hilary. "At Christian holidays I will discuss their Pagan origins with my friends, and I tend to look for the nature-based aspects of the Christian holidays—

that is, the aspects of them that are relevant to the Wheel of the Year. Like Blaine, I also have not written any rituals or prayers for myself, but would like to."

"My practice is mostly private and personal," Brighid says. "My husband and I share a daily practice of meditation, centering prayer, tai chi, personal reading, and journaling. We attend a Christian church about once a month. We honor all the Pagan Sabbats using simple ritual. On some occasions we have been present for public ritual on a Sabbat and have welcomed the opportunity to celebrate and reflect with others. We don't look for such interaction on an ongoing basis, however, since we are not 'out' about our dual-faith practice. We also keep a day of contemplation we call 'Seasonal Silence' about halfway between the holy days," Brighid notes. "On those days, we intentionally reflect on our personal lives in regard to the rhythm of the season. We sometimes observe this day with other Christians, and I have developed reflection materials for use then.

"It was during my graduate work in feminist studies," continues Brighid, "that I became interested in earth religions. As my interest grew, it became harder for me to be comfortable with the liturgy in church. Unfortunately, inclusive language became the focus of much conversation and change in the church. I say unfortunately because language became the focus rather than the underlying meanings and metaphors. I believe we explain the unknown in terms of the known. Then the process reverses and the known has increased value because we have used it to explain the mysterious. When we use only a single set of metaphors, such as 'God the Father' or 'Jesus Christ the Son,' then our concept of mystery and the sacred becomes very narrow.

"Some liturgy, even high-church Episcopal, which I like, becomes a real stretch for me at times," observes Brighid. "I am constantly enlarging the metaphors and translating the language for myself. However, in other ways, the familiar metaphors, the music, and the community are comforting."

"I observe the eight Pagan holidays and the full moons," states Cern. "I only celebrate Christmas in the secular sense with my extended family. I also have an interfaith calendar and try to be aware of the holy days of other faiths. I don't observe them, however, unless I'm invited by people of that faith. This year I had the opportunity to celebrate Hanukkah with my Jewish friends.

"I have written many rituals," Cern notes. "When I was still pastoring, I wrote an Ash Wednesday service that focused on being part of Mother Earth. 'Know that you are of Mother Earth and to Mother Earth you will return.' None of the rituals I write now incorporate Christian prayers or practices. I have 'Paganized' a number of Christian hymns and prayers, however. Would you like some examples?"

"Yes, please," says Joyce.

"Okay, here is my adaptation of the Lord's Prayer. I kept the meter the same so I could pray this prayer in church while others were praying the traditional one. Also, by keeping the meter the same, it can be sung to the traditional Malotte tune."

> THE LADY'S PRAYER
> Our Mother
> Who lives within us
> Wonderful is thy name.
> Thy blessings come,
> To everyone on earth,
> O Queen of heaven.
> Bless now this day our daily food
> And help us enjoy the pleasures
> That you bestow upon us.
> And guide us so we may harm none
> And show us the way to the balance.
> For thine is the laughter,
> And the love,
> And the moonlight forever. Amen.

"Here are some examples of Paganized Easter hymns I wrote when I first became interested in Paganism," says Cern.

> KING OSIRIS, HE AROSE [CHRIST AROSE]
> Low in the Nile he lay,
> Osiris, my King.
> Waiting the coming day
> Osiris, Lord!
>
> *Refrain:*
> And up with the Nile he arose!
> With a mighty triumph o'er his foes,
> He arose a victor from the dark domain,
> And he lives forever
> With his Queen to reign.

He arose! He arose!
King Osiris, he arose!

Seth could not keep his prey,
Osiris, my king.
He tore the bars away,
Osiris, Lord! (*Refrain*)

Isis, she made a kite,
Osiris, my king.
Her breath gave him new life,
Osiris, Lord! (*Refrain*)

OSIRIS IS RISEN TODAY [CHRIST THE LORD IS RISEN TODAY]
Osiris is risen today! O-si-ris!
Mortals and the gods all say: O-si-ris!
Raise your joys and triumphs high! O-si-ris!
Sing ye heavens and earth reply: O-si-ris!

Lives again our glorious king! O-si-ris!
Where O Seth is now thy sting? O-si-ris!
Isis brought him back again. O-si-ris!
And the Nile did rise with him! O-si-ris!

Sing we now the power of O-si-ris!
Ris'n by Isis's faithful love. O-si-ris!
Praise Him all ye starry host! O-si-ris!
Praise the Queen whose love we boast! O-si-ris!

"Thank you for sharing those," says River. "I found myself singing along! Kirk, tell us how you observe the holy days."

"I celebrate the eight Pagan/Wiccan holidays plus the full moons," answers Kirk, "and Christmas and Easter. I also observe some of the saint's days and some Druid days, such as the sixth day after each new and full moon. I celebrate some Hindu holidays, particularly Navaratri, Diwali, Durga Puja, and Ganesha's birthday. Usually I celebrate the Christian holidays with a Mass, often the Western Rite Orthodox. The Wiccan ones I observe with an eclectic Gardnerian-style ritual, and the Druid ones with an eclectic mix of British Revivalist and Celtic Reconstructionist. I do create prayers, rituals, and ceremonies on a fairly regular basis. Since I am a polytheist rather than a pantheist, I do not mix and match traditions or rituals. I do each one in its own context, symbolism, and style."

"I observe the eight Pagan holidays and also attend Mass several times a year," says Paul. "I celebrate the Pagan holidays with my own personal ceremonies and mix them with the Minoan Brotherhood rites, as I learn them."

"As for myself," comments David, "I celebrate the solstices and equinoxes, and since I am a priest in Nova Roma, I also observe several of the Roman festivals. I begin with the Pagan Wheel of the Year and adapt it, which is easier for me since I identify with the Wheel more than I do with the Christian liturgical year. I have created a number of rituals in my roles as both a Gnostic Christian bishop and a Druid Adept/archpriest. One ritual I've shared with others, called the 'Gnostic Divine Liturgy of Peace,' can be found at www.gnosticdruid.com/devotions.htm. I have used that particular liturgy to ordain several people in the past few years."

"I find as time passes that I tend to go with the flow," Barb says, "and I don't tend to celebrate the holidays as such anymore. It has also become more difficult due to my disabilities when I am living alone. However, I did rewrite the Hail Mary and the Glory Be for my own use, as I wanted to pray a more Goddess-centered rosary, using the standard beads. Would you like me to share those prayers?"

"Yes we would," encourages Joyce.

HAIL GODDESS
Hail Goddess, full of Light,
The Lord is with you.
Blessed are you among women,
And blessed is the fruit of your womb, the Earth.
Holy Goddess, Mother of All,
Shine on your children now and forever more.
Blessed Be.

GLORY BE
Glory be to the Maiden, Mother, and Crone,
As it was in the beginning, is now, and ever shall be.
Blessed Be.

"I cannot find the prayer I used instead of the Our Father, which I found online, but Cern's version is very nice," observes Barb.

"Yes, thank you for sharing these," says Joyce.

"I celebrate the solstices, equinoxes, and eight Pagan holidays," comments Victoria. "I don't tend to observe the new and full moons unless I find I need the energy or I am with a group. I also celebrate Christmas/Yule, Easter/Ostara, and Samhain/All Saints Day. A special day I observe is Brigid's Day, which is one of my favorites due to my Irish ancestry, and because it's such a big cross-over feast.

"Like Barb, I also like praying the rosary and other prayer beads I have made for myself," Victoria continues. "The prayer beads I have made most recently are for meditating on the light and dark aspects of myself. This rosary contains light and dark beads in groups of five. I've also made prayer beads for the cycles of the moon, and I pray each phase while focusing on the increasing light or increasing dark. Sometimes I pray the traditional rosary with the traditional prayers, but use nontraditional mysteries, like 'I pray this decade for the mystery of my day.' And on occasion I go to a very conservative Catholic church and pray the rosary with some very traditional Catholic ladies. What I like about praying the rosary," reflects Victoria, "is that it disconnects me from my intellect, and this allows me to let go and enter into a deeper and broader part of myself."

"I celebrate both the Pagan and Christian holidays," notes Raven.

"I do as well," says Charlene. "I celebrate all the Catholic holidays as well as the Pagan ones, and really, some of the traditions are so old that they've already been blended. I have developed some basic rituals for myself that combine Catholicism, Buddhism, and Paganism. I don't have any to share, though, because they are personal, short, and change as my needs change."

"That's okay," affirms River.

"However, I can give examples of what I do at various holidays," Charlene continues. "I celebrate Christmas by burning a Yule log. I celebrate Easter by going to a Catholic sunrise service, then do Easter baskets and an Easter egg hunt with my family. I celebrate Lent as a prelude to spring, and in that time try to read one new book or complete a course of study. The coursebooks I follow are from the United Methodist Church Lenten Series. When I attended Methodist services, their ashes for Ash Wednesday were made from burning slips of paper on which had been written trangressions and wishes for improvement. I have continued that practice for myself."

"Francis, that brings us to you," states River.

"I celebrate the eight Pagan/Wiccan holidays and honor the full moons with my Wiccan community whenever possible," Francis notes. "I try to attend church services during

Holy Week and at Easter, and also celebrate Vesak, which is the commemoration of Buddha's birth, enlightenment, and death, and also Rumi's Urs. And in good Pagan fashion, I celebrate Mardi Gras!

"To give you an idea of what this might look like in actual practice," Francis continues, "I observed the past Easter season in this way: On the spring equinox I greeted the sunrise at a service hosted by Native Americans at a sacred site in my area. Then I went on an Ostara retreat with my Wiccan group, followed by Good Friday services at the Catholic church. For Easter Vigil on Saturday night I attended a Lakota sweat, and on Easter Sunday I performed music and hosted a gathering of the Sufi Dances of Universal Peace."

"Good grief, I think I need to take a nap now!" Joyce exclaims. "I see what you mean about running out of hours in the day."

"I'd like to share my experience of Paul's ordination," comments Francis. "Although it's not a holiday as such, it is a celebration of a rite of passage. Would that be okay?"

"Yes, please do," answers River.

"Well, Paul was ordained at the Pagan festival called Pagan Spirit Gathering, and I was there because I attend every year and serve as the event's volunteer workshift coordinator. David came to me and asked if I could participate in the ordination service. It was a beautiful morning for the service," continues Francis, "and we had a lovely setting—a little grove with a large rock that served quite nicely as an altar. The Quarters were called in each direction, and the Spirit of Peace was also called to join us from each direction. The God and Goddess were also invited, but they were described in very cosmic terms. The service was a Mass, and although it was not quite in the Roman Catholic style I am most familiar with, it was a service of great power and beauty. I was able to use my voice and lectoring abilities to serve as the Deacon. The consecration itself took the service to another level for me, as another Messenger of the Word was created and blessed in a sacred way. As we closed, everyone present was given the opportunity to offer Paul a blessing, and I sang my blessing to him, the Sufi benediction of Hazrat Inayat Khan.

"But it was the feeling of the service," muses Francis, "that was the most important to me. The reality of ChristoPaganism as a spiritual path gained more meaning for me. Beyond my own personal path, I was able to stand in community with people who really understood and practiced in a way that honored both traditions. I had not expected to be strengthening my connection to the church in the middle of a Pagan event, but that is what happened. I felt as though a gap in my spirituality had suddenly, after more than ten years, been bridged."

"We were glad you could be there and be a part of the service," notes David, "and we're honored that it had such meaning for you."

"Thank you, Francis, for sharing this experience and how moving it was. Thanks to all of you as well for sharing the holidays you celebrate and how you celebrate them," Rives acknowledges. "Next, we want to know what contradictions and similarities you see between Christianity and Paganism, and how you incorporate them or reconcile them in your spirituality."

Chapter 14

CONTRADICTIONS

"Perhaps you have heard someone say that you cannot be a Christo-Pagan because the two traditions are irreconcilable," remarks Joyce. "Do you agree with that? What similarities and contradictions do you see between Christianity and Paganism, and how do you address them in your spirituality?"

"In my heart," says Eleanor, "there are no contradictions. There are aspects of Christianity that resonate with me and aspects that do not, and I choose to focus on those that do. Several years ago, my mother asked me if I still believed in Jesus Christ as my savior and I said 'yes, because I believe that it is God who heals us and provides salvation.' I didn't tell her that I don't believe in heaven, hell, or the devil anymore.

"I realize that others might see my amalgamation of beliefs as irreconcilable," continues Eleanor. "As an example, I was at a Bible study at Campus Ministries last year, watching a U2 concert video. Afterward we talked about whether the crowd's ecstasy with Bono could be described as a spiritual experience or even worship. Coming from my years of ecstatic ritual work at Diana's Grove, I know that ecstasy can be spiritually powerful and can connect us to the divine. So I answered yes to the question and was scoffed at by someone in the group. To me, worshipping the divine that expresses itself through Bono and his performance is still worshipping the divine; it is not a worship of Bono. But then I have a very wide and embracing view of where God can be experienced.

"Probably the main point of similarity between Christianity and Paganism that I work with spiritually," concludes Eleanor, "is the cycle of birth and rebirth. This is found in Paganism in the Wheel of the Year and stories of the gods who die and return. It is found in Christianity in Jesus's life from birth to resurrection. Letting the old die so that the new may be born is central to my belief system."

"I have to agree with Eleanor in that I don't focus on the perceived differences between Paganism and Christianity," Blaine says. "If a belief doesn't strike me as true—whether it's from Christianity or Paganism—I just don't incorporate it into my spirituality."

"I can't disagree with this either," speaks up T.J. "I personally don't find any differences in the *philosophies* of Paganism and Christianity. It is true that not everyone believes Jesus is the Christ, but frankly I find his teachings to be quite similar to Pagan beliefs."

"I believe that the 'spirit' Pagans refer to is the same as the Holy Spirit," notes Hilary. "I believe that the tales told in the Bible and tales told in mythology are both human ways of getting closer to and understanding God. Most of the time I find that divergences between Paganism and Christianity are a matter of dogma and interpretation."

"As you know from the earlier discussion of the word Pagan," observes Brighid, "I still struggle with what the words *Pagan* and *Christian* mean exactly. It seems that the very name *Christian* demands the affirmation of the Christ, which traditionally means affirming Jesus as Lord and Savior. Doesn't this deny the possibility of being both Christian and Pagan? So, for the time being, I live with the tension and the cognitive dissonance created by my understanding of these words, while living with as much integrity as I can."

"I've thought about these issues a lot," muses Cern, "and have written several articles about them. Can I share some websites with you?"

"Of course," says River.

"I have written a discussion of the commonalities between the two traditions, and I also explore sixteen specific differences between Paganism and Christianity in depth on my website at www.cernowain.com. Perhaps these will help Brighid or other readers clarify some issues."

"Thank you for sharing these resources," Joyce says, "and I hope others do find them helpful. They are extensive enough, however, that we are not going to be able to include them here as they could fill an entire book themselves. Actually, *you* might want to consider making a book of them."

"Perhaps I will," says Cern, smiling. "How a person answers Brighid's question seems to me to be related to a person's understanding of Christianity. One Pagan I know came from a Baptist tradition that emphasized 'no other way,' relying on John 14:6 and Acts 4:12. Even though this person became a Pagan, he brought that understanding of Christianity with him and never challenged it. So for him Christianity remains a religion that sees itself as the only way and cannot be blended or incorporated into Paganism or anything else. By the same token," continues Cern, "whether Christians can conceive of Paganism and Christianity combining may depend on their view of Paganism. A Methodist preacher I know declined to marry one of his members who was engaged to a Wiccan. His sole understanding of Wicca came from a book about Satanic witchcraft. All of the rest of his theology is really quite liberal, but because he got bad information regarding Wicca, he cannot see it as anything but evil."

"When I look around at the various religions," notes Kirk, "what I see in them all is a similarity in their search for meaning and connection with the divine. All the rest, as I see it, is cultural details. Because of this, I don't try to 'reconcile' religions, but rather recognize that each is appropriate in its own context."

"My approach is similar to Kirk's," observes Paul. "When I'm functioning in one tradition's context, I stick to that context. I stopped worrying about contradictions when I realized that I was responding to the divine in many forms. Now I trust that each form has validity in its own right and its own place, and I am able to shift contexts fluidly. I see myself as a mystic whose main font of spiritual inspiration is the experience of going beyond the contradictions, and enjoying the divine presence in silence. This is beyond language, beyond concepts, beyond contradictions, and yes, even beyond logic. Awe and wonder at the mystery of life is the one thing I repeatedly experience in all the traditions that feed into my spiritual being. I have decided not to deny any of them, despite their seeming contradictions."

"At a deep philosophical level," speaks up Barb, "I believe that all religions are pretty much the same. The differences seem to be found mostly in dogma, and one of the reasons I appreciate Paganism is that it has less dogma."

"Like many others here," says Victoria, "I don't try to 'reconcile' differences or contradictions. I accept that I am working in two different systems. If I encounter contradictions, I simply hold them and look for a third way. For me the ChristoPagan path is definitely two separate paths that come together inside of me. I hold both realities equally and honor both equally. Then I allow them to overlap and integrate."

"Personally, I see more similarities than differences between the two paths," states Raven. "Where I run into trouble is with the very conservative, fundamentalist views about homosexuality, marriage, and the control of nature. I do not know how to reconcile their positions with what I see as Paganism's more life-affirming stance on those issues."

"I have to say I don't get caught up in contradictions either," notes Charlene, "and I tend to disregard what does not feel right or true to me from any religion. I also see no reason why the two paths cannot be extensions of each other. God made both Jesus and the earth—both are to be revered."

"I see we are near the end of going in order," observes River, "which means we come to you, Francis."

"My life has led me to conclude that there is truth to be found in many places," Francis begins. "I think a number of Pagans would agree with me. Although many traditions of Paganism derive from European roots, Pagans generally seem open to a universal cosmology—that is, the idea that many traditions have value and that a contemporary spiritual practice contains elements from all around the planet. In contrast, it seems that much of Christian evangelization has been focused on demonizing other religions. This tends to make Pagans less open to incorporating Christianity into their spirituality than say, the Asian, African, and Native American traditions. It is hard to be open to a group that is convinced of its own superiority. I understand that. But at the same time," Francis notes, "this makes it even more important to acknowledge truth wherever we find it. Both Pagans and Christians need to practice reconciliation or they will continue to create more conflict by reason of their mutual disdain. I really do not believe that the universe wants the spiritualities of the earth to be in conflict with each other. While it sounds like a cliché, I believe the evolution of humanity is contingent on finding ways for spiritualities to cooperate with each other. It seems to me that those who follow Paganism and other spiritual paths, who acknowledge the importance of Christianity without bowing to its claims of exclusivity, are helping to heal the world.

"Furthermore," Francis continues, "someone centuries ago decided what was spiritually proper, who would be a heretic, and who would not. Should I be constrained by such ancient decisions? In my spiritual development, I have come to feel an affinity for Mercury, Thor, Ellegua, and the four elements, but this does not diminish the value and influence the story of Jesus has for me. In fact, as I continue to experience his story and the celebration of the Mass, I feel as though my Catholic path is part of my Pagan path. For many years," he concludes, "I spent three hours each Sunday before Mass in traditional Buddhist meditation as a preparation to experience the Mass more deeply. I know from personal experience that bridging the religious 'divide' is not only possible but has great benefits. I never felt any contradictions at this depth of experience."

"May I share something in response to Francis?" asks Victoria.

"Please do," says River.

"A couple of years ago I embarked on a two-year training program in the tradition of Anderson Feri witchcraft," remarks Victoria. "As I worked with this tradition and met with my group, I found myself plunging deeper into the mysticism of Catholicism. My Feri work took me deeper into my Catholic path. I have also studied tarot for many years and I began to find myself at Mass frequently feeling as though I were a living tarot card."

"For those who are not familiar with it, the tarot is a deck of cards used for divination and for personal and spiritual growth," comments River. "The images of the cards refer either to qualities—like abundance, struggle, accomplishment, and so on—or to universal archetypal patterns. So, for example, the Magician card is an archetypal figure that represents the magician in each of us, who with one hand reaching to heaven and spirit, and one hand pointing to the earth, brings together the blessing and skills of each to create lived reality."

"During Mass, it is as though I can sometimes see and become those archetypes," says Victoria. "At the consecration, for example, when the priest lifts the chalice and on the altar is the paten, the book, and the candles, I feel like I am in the Magician card and know I have all the tools I need at my disposal. At communion, sometimes I feel that I have become the Six of Pentacles and am receiving everything."

"Oh wow, Victoria!" exclaims Eleanor. "Your images of the tarot are so inspiring to me. But what do you mean by the 'mysticism of Catholicism'? I've had experiences with shamanic journeys, I've sensed spirits, and felt like I could talk and listen to things in nature, like the trees, moon, and sky. I also talk to God a lot and listen to what he or she has to say. Is that mysticism, to hear what God is saying?"

"For me, mysticism is an experience of union with the divine," answers Victoria. "I believe that a number of spiritual practices from many different traditions can lead us there. When I say *Catholic* mysticism, I mean two things. The first is the mystical experiences I have that come through the church. This includes the experiences I have in Mass, as when I see the host glowing luminously, and in Eucharistic Adoration am transcended into that other world through the host. I've also had moments of union at shrines of Mary, and in nature, and while doing labyrinth work. The second is the example set by the Christian mystics. I am in the midst of a three-year course of study on the mystics. We study the saints and mystics such as Hildegard, Julian of Norwich, Catherine of Siena, Francis of Assisi, and Meister Eckhart. These people never settled for the status quo of the church; their mysticism led them to introduce new ideas. In fact, I believe they would all be at home in Pagan circles."

"I'd like to add that while at first glance they seem completely at odds," says Francis, "Pagan ritual and Catholic ritual actually share many similarities, such as presenting the fruits of the earth, blessing them, and distributing them to those present."

"Not only is this true of Catholicism," adds David, "but the Independent Sacramental Movement also interfaces well with Paganism. Really, sacramental Christianity is so magickal that it seems to me like a wonderful fit."

"Are you saying that you believe Christianity has magickal aspects, and I mean magick as Pagans understand it?" asks Joyce.

"Yes, I am," responds David. "If magick is 'the science and art of causing change in conformity with will,' which is the classic definition of magick given by Aleister Crowley, then sacraments are definitely magickal acts. Every sacrament is a ritual intended to cause some kind of change."

"I think that Jesus is magick," offers Hilary, "and that the power of prayer is the same transforming power as spellcrafting."

"I completely agree," affirms David. "Any prayer, whether for yourself or someone else, is a form of magickal act. As an example, when I was a Benedictine monk, we arrived in chapel at 4:20 every morning and were there until about 8:30. Oftentimes the superior would inform us of a prayer request, would light a candle on the altar, and would advise us to focus our prayer on the request, of which the candle was a visible sign. This is no different from candle magick or the act of sending energy directly to someone who needs it, as many Pagans do."

"I agree that the sacraments are types of magickal acts," says Paul, "because the goal of all ritual is some sort of magickal transformation—to move the participants from living in the mundane world to an experience with the divine. In classical magickal theory, there are two types of magick: *theurgy*, which seeks direct communication with the divine, and *thaumaturgy*, which seeks the intervention of the divine in human affairs. Since many of the sacraments have a practical purpose (healing, sacralizing unions, memorializing the dead), they are thaumaturgical in nature. Others, like the Eucharist, are primarily theurgic. What can be more magickal than the transformation of bread and wine into the body and blood of Christ? For those Christians who believe that communion is more than a symbolic psychological remembrance and is actually the presence of the divine in the elements of bread and wine, I believe it is an act of very high magick."

"I also strongly agree," adds Francis. "The Mass is a type of metaphysical alchemy; as the bread and wine are transformed into the body and blood of Christ, so too are we transformed and connected across time to the Last Supper. This transformation results in a heightened awareness of ourselves as spiritual beings and hopefully, an outpouring of love for our fellow beings. I would call this ritual magick of the highest order. As I continue to practice Pagan and other non-Christian ritual, I have witnessed the similiarities that the Mass has in common with other magickal practices."

"I can think of one high-school teacher who will strongly disagree with you," Joyce wryly observes.

"For those of us who see the continuity between pre-Christian religious traditions and later Christian ones," notes Paul, "there is no difficulty with acknowledging the deep and ancient roots of magick that permeate our modern sacramental lives."

"I believe the sacraments can easily be accommodated to ChristoPagan practices," agrees David. "A nondogmatic sacramental tradition . . . what a wonderful idea."

"This is so interesting," says River. "Conversations like these are one reason we enjoy this project so much. I imagine some of our readers have no idea that entire theories of magick exist, let alone theories that have been around long enough to be called 'classic.' I am sure you have given them much food for thought. This subject alone could fill a book, I think. Unfortunately, there are other topics we would like to cover. We want to learn what your views of God and Jesus are, as well as your views of the realms of spirit and the afterlife."

Chapter 15

GOD AND JESUS

"Your journey into ChristoPaganism has probably brought with it many changes to your views of God and Jesus," notes River, "as well as your views of the afterlife and the realm of spirit generally. Share with us what you believe now on these topics, if you will. Michael, let's begin with you."

"I'm not so sure I have changed my views that much," observes Michael. "I have always believed and do still believe that Yeshuah (Jesus) is the Christ and the Messiah, and the divine Son of God."

"Okay, how about you, Eleanor?" asks Joyce.

"I think that God is present everywhere in everything, embodied in everything," says Eleanor. "I think that humans are a part of God, but we forget that sometimes. I'm not very interested in transcendent religious experience, but experiencing divinity *in* my body—now that's more challenging and satisfying for me. I feel a big difference between the escape-the-body Christianity I've been exposed to, and earth-based practices where divine immanence is very much valued. Another interesting issue for me is how to reconcile religion and science, although in my earth-based practice they seem compatible. I tend to see God as all the energy in the universe, the building blocks of energy and matter; but if that's so, then how do I go about envisioning the divine as embodied? Even the Christ is an archetype for me, not a god or spirit or a presence."

"If we just die when we die," Eleanor continues, "then where do spirits come in? And I cannot write off the existence of spirit beings because I've had too many experiences with them to do so. Yet I don't really believe in reincarnation or an afterlife. I think this life is a one-shot deal and when it's over it's over, although I'm open to being surprised. Heaven and hell just seem like constructs to control people. Once I'm gone, I want the universe to spin my life energy out and let it come back in many different creatures and structures, all mixed into new possibilities."

"I definitely still hold to the image of the triune God," comments Blaine, "but I also think that God has appeared to other religions in other guises and is called by many names. I feel that the divine is present in everything that surrounds me, from the earth itself to skyscrapers. It is present in *all* creation."

"Despite my roots in Paganism I am very much a monotheist," notes T.J., "but I do not gender-assign the divine. I call it God/dess and believe it to be both our father and mother, and think that Jesus was the God/dess come among us to help us relate better to the divine. I believe all religions lead back to the same source, but that it is important for individuals to follow their own paths to it. I see this life primarily as a learning experience—we're supposed to learn and accomplish certain things while we're here. I believe in an afterlife but don't think it's necessary to understand it fully in this one. Often I feel the presence of those I've been close to who have passed from this life."

"Like Eleanor, I believe that God is the force of life," comments Hilary, "and I believe this force is around us and within us, and in the world and the universe. I do believe that spirit beings exist, and like us can be good or bad, mischievous, grieving, and so on. Humanity is a family in God's eyes, and I think our job here is to learn to love each other despite our differences. The earth is certainly a gift from God that is our home, and we should nurture and support it the way it nurtures and supports us. I guess I am too 'mortal' to understand the universe, but maybe I will when I am part of the spirit world."

"I believe in a divine source that permeates all that is, but is greater than whatever we comprehend about it," remarks Brighid. "Claiming Matthew Fox's idea of 'panentheism' (the divine both transcends all things and permeates all things), I also affirm the divine in all that is inert and alive, visible and unseen. I think the divine is active in all that we know as life and benefits from our awareness and interaction with it. It is still helpful for me to think of Jesus as a human incarnation of the divine. But I do not see his death as significant to my relationship with the divine or my access to the sacred. I don't see his death as impacting my salvation in any way. I do think, however, that following his death, those who believed Jesus to be the Messiah experienced his presence in ways that changed their lives. My journey is my own," continues Brighid, "just as your journey is your own. I cannot and do not judge the validity of anyone else's spiritual life. I can be present to them, however, to 'hear into being' whatever it is they perceive as sacred."

"Like Brighid, I am also a panentheist," notes Cern, "and I do not see Jesus's death as a saving event either. I believe in the unity and interconnectedness of all things and see the divine in everything. It helps me when I'm in worship mode to relate personally to the divine as the Goddess and her consort the God. I tend to view all Gods and Goddesses as archetypes or manifestations of these two prototypes, so I can worship the Divine Feminine as Athena one time and, at another time, as Kuan Yin. The same applies to the masculine. Once I was a pure monotheist, but now I see monotheism as a limited way of understanding the spiritual world. I reason that if this physical world is full of myriad forms of life, then why shouldn't the spiritual world be the same? So I believe that there are many types of entities, spirits, fairies, gnomes, guardians, elements, beings, and so on, in the spiritual realms.

"As for Jesus," Cern continues, "I have a high respect for him though not for the organized church. I do not pray to Jesus as a god, but his teachings and his compassion for others still inspire me. His death was tragic, but I do not agree with the church that it was an atoning sacrifice—I think that is something the church came up with later to explain his death. I don't think Jesus would have wanted us to trust in his death for forgiveness in any case—I think he'd rather we seek forgiveness directly from those we have wronged. I strongly believe, along with Matthew Fox, that people come into this world with an original blessing of love and not an original curse of sin. I no longer view humans as the center of the universe, but as creatures with interesting abilities who are just a part of the whole. I reject the Bible's stories of creation, since we now know that the universe is billions of years old and that we are only one of many galaxies. The earth is our mother, so we must stop destroying her with pollution and start learning to live in harmony with nature.

"Also, I believe in an afterlife but am open to what form it might take," Cern continues. "I think it will be a big surprise for everyone. I don't believe in hell, and I reject the notion that a loving divinity wants to torture people forever. I see all religions as humanity's way of trying to make sense of our existence. They all have good and bad aspects. At its worst, religion breeds hatred, war, competition, corruption, and abuse. At its best, religion brings out love, beauty, compassion, cooperation, wisdom, and respect. Generally, I think religion does promote the good in people and that we can live in peace together if we follow the best our faiths have to offer."

"I consider myself an omnitheist," speaks up Kirk, "and believe everyone is right. I believe there is a great unified field of divine energy, kind of like the big white light behind the child's toy Lite Brite. Like that toy, we put screens over the light so that it shines through only in certain patterns, and these patterns are dictated by culture and belief. Thus, we make God and our reality in our own image. Cultures create consensual realities, but they're still just screens over the light. Whether we accept spirits or not, gods or not, an afterlife or not, all are manifestations created by belief—and each is true if someone believes in it. All potential exists and is true, thus I have no problem working with multiple theologies. In fact, I find that working with multiple ones—*especially* if I don't mix or syncretize them—is a way to get a closer understanding of the truth behind all things. Put one screen on the Lite Brite and see where the light shines though, then put on a different one and see a different pattern. After you've put on dozens of screens, you have seen many parts of the overall light."

"In my own path I begin as a deist or animist," notes Paul, "and believe in an impersonal divine ground of being. To that I add theism. While I don't think it's necessary to personify the divine, if we do then I think we should give it both male and female aspects. Because of my perspective, a commitment to both a God and a Goddess is fundamental to me. Perhaps some of this comes from my Mormon background, since while most Mormons will tell you they don't worship a divine female, their cosmology requires it and it's a whispered secret idea. At the moment I find I hold contradictory positions, both denying the doctrine of original sin and therefore the need for a savior, and denying a substantial soul—that's the Buddhist in me. Yet when I'm in a Christian context I can, with faith, repeat the Nicene Creed and accept Jesus as a savior. As I shift contexts, what I am willing to affirm shifts as well, at least for now."

"God is far beyond anything I can conceive of, and ultimately is incomprehensible," says Barb. "I believe that we are all God, and yet we're not. I think Jesus is divine, but he doesn't have an exclusive on being so. I do believe that spirit beings are real, though not physical. I have two animal guides that I work with, but I see their reality as completely interior to myself."

"I would describe the nature of God as a sea or creative source in which we live and that lives in us," states Victoria. "I balk at the image of God the Father and so prefer the term Mother God. But I realize that God transcends gender and even Mother does not capture what it is. I do see Jesus as God incarnate, as God in human form at a very high vibration. I see the historical Jesus as a great teacher, a wise man, and a radical activist. In contrast to the person of Jesus, I understand the idea of the *Christ* to be the embodied God essence in us—a Christ consciousness, if you will.

"I believe that we are also incarnated spirits," Victoria continues, "and that this world is a stage on which we live in human form. I believe in spirit beings and see them as energy patterns that appear to us in forms we can see and recognize. I think the afterlife is a return to our pure spirit form without our human body. I believe there are many paths to God, and all these paths deserve honor and respect. God comes to us through the eyes of culture in ways that enable us to comprehend God. Oh, and previously Eleanor mentioned she doesn't find church to be a very safe place," notes Victoria.

"No, I don't," agrees Eleanor.

"I don't much either," continues Victoria, "but over the last three years I've developed what I call 'resilience in the church.' I have worked on being a part of the church but not entwined in it. More and more I am able to listen objectively to what is taught in church. I feel clearer about what I think and believe and know that no one—whoever they are—has a monopoly on truth."

"For myself," states Charlene, "I believe that God and humanity are interrelated. While God made creation, we humans have an obligation to protect it. I view Jesus as a great prophet, but one of many. He is an example of a truly unselfish individual. I believe in an afterlife although not in terms of heaven, but a continuation of our spirit's journey."

"God, for me, is the embodiment of all physically created space," Francis says, "and the spirit-force that animates and keeps this reality in existence. I think that religion principally springs from the interaction between humans and this spirit-force. From this overarching principle, it is easy for me to see the threads of truth that connect all religions. I view Jesus as a master teacher, and I do believe in spirit beings of various sorts. They come in forms such as deities and messengers, with varieties and gradations as numerous as we can conceive."

"Thanks, Francis, for bringing us to the end of this topic," comments Joyce.

"Not quite the end," River says. "We should also mention findings by Old and New Testament scholars, some of which support a historical interpretation of Jesus and the Bible, and some of which do not."

"That is true," Joyce agrees. "We want to present this research from both sides of the biblical debate."

"I'm sorry, but my head is just swirling," complains Eleanor. "It never even occurred to me that Jesus might not be a historical figure. I was raised with a literal, fundamentalist understanding of Jesus as a real, historical man. It is very hard for me even to think of those beliefs being uprooted or challenged. I feel like I've been punched in the chest or my heart has been ripped out."

"I can sure relate to your feelings," says Cern, "and know what you are going through. I was raised with a literal and historical view also and was astonished when I first heard of the wide range of scholarly views. Initially I felt as though I had been lied to, but after a while I began to feel liberated."

"I guess I still believe that Jesus existed in history," responds Eleanor, "which I find really comforting. I've done some reading of Sallie McFague's *Metaphorical Theology: Models of God in Religious Language*, and she maintains that the literal understanding of Jesus came about with society's transition to a scientific worldview. In this worldview, truth is based on measurable facts. Sallie postulates that humans didn't think about the world literally until the development of the scientific method. It's an amazing idea to consider that humans at one time *only* thought metaphorically. For them, the question of what was real and what was myth was irrelevant."

"I've also read and enjoyed Sallie McFague's work," observes Brighid, "and she suggests that theology is a two-step process. First, when we speak of the divine or what is sacred, we use things we understand to explain what is a mystery to us. Then, second, we sacramentalize what we have used as a metaphor. I have come to accept that the story of Jesus is at least partly myth. But myth has power."

"I think people can be as fundamentalist and attached to the idea of a 'myth' as they can be to their literal, historical beliefs," Eleanor observes, "although I do think that the way many Christians insist on only one truth prevents interfaith understanding. It's interesting, but I see that while I've considered the Jesus story to be literally 'true,' I've always seen the stories of other traditions as purely mythological and not factual."

"I now realize I also approach the story of Jesus differently than I do other myths," remarks Brighid. "Even as I begin to demythologize the Jesus story, I assume there is validity in the myth for spiritual growth and development. I start with the assumption of its validity and then apply it metaphorically to my life. But with other myths I begin with myself and my own experience and then ask if the story offers a metaphor that relates to me."

"This discussion has led me to think about how I relate to myth," comments Victoria. "The Jesus myth is prevalent in my life because I meet weekly with a Catholic community and participate in the Mass. I keep a nativity set on my mantle, and when I see it I mentally enact the story over again. Plus, I have lived longer with the Jesus myth. But I must say that Persephone is also very close to me. I have a picture of her and think of her often—like in the spring I say, 'Can Persephone come out and play?' I get comfort from her story, living half of the year in the underworld and half above. Her experience of being snatched into the underworld was also my experience in an earlier part of my life. So I feel that I can relate to her; sometimes I talk with her and feel that she understands exactly how I feel.

"For other myths I may attend a ritual about them or study them," continues Victoria. "I may find useful metaphors in them, but they are not embedded in me like the stories of Jesus and Persephone. I probably could embrace other myths as deeply, but really, how many myths can a person get into at one time?"

"Like Francis running out of hours in the day?" asks River with a grin.

"Exactly!" agrees Victoria.

"In a recent sermon at my church, the minister said something that stuck with me," comments Brighid.

"Tell us about it," says Joyce.

"The minister's subject was the phrase 'there is a love loose in the world that can save our souls,'" Brighid remarks. "I believe that is true. There is a love that can help us recreate a world of balance, justice, harmony, and peace. I think it's easier to understand that reality when we use a human being as a metaphor for the divine presence."

"As in Jesus," suggests River.

"Yes, like Jesus," affirms Brighid. "I believe that the divine is incarnate in human form. But a person who believes that the divine is present within us and interacts with us will likely be dismissed by the culture or even persecuted. Meanwhile, the exploration of the historical validity of Jesus continues within the church. This debate has been going on for a long time."

"For several centuries, actually," notes Cern, "although many fundamentalists have been ignoring textual and historical problems ever since they were first raised."

"It was after the birth of science in the 1700s that aspects of the scriptures began to be questioned openly," observes Paul. "As lost languages were recovered, modern hermeneutics began and we evolved more sophisticated understandings of literature. We became aware that books could be interpreted on multiple levels, and perhaps were written from multiple levels as well. Some books appear to be histories while others, like the Wisdom literature, are clearly metaphorical and lyrical. Modernism has created a lot of uncertainties, causing some to cling to a literal interpretation of scripture. But let's not assume this is unique to Christians."

"What do you mean?" River asks.

"In the early days of modern Paganism, Gerald Gardner attempted to establish a line of continuity in the history of witchcraft that many scholars today believe is likely not true," states Paul. "So in both Pagan and Christian communities there are those who can tolerate ambiguity and levels of meaning, and those who can't. Interestingly, archaeology finds evidence supporting some claims of both Christianity and Paganism, while challenging other claims. In the end, my faith is grounded in historical reality. But like science, I know that history is a construction, a narrative woven to make sense of pieces of fact and story."

"I think that if someone relies solely on the historical in their spirituality," Francis observes, "that person could be ignoring the beauty found in the present moment. While I think there are valid historical bases for Paganism, there is also my present reality and the lived experience of being on the earth and enjoying life's seasons."

"I agree with you," says Paul, "and we tend to forget that even the historical narratives were shaped by someone's lived experience and are always evolving. That's part of the great mystery and magic of being human. We retell our oldest stories so that they make sense in our modern times. God and Goddess willing, we will continue this as a species, provided we don't bring about our own end through war, pestilence, or otherwise. Faith always looks to the future, no matter how tawdry the past has been or how grim the future may appear."

"Thanks again to all for another great discussion," comments Joyce. "I think many of our readers will see that they are not alone in their struggles with belief and faith, and their understanding of God, Jesus, and the realm of the divine generally. Next, we're going to continue with these deeper issues and ask you for your views on sin and ethics."

Chapter 16

ETHICS AND SIN

"We are interested in your view of ethics," Joyce says. "Do your ethics blend aspects of Christianity and Paganism? Do you have one system of ethics for relating to human beings and another for nonhumans? Tell us how you have come to develop your system of values." Turning to Michael, Joyce says, "How about getting us started?"

"Sure," agrees Michael. "I use specific words to mean specific things in regard to ethics."

"What words do you use?" asks River.

"I see 'morality' as our duty to the divine being," answers Michael, "whereas 'ethics' are reserved for our duty to other people. I use the word *cosmolity* to refer to our duty to the entire created order. If I hear a better term, I'll switch to it!" Michael says with a grin. "Our first duty is to the divine—to love the Lord and Lady or God/dess with all our hearts and minds, and the second duty is to love our neighbors as ourselves. The question becomes 'Who or what is our neighbor?' As we know from Jesus's parable of the Good Samaritan, our neighbor is not always who or what we expect. When I teach ethics in our order, I instruct the students to 'do the right thing for the right reason because it's the right thing to do.' What is right is right in itself in Truth, and I see Truth as an ultimate reality. Now we may have a number of perspectives and viewpoints on what Truth is, but I see Truth as remaining one thing regardless of our understanding of it."

"I try to treat plants and animals as ethically as I treat other people," comments Eleanor. "I believe in the Wiccan ethic of 'do what you will' but I combine it with the injunction to 'do to others as you would have them do unto you.'"

"I agree with Eleanor," Blaine says, "and try to uphold both the Wiccan Rede, which states 'If it harm none, do as you will,' along with the Golden Rule."

"I believe in 'leading with compassion,' as my mother calls it," remarks T.J., "and trying to be a good person in spite of how others behave. We have a moral obligation to take care of our planet and all that exists on it. As an expression of that in our family, we recycle. If everyone did what they could for others, no matter how small, a great deal would be accomplished."

"I believe deeply in honor and humility," says Hilary, "and doing your best so as to leave the world a better place. I extend my ethical concern to nonhumans also. I don't think animals should be mistreated in order to be used as food, although I'm not a vegetarian. But all life should be treated respectfully."

"Hilary raises an issue I face ethically," notes Brighid, "in that I believe we should do no harm, but that's impossible, isn't it? In the very act of surviving I harm plants and animals and possibly the earth and other people."

"How do you deal with that?" asks River.

"By recognizing and honoring the cycles of life," Brighid answers, "and living in balance as much as possible with people, animals, plants, and the forces of nature. Because of the interdependence and unity of all things, I must live in balance with the systems in which I move, doing as little harm as possible and bringing as much joy as I can. Philosophically, I believe I am responsible for defining my worldview and my ethical system, and then seeing that my behavior reflects my definitions. In other words, I am responsible for the truth I know and for living a life congruent with that truth. Because I define the world based on what I know, I accept that ethics are biased and situational. But I believe that I am responsible for knowing and understanding my biases as best I can."

"I agree with Brighid that ethics are situational," speaks up Cern.

"What do you mean by that?" asks Joyce.

"I mean that I look at each situation individually," answers Cern, "and then try to do no permanent harm to anyone, and choose the path of least harm while having compassion for all who are involved. And yes, I include humans and nonhumans, living and nonliving entities in my ethics, for we are all children of the Mother Goddess. I try to align my ethics with the Wiccan Rede, although like Brighid, I realize it's not always possible never to bring harm. Even the best available choice can harm sometimes."

"How do you see your ethics fitting in, or not, with the Christian view?" asks Joyce.

"I think my ethics are compatible with what Jesus taught," Cern notes, "although not necessarily with legalistic applications of the commandments, or other strict moral codes that a fundamentalist might adhere to. The Golden Rule is basically good, but it can fall apart, since not everyone wants you to do to them what you would do to yourself. I frequently see this in my work as a hospital chaplain. One person might want to stay alive at all costs and be kept going on respirators and feeding tubes. Yet their parent or loved one doesn't want any of that treatment. Should they then apply the Golden Rule and do to their loved one what they want done to themselves, even though their loved one doesn't? Perhaps Confucius's admonition to 'do not to others' would be better."

"I also agree that situations are relative and ethical questions are shades of gray," observes Kirk. "My ethic is simply to do a minimal amount of harm and have a positive impact wherever possible. I apply this ethic to all beings and all reality."

"As a good Buddhist, I work for the enlightenment of all sentient beings," remarks Paul. "As a good animist, I believe that all living beings are sacred and divine creations, and also that nonliving matter has a minimal but nonetheless existent capacity for relationship. Where I am most firmly a Christian is in my affirmation of pacifism. I became a pacifist as a response to the call of Christianity, and even though I've added other reasons for my belief over the years, I've never changed the stance I took back in 1968."

"My ethics are a blend of developing the virtues as described by Aristotle," says David, "combined with modern existential ethics, and a Hindu/Buddhist concept of doing no harm called *Ahimsa*. I haven't yet applied this to food animals because I still eat meat, although someday I hope to transition to vegetarianism. I did take a six-month vow of vegetarianism to the Goddess Pomona once, and I had no problems with it but it caused some discord in the family."

"I am not a vegetarian either," notes Barb. "While I do eat meat, I don't believe in killing animals for sport. I think that the Wiccan Rede and the Golden Rule essentially say the same thing, but we cannot live it 100%. We can only do the best we can."

"I see my ethical system as being congruent with both Paganism and Catholicism," says Victoria. "Basically I try to do no harm and work for the good of all."

"Several have already said what I believe," remarks Charlene.

"That's okay, we still want to hear your perspective," encourages River.

"I feel it is my responsibility to leave the world just a little better than I found it," Charlene observes. "And as best I can, I try to protect all life. For myself, I am comfortable blending Christian and Pagan ethics—I don't feel that any one religion is the only way to lead a fulfilling life. I pull many ideas together and add them into my perspective on things."

"Okay, Francis, I see we have again come to you," says Joyce. "Tell us about your ethics."

"My ethics are constructed from all the traditions I have incorporated into my spirituality," notes Francis, "which include Paganism, Christianity, Zen, and Sufism. Into that mix I throw a dash of Scientology. I do not limit my ethics to humans, but believe our ethical standards should apply to all life. Probably the most significant feature of my ethical system is an acceptance of others."

"I wonder," muses River. "Can we still practice acceptance of others regardless of what they are doing? What if they are engaging in destructive behavior?"

"Perhaps we should expect destructive behavior from people all the time," speculates Joyce. "Doesn't religion see us as inherently bad or flawed, and if that's the case, why wouldn't destructive behavior be the expected norm?"

"You're talking about sin and original sin," observes River.

"Yes," agrees Joyce. "Pagans frequently hear the criticism that they don't 'believe' in sin, yet Pagans recognize destructive behavior as a reality and a choice."

"A choice that an individual makes for potentially many reasons," comments River, "although these don't necessarily arise from an inherently flawed nature."

"Yes, that's what makes Paganism a bit odd compared to many of the major world religions, I think," observes Joyce. "It recognizes the reality of destructive behavior but does not label it as coming from a flaw in human nature."

"Does it matter where it comes from?" River wonders.

"Well, if destructive behavior is seen as a choice, even if unconsciously made, or made under duress, or due to illness, or lack of support in the individual's life," Joyce observes, "then there is some possibility for growth and change. Theoretically, the responsibility for behavior can remain with the individual. But if we are tainted by our natures, always flawed, where is the possibility for change, and how can we truly be responsible for bad choices we are destined to make anyway?"

"Perhaps it's the role of religion to remove that flaw," reflects River.

"I wonder," counters Joyce. "If religion weren't so busy trying to remove an inherent flaw, where might it aim its energies instead?"

"I am very interested to hear what our volunteers have to say about sin, flawed natures, and the role of religion," continues River. "What do you think sin is? Would anyone like to start?"

"I will," speaks up Victoria. "I think that sin is being out of harmony with the flow of the spirit of life."

"And to that statement I would add 'and with our divine natures and thus with nature and deity itself,'" adds Michael.

"I agree with Michael that sin is when we are alienated from the divine," remarks Eleanor, "when we cannot, or do not for whatever reason, feel connected to the divine."

"We all have our ways and moments of being out of harmony," observes Victoria, "and some Christians call that sin. What is repentance? I think it is the effort to move away from disharmony and toward harmony. We could all benefit from that, don't you think?"

"Can't argue with that," agrees Joyce.

"But I think we get stuck on the words," Victoria continues, "and instead we need to think about the *process*. For myself, this year at Lent I am spending time each day clearing away clutter and giving away things I don't need, because being a clutterbug creates disharmony in my life. I also walk the labyrinth with the Dominican Sisters every Thursday. If we want to reconcile with God, then we need to move toward harmony and balance in all parts of our being."

"I like that," comments Michael. "I like the focus Victoria gives here on the experiential nature of the process. An explanation of the process requires words, but actually doing the work is key."

"I don't think we need to have 'sin' to find direction in bettering ourselves," notes Cern, "nor do we need 'sin' to explore and enjoy the goodness of the world. The Greeks used the word *harmatia* for sin and it means 'missing the mark,' like an arrow that doesn't quite make its target. We make mistakes, but then we try again.

"But for many Christians," Cern observes, "the word *sin* has stronger connotations than simply making mistakes. In Paul's theology, sin is a slavery one cannot escape (Rom. 6:20). This view turns the law into a force that exists to make us feel more sinful and guilty (Rom. 5:20). According to Paul, the Law only brings death (Rom. 7:9–10). Sin and death have reigned over the world since the beginning (Rom. 5:12–14). Luther continued this theology in his treatise called *The Bondage of the Will*, and conservative Christians today seem to have the conviction that unless we feel terribly guilty first, we cannot know God.

"Now Jesus, on the other hand, did not seem to have such an overwhelming view of sin in the gospels," Cern continues. "His emphasis was on forgiving rather than condemning (Mark 2:5, John 8:3–11). He instructed his disciples to be the same way (Luke 6:37). The sins for which he seemed to have the most dislike were hypocrisy and injustice (Matt. 6:5, 23:23). If ChristoPagans have a concept of sin, I think they would not adopt Paul's view, but instead adopt Jesus's approach of forgiveness. Pagans don't assume that anything about humanity is broken, so I think most ChristoPagans would also not see human nature as depraved or in slavery to sin."

"I don't know if there has ever been a religious tradition that has held that there is *nothing* wrong with people or the created order," muses Michael, "even Paganism. Although I think Paganism is less concerned with that and more focused on helping people develop themselves and their relationship to divinity. In my opinion, religion can't 'fix' any problem in human nature anyway. All religious institutions have failed miserably when making such attempts."

"I think religion's proper foundations are in mystery, wonder, and trying to understand life and death," responds Cern. "It is a search for meaning. To focus instead on something being wrong with the world is a perversion of religion—its dark side, if you will. Some Christians are beginning to move away from this view and rediscover the 'original blessing' of creation, as Matthew Fox proposes. Unfortunately, I think these folks are still in a minority."

"I think that the real value of many Pagan traditions today is to offer a more 'blessed' perspective of humanity," affirms Michael. "This is especially true in regard to the nature of humanity and its relation to the created order—that is, in working to build a positive relationship with nature and the natural world."

"This is a strength I see as well," Cern agrees, "both in Paganism and ChristoPaganism. In my experience, ChristoPagans are not focused on any perceived 'sinful depravity' of humanity, but instead celebrate the goodness the divine brings us in life and nature."

"No doubt you could say much more on this subject," observes River. "However, we will leave this topic for now and move into a discussion of your relationships with others, especially friends and family."

Chapter 17

FAMILY AND FRIENDS

"**N**ow we would like to talk about your relationships with friends and family, and how your spirituality does or does not affect them," River notes. "We'd like to begin with the young people in your life. Do you have children, and if so, how do you raise them in regard to spirituality?"

"If you don't have children, feel free to include stepchildren or nieces and nephews, as it fits your situation," Joyce suggests.

"As usual, let's begin with you, Michael," says River.

"I am one who does not have children of my own," observes Michael, "but I am engaged to a woman who has a child, currently eight years old. He is active in a small Southern Baptist church, which he attends with his grandmother. His mother and I are also gradually introducing him to the Order of the Astral Star. We try to expose him to a multitude of spiritual traditions and faiths, hoping to encourage him to form an open mind. As he gets older, we will probably involve him more with the work of the order.

"Can I speak to how the order handles the membership and education of children?" Michael asks.

"Yes, please do," replies Joyce.

"The training of children within the order has generally been handled informally," Michael continues. "The parents decide if and when they become involved in the order and its work. The children of active members are called Legacies. We do christen infants and young children, but it has nothing to do with salvation, as children are seen as direct expressions of the God/dess. The christening really acknowledges the parents' intent to raise the child using the perspectives of the order as a starting point."

"Do you baptize?" Joyce asks.

"Actually, we do," answers Michael. "Individuals must be at least thirteen, if they are Legacies, and they must make the request themselves. The baptism is conducted as a public demonstration of Christian faith. If they were Legacies, they can apply to be associate members (Aspirants) at age thirteen. No one can be initiated as a regular active member (First-Degree Adelphon) until they are fourteen, or seek admission to further training as an Adept until they are at least eighteen. We accept applications for non-Legacy candidates only after the age of majority, usually eighteen, mostly for legal reasons."

"Thanks for explaining the structure of your group, and the inclusion of children," Joyce notes.

"I do not have children or stepchildren," remarks Eleanor, "but I intend to teach any children I do have about what I believe. This includes exposing them to a variety of paths and finding a balance between masculine and feminine in the divine. I hope to share my sense that God is everywhere and in every religion."

"I have two small children," states Blaine, "and at their ages I keep it simple but try to relate the meaning of holidays and stress that they should be true to what is right. You can know what is right in your heart. When you think about your actions, are you proud of them or ashamed? If you are proud, then they were probably the right things to do."

"I also have two children, though they are older," T.J. remarks. "I have taught them that there are so many different religions and beliefs because people are individuals and they all have their own relationships with deity, whatever name they give to it."

"Previously, you told us you attend an Episcopalian church, Hilary," observes River. "Do you take your children to church with you?"

"Yes, and actually we're raising them pretty traditionally in the church," Hilary notes. "We also teach them about free will and the importance of caring for the earth and its inhabitants. We teach them nonviolence. We stress that this caring and nonviolence is the path that Jesus taught, but I also do not see these ideals as belonging solely to Christianity."

"My children are grown now," observes Brighid, "and they know I stand between two worlds and respect that. We dialogue about ideas and even celebrated Solstice together at my son's Unitarian church recently. Because Christianity is the normative paradigm in this culture, I think it's essential for children to learn about the Christian myth. For my grandchildren, I also want them to learn about other religion's myths and stories. And I want them to believe in magic until they come to realize they make their own magical reality."

"My wife and I do not yet have children," comments Cern, "but we do intend to raise any we have as Pagans, while exposing them to many faiths. We will frankly discuss the good and bad points of all faiths with them. I do feel it's important, however, to ground a child in one specific faith—which would be Paganism for us—and then let them make choices once they are in their teens. We will certainly teach them that religion is a personal matter and should never be pushed on anyone."

"I agree with Cern about the freedom to choose," adds Kirk. "We are raising our daughter so as to expose her to a number of spiritual practices without pressure to join or practice any of them. She can choose what works best for her when she is ready."

"Although I have no children, I do have nieces and nephews," Paul says. "My brother died during the period of many losses I suffered earlier, and his wife—the mother of the nieces and nephews—considers herself both a witch and an Episcopalian, so that's been nice. She is less spiritually involved and active than I am, however. When my nephew visited me at Christmas a couple years ago, I took him to Mass with me."

"Unfortunately for me," notes David, "my son lives with my ex-wife and I don't see him often enough to have any impact on his spiritual development."

"Well, at least that you're aware of," cautions Joyce.

"That's true," David responds. "Perhaps I will learn otherwise in the years ahead."

"I have generally raised my children to be Pagan," observes Raven, "although we celebrate all the Christian holidays. My oldest child would probably classify himself as an agnostic, but both have been raised to be familiar with various religious myths. We do teach them that the Christian stories are also myths, and I know neither of them relates to concepts such as the devil."

"We decided to raise our children in the Methodist church," Charlene notes, "but at the same time tried to expose them to other ideas, religious ideas among them. When I taught the confirmation class for this church, I exposed the students to other religions. We never taught our kids that there was only one way to do something, to feel, or to think."

"When my son was eight years old, I exposed him to Catholicism and encouraged him to attend a weekend of religious education," Francis notes. "This resulted in him becoming baptized and confirmed, with First Communion when he was ten. This was years before I encountered either Buddhism or Paganism."

"Since you've learned about Buddhism and Paganism, have you involved him in those traditions?" asks River.

"I have taken him to a few Pagan events, and not as many Buddhist events," answers Francis. "He is twenty-five years old now and making his own decisions about spirituality. Having a religious affiliation and practice do not seem to be of great importance to him, at least for now."

"Shifting focus just a bit, what about the rest of your family, friends, and co-workers?" asks Joyce. "Do they know about your spirituality, and if so, how have they reacted?"

"My parents know about my alternative views and practices," Michael states. "They are both conservative Christians who are getting more conservative as they get older. My mother tries to understand why I believe what I believe but just cannot, and she often expresses concern for my soul. My father cannot fathom any ideas about God that do not come through his church. They have attended two public services I performed—one the funeral of my grandmother and the other the wedding of a friend. They didn't understand some of it but they weren't put off either. Both of them think I am wasting my time and talent and should join a mainstream church. I am sure that they love me," Michael observes, "but when it comes to matters of faith, we've had to agree to disagree."

"What about your friends and co-workers?" asks River.

"My friends all know of my spirituality and are tolerant," Michael says. "Some are in the order with me. I am a member of the local lodge of the Fraternal Order of Police and have served five years as its secretary and four years as its chaplain. The lodge members all know me as an alternative Christian. The local police consider me to be their 'wizard,' and consult me on investigations if they involve anything unusual. Some of my co-workers know about my spirituality, although many only know I am not mainstream. I don't hide who I am but am not outspoken about it either. If the topic comes up, I will share my views. My boss knows about my spirituality and had no problem appointing me chaplain for the department. Most of my co-workers are comfortable coming to talk to me as a chaplain. I can think of only two who are negative toward me, and they are very conservative Christians."

"Most of my friends know of my spirituality," comments Eleanor, "and are comfortable with it, but then the issue of spirituality is central to many of those friendships. My family I am not so sure about. We don't really discuss it, but I think they would be more comfortable with me if I were more like them. As for co-workers, I don't go there at all. In fact, I pretend to be Christian so I don't have to debate with anyone about it."

"Some of my friends know, and some do not," notes Blaine, "and they all react differently. Some are curious and want to know more, and others try to show me the error of my ways."

"My family and close friends know about my path," T.J. comments, "but my co-workers—absolutely not!"

"When I was solely a Pagan, some people thought it was weird, others thought it was cool," remarks Hilary.

"And now that you attend the Episcopal church regularly?" asks River.

"Now the folks who were worried about my salvation are happier," replies Hilary. "Those at the church who know about my Pagan background seem open to it. One lady there calls me an Episco-Pagan."

"Most of our friends know me as a 'liberal Christian' and are comfortable with that," Brighid states. "As I have worked with some people as a Spiritual Companion, or advisor, I have on occasion revealed more of what I believe to them. The acceptance of those my husband and I encounter is demonstrated by the growing numbers of them who attend a program of spiritual well-being that we teach. One ongoing series of classes that we offer uses the four directions and the qualities related to them as a core model. These classes are an interesting blend of Christianity, 'indigenous Indo-European thought,' and Native American ideas, and are well received."

"Both of my wife's sisters know we are Wiccan," observes Cern, "but no one in my family knows, even though I think they would be accepting of it. The problem is that I don't think they could keep it to themselves, and I'm not ready for the world at large or my co-workers to know. Plus, we have a niece who is married to an evangelical preacher, and I know they would react very negatively if they learned of it. I would prefer to keep peace in the family."

"I've been fortunate that I can discuss my spirituality with my family," Kirk comments, "and they are fine with it. I noticed over the years that although my old friends were tolerant of my beliefs, those who were non-Pagan gradually drifted away to be replaced by Pagan ones. This seems to have been related more to changes in my lifestyle than my spirituality. Since I have my own business, I work alone and do not have co-workers."

"My friends humor me and generally accept me, even though they may not understand my spirituality," notes Paul. "Professionally, I'm beginning to be open to others about having multiple spiritual identities, and have even begun to do some teaching about it."

"I am fully open about my spirituality, and in my circles at school and the Unitarian (UU) church, no one seems to object," David remarks.

"Generally I do not share my views with others," says Barb, "although my roommate knows and doesn't seem to mind. She is a Christian and doesn't really understand what Paganism is. I have not kept my old acquaintances informed of my spirituality as I don't think they'd be comfortable with it. Since I'm retired now, I do not have co-workers."

"I guess I'm similar to Barb," says Victoria.

"How so?" asks Joyce.

"Because I don't usually share much about my path with others," Victoria replies. "Most people don't understand it, although I have friends who say they admire me for my courage."

"Both my family and my friends are aware of my beliefs," notes Raven. "It hasn't seemed to negatively affect our relationships, maybe because I try not to be inflammatory when discussing religion, and I respect differences in opinion."

"My co-workers know absolutely nothing about my spirituality," observes Charlene, "and I even avoid discussing it with my friends. If they ask me a question, I will answer it, but I never initiate a discussion. I remember the day I told some friends I could see auras, and they actually moved several feet away from me! That was disheartening."

"I imagine so," sympathizes River.

"Since I settled into my current spiritual practices in 2001," remarks Francis, "my employment has changed and I now work with a young, progressive group of people. In prior jobs I never discussed my spirituality, but now I feel like my practices are honored by my co-workers."

"Thank you for sharing about your relationships and how others have responded to you," comments Joyce. "I know that readers might recognize some of their own relationships in what you have shared. We will continue the general thread of this topic, as we ask you to tell us about debates and conversations you have had with others about your beliefs."

Chapter 18

DISCUSSIONS ABOUT SPIRITUALITY

"Have you ever gotten into a discussion or debate about your beliefs or spiritual path with someone, and if so," Joyce adds, "what happened during your exchange?"

"I bet you're going to begin with me," says Michael.

"How did you guess?" asks River.

"Do you want to know about discussions with Pagans or with Christians?" Michael asks.

"Either one or both, as it applies to you," answers Joyce.

"I have had discussions many times with both Pagans and Christians," observes Michael. "When topics come up with my co-workers, some of them are scandalized, but most are intrigued. I've invited a few to visit the order, and some have even joined. In regard to Pagans, many of them seem put off by anyone claiming to be part Christian. They don't much care for ceremonial magicians either, finding them egotistical and arrogant. Since I claim both affiliations, I've gotten some unique reactions. I have found it helps if we each define our terms before having a discussion. After a few experiences with the order," Michael notes, "they realize we're not out to cause any trouble. We've made several Pagans honorary members, and that has surprised them."

"I generally try to avoid getting into discussions with people," Eleanor says, "unless I think my sharing will be well-received."

"I've had a number of discussions with both Christians and Pagans, and I've found that the Pagans can be more intolerant of my views than the Christians are," remarks Blaine.

"In all the discussions I've had," observes T.J., "I can't remember a time when it didn't turn out to be a growing experience for all involved. With enough patience and effort to be understanding, one can discuss just about anything with anybody."

"I once got into a discussion of Christianity with a Pagan friend," remembers Hilary. "He had been badly treated by the church when he was young. His family were members of a very strict church. His father was abusive, but when he complained, the church backed the father and ostracized the son. He was so hurt by this experience that I wondered if he would ever heal from it. It seems that he has, but he remains very negative toward Christianity."

"There was another time I was in a book review class," continues Hilary, "and I offered my perspective on the topic we were discussing as a non-Christian. Even though my perspective was opposite of what everyone else was presenting, they thanked me later and said my views were valuable to them."

"One time a Catholic told me he thought that Paganism meant a primitive with a bone in his nose," recalls Cern. "I explained that Socrates and Ovid were both Pagan and intellectuals. I worked at a Catholic hospital for a while and there was quite a negative reaction to my Pagan leanings by some of the staff. I decided that hospital was not for me. Then a guy I know who is Assembly of God and usually Pagan-friendly got into a debate with me about whether America is a Christian nation. He said the Founding Fathers were all Christians, and I said Thomas Paine wasn't."

"A number of them weren't," remarks Joyce, "although several of them were Deists. I recommend the book *The Religious Beliefs of Our Presidents* by Franklin Steiner for those interested in this issue as it relates to early Presidents."

"Well, he told me he didn't consider Thomas Paine a Founding Father anyway," notes Cern, "although we did have quite a debate on the subject."

"I am not very confrontational," observes Kirk, "but I've found that being clear and concise really helps people in understanding my point of view, even if they don't agree with it."

"I've never gotten into a debate as such," Paul notes, "although I do speak publicly about my multiple spiritual paths. I gave a talk at an evangelical counseling center last year and have been invited back."

"My Unitarian (UU) friends seem to be more understanding of my spirituality than my Pagan friends," remarks David, "although I've done workshops on Gnosticism and ChristoPaganism with Pagan groups and the response has been good. I facilitate a discussion group at the UU church and sometimes articulate my beliefs as part of the class. But generally I do not raise the issue of spirituality with others, except that I have started talking about it with my wife more. She is a Pagan and really doesn't understand my interest in Jesus. It can be a rough subject, but I'm trying not to avoid talking about it. However, I absolutely feel no need to evangelize."

"I don't usually get into discussions with people about religion," Barb says, "although I did one time with a door-to-door minister. We talked about Paganism and I loaned him your first book."

"You loaned him one of our books?" asks Joyce.

"Yes, your first one, the introduction book," Barb replies, "and I never got it back either."

"I think we can get you another one," laughs River.

"When people ask me about my path, I share what feels appropriate," notes Victoria, "but I am not an in-your-face person about it. I feel no desire to proselytize either for Catholicism or Paganism. Because of my work as a healer, I try to support people in finding the spiritual connection that works for them. I might make simple suggestions, like to go out into nature or to walk the labyrinth. The jewelry I wear is also inclusive," notes Victoria. "I don't wear either a cross or a pentacle. I often wear a silver circle with a tree in the middle, which is the Tree of Life. My Pagan friends think it's a Pagan symbol, and my Catholic friends think it's a Christian symbol."

"The times I have gotten into discussions about my spirituality," observes Raven, "I've been informed that I really am a Christian, even if I don't think I am."

"I have had discussions with Pagans about spirituality, and they were all interested in what I had to say," remarks Charlene. "They were not judgmental, and I enjoyed those talks very much."

"I've engaged in a number of debates about spirituality with many people over the years, but the biggest reaction I remember was on September 13, 2001," Francis recalls. "A person with whom I was partnered in an environmental studies group began to rage about 'what the damn Muslims had done.' This person knew I honored many spiritual traditions, including Sufism, which is Islamic, but he could not control his anger. I had to leave or lose my own temper. Later, he and I were able to work though our differences online, but this incident unfortunately ended the group."

"What about discussions regarding ChristoPaganism?" inquires River.

"Several Pagans I have talked to are puzzled as to why, having found Paganism, I would continue my affiliation with the Christians, Buddhists, or Sufis," responds Francis. "They assume that just as Paganism replaced their Christian model, all those who come to Paganism leave other models behind. Some of them simply cannot relate to me, while others begin to consider the unity of human spiritual experience."

"A couple of volunteers have mentioned their view of proselytizing," Joyce notes. "Since you combine several traditions, each of which has a different perspective on proselytizing, what are your views?"

"I have pondered this question for myself," Francis answers, "and have decided that just being 'out' about what I do does more to open minds and hearts than if I were knocking on doors. Just admitting you are Pagan, for example, and holding a responsible job, taking care of your family, and treating people with respect, says a lot about Paganism in my opinion. Publicly, I find that people come to me with their spiritual concerns because they 'have a feeling' that I will listen. Sometimes I do suggest to people that they meditate," Francis observes, "but there's nothing particularly Pagan about that. Meditation is a practical way of dealing with some types of problems. I guess I do consider the Dances of Universal Peace, which I have hosted for the past six years, to be a type of public statement of who I am as a Pagan, as this musical offering celebrates the divine in many of its aspects."

"Listening to your stories about discussions with others, especially non-Pagans, has made me curious about what you perceive to be the current views of Pagans toward ChristoPaganism," River wonders. "What has been your experience of this?"

"I don't think the term 'ChristoPagan' itself is particularly liked in the Pagan community," Michael answers, "although it is making some inroads. It's certainly a more accepted term than Christian Witch, I think. I urge everyone who blends some aspect of Christianity and Paganism and/or Wicca to give serious thought to how they choose to label themselves, both inside and outside the Pagan community."

"Do you find the Pagan attitude constructive?" River asks.

"No, and I think it's purely reactionary," Michael responds. "If Pagans aren't careful, they are in danger of becoming what they dislike about other religions. It's hypocritical to demand something for yourself and then not grant it to others. If Pagans and Wiccans want the freedom to identify and label themselves as they wish, then they must give other people the same freedom and respect."

"I think many Pagans think that a Christian cannot also be a Pagan—or incorporate Paganism into their spirituality," observes Eleanor. "This attitude doesn't seem constructive to me, because it's discriminatory and doesn't open up the possibility of bridge-building between the two communities."

"Do you find this attitude everywhere?" asks Joyce.

"No, not everywhere, and certainly not at Diana's Grove, which I've found to be respectful and affirming," responds Eleanor.

"I find it interesting that a group of people who feel so strongly about Christian intolerance can be so intolerant about my beliefs," adds Blaine. "They want to believe as they wish, but if I include the 'Christo' part in my spirituality, they doubt my sanity. This does not help Paganism stay inclusive."

"My experience doesn't really match the others, I guess," says T.J.

"What have you experienced?" asks River.

"Most Pagans I know don't have a negative reaction to my path," T.J. notes. "They just consider me another Pagan with my own path."

"Since I haven't been active in the community for a while," observes Hilary, "I'm not sure what the prevalent view is. However, my own friends who are Pagan respect my path."

"I'm not sure that some skepticism and antagonism from Pagans is an inappropriate response," observes Brighid. "Pagans have been shunned and worse by the church historically, which could be good reason for antagonism."

"It is true that some Pagans have been spiritually, emotionally, or sexually abused by Christians, and have brought an anti-Christian bias with them," Cern agrees. "When I was becoming a Pagan I was still a pastor of a Christian church, and Pagans were very leery of me. Even so, the leaders of Pagan groups were inviting and curious about me. They encouraged me. I think if Pagans could see that ChristoPagans mean no harm and are not agents of the Inquisition, they would be more accepting. ChristoPagans also need to listen to Pagans' bad experiences with Christianity and try to understand the ugliness they have endured."

"In my experience, it is newer Pagans or those who have been injured by their faith of origin who react against all things Christian," observes Kirk. "Thus they tend to dismiss ChristoPaganism as a futile effort to combine irreconcilable faiths. Pagans who have been around longer begin to see that all paths to the divine are valid and can be mutually supportive."

"Unfortunately, most of the Pagans I know haven't yet gotten over their issues with Christianity," comments David.

"In contrast, most reactions I've had are generally favorable," Paul reports, "with only occasional discomfort or uncertainty."

"I see some negative comments about ChristoPaganism on Pagan e-lists," notes Barb, "but I see it as a normal human reaction. Some indeed have been hurt by Christianity, but many people don't look into the depths of religion and I include both Pagans and Christians in this. They just tend to follow along, and they don't look deeper to see the correlations."

"I agree with Barb on this," Victoria says. "I have found that the more deeply spiritual people are, the greater the understanding they can have for my path."

"We are nearing the end once again," says Joyce, "which brings us to you, Francis. What has been your experience?"

"I have perceived a real bitterness among Pagans toward Christianity, with hatred for specific Christians who have committed acts of cruelty under the guise of religion," comments Francis. "It's like hating all African Americans because of the acts of a few. This attitude undermines Paganism, in my opinion. If we want this movement to be sustainable and to survive, then we must learn to focus on being engaged in positive action. Indulging in sustained bitterness and negativity does not support such a goal."

"Well, all of you have certainly offered both communities much to think about," observes River. "There is obviously much growth and healing needed, although I am heartened to hear of the many positive experiences you have had as well. The final topic we will discuss will examine what you think blended spiritualities add to religion generally, and where you think Christianity and Paganism are headed in the future."

Chapter 19

THE FUTURE

"Do blended spiritualities like ChristoPaganism bring anything of value to the religious landscape?" asks River. "What value do you see in a path such as yours for Christians and Pagans and the culture at large?"

"Its value is pure evolution," Michael states. "As a species, we are always developing our senses to perceive the spiritual cosmos in new and exciting ways. We are at the brink of a new beginning. People are starting to get the idea that maybe there is more, a lot more, buried in their tradition. Paganism and Christianity also give us both strengths and weaknesses. The well-trained clergy and leaders that Christianity has are a strength, while a formal structure can also be a weakness. Paganism's strength here is that it gives back some of the freedom of spiritual expression to individual members.

"On every altar of every temple in the order sits a crystal cut like a gemstone," continues Michael, "a diamond with different facets. That gem represents our vision of the divine—it is multifaceted, and we can see only a couple faces of it at a time. Every religious faith sees and understands one—or perhaps several—facets of the whole that is divinity, and so contains a genuine perception of the divine. We honor this in our initiatory rituals when we say to the new member, 'Remember that you hold all religions in reverence, for there is none but contains a Ray from the Ineffable Light that you yourself are seeking.'"

"Blended spiritualities make room for the reality of people's lives, where they need to find ways to work with spirit now, while incorporating what they need from their past," observes Eleanor. "They allow people not to have to throw the baby out with the bath, so to speak. I believe the culture at large always benefits from greater diversity, just as exposure to a variety of ideas and beliefs opens an individual's mind."

"I think blended spiritualities will be very advantageous to society," notes Blaine, "because they help foster tolerance."

"It is my hope that it will have the effect of making people more open and accepting of one another," T.J. observes, "and allow people to pursue individual paths without fear of prejudice or persecution."

"I believe that each person has a unique and individual path to God," Hilary remarks. "When people can pull together several spiritualities, then they have more paths to choose from. I think such choice gives us more opportunity to grow and change spiritually, without feeling lost or 'wrong.' I think I have learned to value both Christianity and Paganism, and can see the light and love in both. I also think that interspirituality has made me more open-minded about faiths and practices I'm not familiar with because I've walked a broad path myself. My blended spirituality feels more valuable to me because it is founded upon all the paths I traveled before."

"The fact that ChristoPaganism exists shows that there are things Christians and Pagans have in common," Cern notes. "As for me, living in more than one religion helps me to understand others better, to see diferrent points of view, and to have respect for others' paths."

"As I've mentioned before," Kirk states, "I do not practice a blended spiritual path— I practice several paths in parallel. I do not mix them."

"I recall that," agrees River. "Given your perspective, what value do you see in paths such as ChristoPaganism?"

"One value ChristoPaganism has is that it can hopefully bridge the gap that exists on both sides," Kirk observes. "The development of ChristoPaganism both allows and requires a deeper dialogue and awareness by people in both faiths. And that is a good thing."

"I think the study of comparative religions is vital to our times," comments Paul, "but not study in order to convert people to one's own view, but study that leads to an experiential touching of other faiths. Peace and understanding can only come about through listening, hearing the other, and seeing in the other the spark of the divine."

"How has your blended spirituality helped you do this?" asks Joyce.

"Blending Christianity, Buddhism, and Paganism together is my attempt to build bridges," replies Paul. "This is vital because our times seem to be set on blowing up bridges and polarizing our various communities throughout the world."

"Part of the growth process, it seems to me," muses Barb, "is to grow the ability to see patterns and similarities, to see outside the box. Blended paths are one way to allow this to happen through a type of merging. For myself, it has brought me to a respect for all religions."

"Blended spiritualities allow people to open their minds and hearts to the fact that there is more than one way," observes Victoria.

"I see blended spiritualities as having an important value now and into the future, for two reasons," Francis remarks. "First, because individuals who openly practice a blended path can demonstrate that people really are free, and that they can create a path for themselves that is fulfilling. Second, I think those with blended spiritualities may be best suited to act as peacemakers and help bring communities together."

"What has your blended path given to you that you needed spiritually?" asks River.

"I've learned a number of things about my spiritual needs over the years," Francis observes. "Among them is that I need a meditative practice; I need to create and connect with a personal and flexible concept of deity (or deities); I need to publicly express the importance of love, sacrifice, community, and the history of those things within a tradition, to celebrate the ecstasy of existence, to find God in nature; and I need to see the world as one. These are some of my primary spiritual needs, and I have found no one spiritual tradition that provides for them all."

"You have all answered what you see as the value of blended paths in today's world," acknowledges Joyce. "But what about tomorrow's world? What do you think the future of Paganism is? And the future of Christianity? Then, putting the two together, is there a future for ChristoPaganism?"

"I am not sure about the futures of Paganism and Christianity individually," speaks up Michael, "although I think Paganism will continue to grow, at least in the short term. As for ChristoPaganism, I believe it will continue to grow, and significantly so. This growth may force many mainstream Christian groups to re-evaluate what they are doing that is not effective. ChristoPaganism will probably continue to express itself mostly in smaller groups, which can be good in a number of ways. People can more actively participate in smaller groups. However, I can foresee that these small groups may affiliate themselves with a larger organization that may be mostly administrative and educational.

"I am encouraged to see how the ChristoPagan movement has developed so far," Michael continues. "I like the fact that so many people are exploring self and relationship to deity, and are using magick as a means of practical mysticism. I'm happy that so many people are getting to know each other and are finding each other on the Internet. Our own order has grown exponentially. We cannot handle the growth with the resources we have, but we're getting better at it!"

"I don't really know what the future holds," comments Eleanor, "but I agree that both Paganism and ChristoPaganism will continue to grow."

"At the moment ChristoPaganism seems such a personal and private path that I'm not sure if it will grow into its own movement," Blaine ponders. "I will have to think about that."

"I agree that Paganism will continue to grow," says T.J., "and that people will come to it by means of a variety of paths."

"I also believe that Paganism will continue to grow, because it is a wonderful, positive, affirming practice that heals and empowers," observes Hilary. "I would like to see Paganism be more accepted by society and see more recognition given to its fundamental goodness. If ChristoPaganism changes either faith, I think it will be to broaden the concept of God and the ways in which God can be praised and worshipped."

"Paganism will continue to grow, especially if Christian churches continue to become more conservative," Cern says. "People are looking for alternatives, and they are finding them—on the Internet, at local gatherings, festivals, and so on. I think other minority religions, like Buddhism, will also continue to grow, and America will become increasingly diverse. The day is coming that Wicca—the largest tradition in Paganism—will be recognized as a legitimate faith choice, in spite of, or maybe because of, Christianity opposing it."

"What about ChristoPaganism?" asks Joyce.

"I'm not sure I see it becoming a movement in itself," Cern responds, "since it seems for the moment to be a path people explore as they are transitioning from Christianity to Paganism. At least that has been my experience. Pagans can learn to be more accepting of ChristoPagans and where they are on their journey. As for ChristoPaganism impacting Christianity, I'm afraid it may just strengthen the cult hunters and those looking to punish heretics. If ChristoPaganism becomes more widespread, Bible-oriented Christians are likely to recoil from it, and unfortunately, they may become less tolerant."

"I believe Paganism will continue to grow and mature," notes Kirk, "and it will be interesting to see how well we retain our second and third generations—our kids and grandkids. ChristoPaganism will probably continue as a subset of Paganism that appeals to those who still feel connected to Christianity but reject some aspects of it. I don't see ChristoPaganism changing Paganism overall, except to stimulate dialogue about why Pagans react negatively to Christianity. This may fade over time as we grow future generations of Pagans, fewer of whom are Pagans as a reaction to a Christian upbringing. I think mainstream Christianity may be too large and megalithic to be affected much," Kirk observes, "and the alternative Christians already have no problem with Paganism. Many of them are in fact ChristoPagans or at least Pagan-friendly."

"The apocalyptic Latter Day Saint in me tends to see only war, economic conflict, and climatic catastrophe in our future," warns Paul. "Yet I go forward with faith that somehow we will turn the corner and roll back the forces working against peace, understanding, social justice, and a sustainable human civilization."

"I also agree that Paganism is growing," adds Barb, "and it may even become more Christianized as it becomes more popular. I do see Paganism and Christianity blending in some fashion in the future, but I don't think it will be called ChristoPaganism—whatever is created will be unique in itself. I believe that both Christianity and Paganism will influence each other and because of that, both will change."

"I am not sure that I see the two paths changing each other, but I do agree with Barb that as each path drifts, it will form a growing third way," notes Francis. "I do not know if this third way will develop independently or if it will join with eclectic groups already in existence."

"Thanks for wrapping up this topic for us, Francis," concludes Joyce.

"If I may," speaks up Barb.

"Of course," says River.

"All this talk of the future and our concerns and doubts about it can be unsettling, especially for young people," notes Barb, "and so I'd like to say something to them, as one of the oldest of the volunteers on this project. I would like to encourage those reading this, especially those who are new to ChristoPaganism or young, to let your spirituality touch all parts of your life. Let it be real in the world. Live by example. Know that seeking the divine is what is important, not the path you choose to walk there. The future will be fine—simply follow spirit wherever spirit leads. Like myself and others have come to accept, I hope you can accept that you're on a journey. You may not know where you're going, but it's good."

"Amen to that," says Francis.

"Thank you, everyone," says Joyce, "for being willing to share yourselves and your views with others, and for making this project a success."

"Yes indeed," agrees River. "Thank you. We hope that your experiences and reflections are helpful to those who read this book, perhaps someone who is struggling with his or her path and doesn't know how to go forward. If it speaks to even one person, you can be assured your time has been well spent."

Victoria's Poem

What I want people to know is
I am a seeker and I seek hard
Something inside of me is compelled to seek

I am drawn to the mystery

I want my own spiritual experience
And I don't want it second hand

I want to feel it and have it make sense
If it doesn't make sense, I will say,
"I want to go deeper"

I believe no one has the monopoly on truth
You and I are just looking out of different windows
I am blessed because I can look out of two windows
Or more than two

Sometimes I walk in fear and dread because I am misunderstood
And some don't want me to be on my path

But if you are curious and want to understand my journey
I will spend time with you

ENDNOTES

Introduction

1. Nancy Chandler Pittman, author of *Christian Wicca: The Trinitarian Tradition*, gives the following list of names people have used to describe their ChristoPagan path: Trinitarian Wiccans, ChristoWiccans, Goddess Christianity, Eco-Christianity, Green Christianity, Eclectic Christianity, Kabalistic Wiccans, Gnostic Christianity, Gnostic Wiccans, Grail Priests, WicCatholics, EpiscoPagans, Pagans for Jesus, Jewitches, Christian Craft Practitioners, and Christian Witches (1st Books, 2003), 13.

2. Ken Wilber, *Integral Psychology* (Boston: Shambhala Publications, 2000), 163.

3. Ibid., 21, 22.

4. Don Edward Beck and Christopher C. Cowan, *Spiral Dynamics: Mastering Values, Leadership, and Change* (Cambridge: Blackwell Publishers, Inc., 1996), 51.

5. James Fowler, *Stages of Faith: The Psychology of Human Development and the Quest for Meaning* (San Francisco: HarperSanFrancisco, 1995), 186.

6. Beck and Cowan, *Spiral Dynamics*, p. 301.

Chapter 1

1. Wayne Teasdale, *The Mystic Heart: Discovering a Universal Spirituality in the World's Religions* (Novato, CA: New World Library, 2001), 27.

2. Ibid.

3. Ibid., 26.

4. Ibid., 236.

5. James Fowler, *Becoming Adult, Becoming Christian: Adult Development and Christian Faith* (New York: Harper & Row, 1984), 2, 51.

Chapter 2

1. Danny L. Jorgensen and Scott E. Russell, "American NeoPaganism: The Participants' Social Identities," *Journal for the Scientific Study of Religion* 38, no. 3 (September 1999): 333.

2. Dennis Carpenter, Selena Fox, and K. M. Scott, eds., "Pagan Spirit Gathering 1994 Tribal Survey Results," *Pagan Spirit Gathering Village Guide 1995* (Mt. Horeb, WI: Circle Publications, 1995), 21, 22.

3. John Dart. "Surveys: 'UUism' Unique Churchgoers from Elsewhere." *The Christian Century*, December 5, 2001. Survey results taken from the UU 1997 survey "Fulfilling the Promise," presented at the General Assembly in Rochester, NY, June 1993, p. 48, question 30.

4. Wilber, *Sex, Ecology, Spirituality: The Spirit of Evolution* (Boston: Shambhala Publications, 2000), 127.

Chapter 3

1. Jonathan Kirsch, *God Against the Gods: The History of the War Between Monotheism and Polytheism* (New York: Penguin Group, 2004), 11.

2. Ibid., 16.

3. Elaine Pagels, *The Gnostic Gospels* (New York: Random House, 1981), xxiii.

4. Burton L. Mack, *The Lost Gospel: The Book of Q and Christian Origins* (New York: HarperSanFrancisco, 1993), 229.

5. Ibid., 229, 230.

6. Pagels, *The Gnostic Gospels*, xxiii.

7. Mack, *The Lost Gospel*, 2.

8. G. A. Wells, *Can We Trust the New Testament? Thoughts on the Reliability of Early Christian Testimony* (Chicago: Open Court, 2004), xi.

9. Mack, *The Lost Gospel*, 5, 9.

10. Ibid., 3, 4.

11. Ibid., 20, 21.

12. Ibid., 26, 34.

13. Ibid., 149–163, 172–176.

14. Graham Stanton, *Gospel Truth? New Light on Jesus & the Gospels* (Valley Forge, PA: Trinity Press Intl, 1995), 74.

15. Mack, *The Lost Gospel*, 4.

16. Ibid., 9.

17. Ibid., 214.

18. Ibid., 4, 5.

19. Ibid., 213.

20. Wells, *Can We Trust the New Testament?* xi.

21. Mack, *The Lost Gospel*, 2.

22. Ibid., 216.

23. Rebecca Merrill Groothuis, *Good News For Women: A Biblical Picture of Gender Equality* (Grand Rapids, MI: Baker Book House, 1997), 23.

24. Mack, *The Lost Gospel*, 5.

25. Ibid., 5, 247.

26. Ibid., 233.

27. Ibid., 234.

28. Pagels, *The Gnostic Gospels*, 59.

29. Ibid., 61.

30. Ibid., 62.

31. Ibid., 68.

32. William Foxwell Albright, *From the Stone Age to Christianity: Monotheism and the Historical Process* (Garden City, NY: Doubleday & Co., 1957), 397.

33. Ibid., 398.

34. Elizabeth Johnson, *She Who Is: The Mystery of God in Feminist Theological Discourse* (New York: Crossroad, 1992), 91.

35. Ibid.

36. Marcus J. Borg, *Meeting Jesus Again for the First Time: The Historical Jesus & the Heart of Contemporary Faith* (San Francisco: HarperSanFrancisco, 1995), 102.

37. Johnson, *She Who Is*, 97.

38. Ibid., 98.

39. Borg, *Meeting Jesus Again*, 16.

40. Johnson, *She Who Is*, 99.

41. Mack, *The Lost Gospel*, 212.

42. Ibid., 218.

43. Ibid., 219.

44. Albert Nolan, *Jesus Before Christianity* (Maryknoll, NY: Orbis Books, 1999), 150.

45. Ibid.

46. Ibid.

47. Borg, *Meeting Jesus Again*, 24.

48. Ibid., 29.

49. Mack, *The Lost Gospel*, 247.

50. Borg, *Meeting Jesus Again*, 30.

51. Ibid., 15.

52. Ibid., 12.

53. Ibid., 32.

54. Ibid., 37.

55. Ibid.

56. Tom Harpur, *The Pagan Christ: Recovering the Lost Light* (New York: Walker & Co., 2004), 162.

57. Pagels, *The Gnostic Gospels*, 10.

58. Ibid.

59. Ibid., 11.

60. Borg, *Meeting Jesus Again*, 16.

61. Pagels, *The Gnostic Gospels*, 14.

62. Ibid., 30.

63. Ibid., 49.

64. Riane Eisler, *The Chalice and the Blade: Our History, Our Future* (San Francisco: Harper & Row, 1979), 121.

65. Ibid.

66. Pagels, *The Gnostic Gospels*, 73.

67. Ibid., 4.

68. Mack, *The Lost Gospel*, 232.

69. Ibid.

70. Pagels, *The Gnostic Gospels*, 54.

71. Ibid., 81, citing Clemens Alexandrinus, *Paidagogos* 1.6 and 1.4.

72. Elisabeth Schüssler Fiorenza, *In Memory of Her: A Feminist Theological Reconstruction of Christian Origins* (New York: Crossroad, 1983), 54.

73. Ibid., 55.

74. Eisler, *The Chalice and the Blade*, 131, 133.

75. Mack, *The Lost Gospel*, 239.

76. Ibid., 230.

77. Ibid., 208.

78. Ibid.

79. Fiorenza, *In Memory of Her*, 55.

80. Pagels, *The Gnostic Gospels*, xxiv.

81. Ibid., xxxviii.

82. Fiorenza, *In Memory of Her*, 56.

83. Pagels, *The Gnostic Gospels*, 169.

84. Ibid.

85. Ibid.

86. Martin Palmer, *The Jesus Sutras: Rediscovering the Lost Scrolls of Taoist Christianity* (New York: The Ballantine Publishing Group, 2001), 44.

87. Ibid., 49.

88. Ibid., 42.

89. Ibid., 43.

90. Ibid., 114, 115.

91. Ibid., 1, 2.

92. Ibid., 50.

93. Ibid., 48.

94. Ibid.

95. Ibid., 175.

96. Ibid.

97. Ibid., 211.

98. *Time Almanac 2006* (Boston: Pearson Education, 2005), 360.

99. *Our Sunday Visitor's Catholic Almanac 2006* (Huntington, IN: Our Sunday Visitor, 2005), 432, 599–601.

100. Paul J. Niemann, *The Lent, Triduum, and Easter Answer Book* (San Jose, CA: Resource Publications, 1998), 9.

Chapter 4

1. Charles Guignebert, *Christianity, Past and Present* (New York: The MacMillan Co., 1927), 27.

2. Ibid.

3. Ibid., 67.

4. Ibid., 66.

5. Ibid., 76.

6. Ibid., 77.

7. Ibid., 67, 69.

8. Ibid., 67.

9. James Bonwick, *Egyptian Belief and Modern Thought* (London: C. Kegan Paul & Co., 1878), 40.

10. Guigenebert, *Christianity, Past and Present*, 70.

11. Ibid., 70–71, quoting Firmicus Maternus, *De Errore Profanarum Religionum*, xxii.1.

12. Ibid., 74.

13. Ibid.

14. Ibid., 27.

15. Ibid.

16. Regarding Cybele, see Eugene N. Lane, *Cybele, Attis and Related Cults* (Leiden, Netherlands: E.J. Brill, 1996), 40. Regarding Dionysus, see Joseph Campbell, *The Masks of God: Occidental Mythology*, (New York: Viking Press, 1964), 26. Regarding Aion, see Campbell, 339, citing St. Epiphanius who says, "Today at this hour the virgin Kore has given birth to Aion." Regarding Neith, see Sir James George Frazer, *Adonis, Attis, Osiris*, 282, n. 6, citing E. A. Wallis Budge, *The Gods of the Egyptians* (London: Methuen & Co, 1904), 457–462.

17. Thomas William Doane, *Bible Myths and Their Parallels in Other Religions* (New York: University Books, 1971), 364–365.

18. Plutarch, *Isis et Osiris*, 65, as cited by Sir James George Frazer, *The Golden Bough* (New York: Dover, 1922), 9, n. 2.

19. Joseph, Campbell, *The Masks of God: Occidental Mythology* (New York: Viking Press, 1964), 339.

20. Manfred Clauss, *The Roman Cult of Mithras: The God and His Mysteries*, trans. Gordon Richard (New York: Routledge, 2000), 66, quoting from *Corpus Inscriptionum Latinarum*, I 338–339.

21. Alvin Boyd Kuhn, *Who Is This King of Glory? A Critical Study of the Christos-Messiah Tradition* (Elizabeth, NJ: Academy Press, 1944), 415.

22. Joseph Wheless, *Forgery in Christianity* (New York: Alfred A. Knopf, 1930), 147, quoting Tertullian's *Ad. Nationes*, xiii.

23. Doane, *Bible Myths*, 328, citing James Bonwick, *Egyptian Belief and Modern Thought*, 141.

24. Ibid., 328.

25. J. P. Lundy, *Monumental Christianity* (New York: J.W. Bouton, 1876), 219.

26. Kuhn, *Who Is This King of Glory?* 265–266.

27. Ibid., 270.

28. E. A. Wallis Budge, *The Egyptian Book of the Dead* (New York: Dover Publications, 1967). See page liv for source papyri and images of the translated hieroglyphics.

29. Peter le Page Renouf, *Lectures on the Origin & Growth of Religion as Illustrated by the Religion of Ancient Egypt* (London: Williams & Norgate, 1880), 162.

30. Ibid., 190, 193–194.

31. Margaret A. Murray, *Egyptian Religious Poetry* (London: John Murray, 1949), 46, quoting *Zeitschrift für Aegyptische Sprache*, xlii: 32.

32. Ambroise de Milan, *Traité sur L'Évangile de S. Luc II*, Livres VII–X, trans. Dom Gabriel Tissot (Paris: Les Editions du Arf, 1955), 193–194, and cited in E. A. Wallis Budge, *The Mummy* (London: Collier MacMillan Publishers, 1972), 233 n. 2.

33. Wheless, *Forgery in Christianity*, 155.

34. Ibid., 154, quoting Lactantius, *The Divine Institutions* IV, viii–ix.

35. Ibid., 156, citing the Catholic Encyclopedia ix, 328–329, 1907.

36. Doane, *Bible Myths*, 203, citing Mrs. Jameson, *The History of Our Lord as Exemplified in Works of Art* (London: Longmans, Green & Co., 1864), vol. 2, 340.

37. Murray, *Egyptian Religious Poetry*, 46, quoting *Zeitschrift für Aegyptische Sprache*, xlii: 35.

38. Joseph Campbell, *The Masks of God*, 349–350.

39. Ibid.

40. Ibid.

41. Berossus, quoted in Isaac Cory, *Ancient Fragments* (Whitefish, MT: Kessinger Publishing, 2003), 23.

42. Doane, *Bible Myths*, 318, 319.

43. Joscelyn Godwin, *Mystery Religions in the Ancient World* (San Francisco: Harper & Row, 1981), 111, and Sir James George Frazer, *Adonis, Attis, Osiris* (New York: University Books, 1961), book 2, 275.

44. Godwin, *Mystery Religions in the Ancient World*, 111.

45. Ibid., 54, and Robert Turcan, *Cults of the Roman Empire* (Oxford: Blackwell Publishers, 1992), 226.

46. Godwin, *Mystery Religions in the Ancient World*, 24.

47. Ibid.

48. Kuhn, *Who Is This King of Glory?* 208–210.

49. Wheless, *Forgery in Christianity*, 11.

50. Charles B. Waite, *History of the Christian Religion to the Year Two Hundred* (Chicago: C.V. Waite & Co., 1881), 388.

51. Wheless, *Forgery in Christianity*, 13.

52. Doane, *Bible Myths*, 268–269, citing *The History of Cornelius Tacitus*, trans. Arthur Murphy (London: Jones & Co., 1831), lib. iv, ch. lxxxi.

53. E. A. Wallis Budge, *The Egyptian Book of the Dead* (New York: Dover Publications, 1967), chapter 17.

54. Doane, *Bible Myths*, 273, and Lundy, *Monumental Christianity*, 100, 402–405.

55. Lundy, *Monumental Christianity*, 8.

56. Ibid., citing Proclus's First Apology, c, lx.

57. Ibid., 8.

58. Lundy, *Monumental Christianity*, 124–125.

59. Robin Lane Fox, *Pagans and Christians* (London: Penguin Books, 1986), 39, and Frazer, *The Golden Bough*, 349, and Frazer, *Adonis, Attis, Osiris*, book 2, 267.

60. Frazer, *Adonis, Attis, Osiris*, 272–273, and Turcan, *The Cults of the Roman Empire*, 20.

61. Euripides, *The Bacchae* (London: Penguin Classics, 1954), 205–209.

62. Manfred Clauss, *The Roman Cult of Mithras*, 108–110.

63. Godwin, *Mystery Religions in the Ancient World*, 28.

64. Justin Martyr, *First Apology*, chapter 66.

65. Clauss, *The Roman Cult of Mithras*, 137.

66. Wells, *Can We Trust the New Testament?* 18.

67. Lucian, *The Syrian Great Mother*, 4.262. See also *On the Syrian Goddess*, edited by J. L. Lightfoot (New York: Oxford University Press, 2003) 309–311.

68. Frazer, *The Golden Bough*, 335.

69. Bonwick, *Egyptian Belief and Modern Thought*, 174.

70. Ibid., citing Franz Cumont, *The Mysteries of Mithra* (New York: Dover Books, 1903), 138, 146.

71. Ibid., 419.

72. Ibid., 408.

73. Guignebert, *Christianity, Past and Present*, 116.

74. Ibid., 121.

75. Edward Carpenter, *Pagan and Christian Creeds* (New York: Harcourt, Brace & Co., 1920), 12.

76. Wheless, *Forgery in Christianity*, 131.

77. Ibid.

78. Ibid., 131–154.

79. Lundy, *Monumental Christianity*, xvi, xvii.

80. Ibid., xvii.

81. Carpenter, *Pagan and Christian Creeds*, 164.

82. Alvin Boyd Kuhn, *Shadow of the Third Century: A Revaluation of Christianity* (Elizabeth, NJ: Academy Press, 1949), 65.

83. Ibid., 69.

84. Ibid., 94, quoting Johann von Mosheim, *History of the Christian Religion*, Vol. 1, 18.

85. Lundy, *Monumental Christianity*, 81.

86. Kuhn, *Shadow of the Third Century*, 125, 126.

87. Lundy, *Monumental Christianity*, 82.

88. Kuhn, *Shadow of the Third Century*, 125, citing St. Basil's *De Spiritu Sancto*, c. 27, 311–312, Lipsiae, 1854.

89. R. P. C. Hanson, *Allegory and Event: A Study of the Sources and Significance of Origen's Interpretation of Scripture* (Richmond, VA: John Knox Press, 1959), 186.

90. Kuhn, *Shadow of the Third Century*, 124, quoting Origen's *Contra Celsum*, Book LCVII.

91. Hanson, *Allegory and Event*, 117–118, quoting Clement of Alexandria's *Strom*, VI.15.129, PG9.349.

92. Ibid., 242.

93. Ibid., 127.

94. Hanson, *Allegory and Event*, 149, quoting Origen's *Comm. on Matt.* Comm. Ser. 15.

95. Ibid., 348, quoting Origen's *Comm. on Matt.* Comm. Ser. 29.

96. Kuhn, *Shadow of the Third Century*, 127.

97. Ibid., 200.

98. R. Joseph Hoffman, trans., *On the True Doctrine: A Discourse Against the Christians*, by Celsus (New York: Oxford University Press, 1987), 57.

99. Hanson, *Allegory and Event*, 238, citing *Contra Celsum*, VII.60.

100. Hoffman, *On the True Doctrine*, 128 n. 6, citing *Contra Celsum* I.10.

101. Wheless, *Forgery in Christianity*, 358.

102. Gerald Massey. *The Historical Jesus and the Mythical Christ* (Escondido, CA: Book Tree, 2000), 178.

103. Harpur, *The Pagan Christ*, 79.

104. Hoffman, *On the True Doctrine*, 98.

105. Ibid., 95.

106. Ibid., 64.

107. Harpur, *The Pagan Christ*, 7.

108. Kuhn, *Who Is This King of Glory?* ix.

109. Harpur, *The Pagan Christ*, 79.

110. Ibid.

111. Wheless, *Forgery in Christianity*, 147, citing Tertullian's *Ad. Nationes*, xiii.

112. Justin Martyr, *First Apology*, chapter 21.

113. Kuhn, *Who Is This King of Glory?* 204.

114. Kuhn, *Shadow of the Third Century*, 3, quoting Augustine's *Retractt. I*, xiii.

115. Wheless, *Forgery in Christianity*, 140, quoting from Justin Martyr's *Dialogue with Trypho the Jew*, chapter 69.

116. Frazer, *The Golden Bough*, 361.

117. William Kingsland, *The Gnosis* (London: Phanes Press, 1937), 99, and C. W. King, *Gnostics and Their Remains: Ancient and Medieval* (London: David Nutt, 1887), 123.

118. Wells, *Can We Trust the New Testament?* 3.

119. Ibid., 18.

120. Ibid., 34.

121. Kuhn, *Who Is This King of Glory?* 257.

122. Ibid., 258.

123. Waite, *History of the Christian Religion*, 296.

124. Ibid.

125. Ibid., 302, 304, and Wheless, 189, citing Irenaeus's *Adversus Hareses*., chapter 22, book 2.

126. Earl Doherty, *The Jesus Puzzle: Did Christianity Begin with a Mythical Christ?* (Ottawa, Canada: Canadian Humanist Publications, 1999), 268 and n. 118.

127. Ibid., 269.

128. Graham Stanton, *Gospel Truth? New Light on Jesus and the Gospels* (Valley Forge, PA: Trinity Press Intl, 1995), 35, quoting from Léon Vaganay and Christian-Bernard Amphoux, *An Introduction to New Testament Textual Criticism* (Cambridge: Cambridge University Press, 1991), 96.

129. Ibid., 34.

130. Burton L. Mack, *Who Wrote the New Testament? The Making of the Christian Myth* (New York: HarperSanFrancisco, 1995), 6.

131. Ibid., 7.

132. Ibid.

133. Ibid.

134. Kuhn, *Who Is This King of Glory?* 340.

135. Ibid., 347–348.

136. Harpur, *The Pagan Christ*, 119.

137. Ibid., 189.

138. Ibid., 187, 189.

139. Ibid., 187.

140. Richard N. Potter, *Authentic Spirituality: The Direct Path to Consciousness* (St. Paul: Llewellyn, 2004), xix.

141. Kuhn, *Shadow of the Third Century*, 75.

142. Ibid., 76.

Chapter 5

1. Donald B. Redford, *Akhenaten: The Heretic King* (Princeton NJ: Princeton University Press, 1984), 58.

2. Ibid.

3. Ibid., 62, 139, 144.

4. Ibid., 207.

5. Ibid., 170, 177.

6. Ibid., 175.

7. Ibid., 177–179.

8. Ibid., 175–176.

9. Jan Assmann, *Moses the Egyptian: The Memory of Egypt in Western Monotheism* (Cambridge: Harvard University Press, 1997), 191.

10. Ibid., 172–173.

11. Ibid., 176.

12. Ibid., 25, and Redford, *Akhenaten*, 187.

13. Redford, *Akhenaten*, 187, 207.

14. Assmann, *Moses the Egyptian*, 26.

15. Ibid., 27, quoting from Wolfgang Helck, *Urkunden IV: Urkunden der 18. Dynastie*, vol. 22 (Berlin: Akademie Verlag, 1958), 2025ff.

16. Redford, *Akhenaten*, 219, 225–227.

17. Ibid., 65–67, 227–230.

18. Kirsch, *God Against the Gods*, 26–27.

19. Redford, *Akhenaten*, 231.

20. Assmann, *Moses the Egyptian*, 216.

21. Ibid., 30–31.

22. Albright, *From the Stone Age to Christianity*, chronological table.

23. Assmann, *Moses the Egyptian*, 31.

24. Ibid., 32–33.

25. Ibid., 23.

26. Ibid., 39.

27. William G. Dever, *Who Were the Early Israelites and Where Did They Come From?* (Grand Rapids: Wm B. Eerdmans Publishing Co., 2003), 110–114.

28. Philip R. Davies, *In Search of 'Ancient Israel'* (Sheffield, England: Sheffield Academic Press, 1992), from the *Journal for the Study of the Old Testament Supplement Series 148*, 64.

29. William G. Dever, *What Did the Biblical Writers Know and When Did They Know It?* (Grand Rapids: Wm B Eerdmans Publishing Co., 2001), 118.

30. Davies, *In Search of,* 66.

31. Ibid., 67.

32. William G. Dever, *Who Were the Early Israelites,* 41–50.

33. Ibid., 71.

34. Ibid., 228.

35. Ibid., 170, 174–175.

36. Ibid., 176, 179.

37. Ibid., 181–182.

38. Ibid., 196.

39. Bernhard Lang, *Monotheism and the Prophetic Minority* (Sheffield, England: Almond Press, 1983), 20.

40. Ibid., 20–21, and Morton Smith, *Palestinian Parties and Politics that Shaped the Old Testament* (New York: Columbia University Press, 1971), 27.

41. Richard Elliott Friedman, *Who Wrote the Bible?* (New York: Summit Books, 1987), 47.

42. Smith, *Palestinian Parties,* 21.

43. Bernhard Lang, *Wisdom and the Book of Proverbs: A Hebrew Goddess Redefined* (New York: The Pilgrim Press, 1986), 129.

44. Ibid., 130.

45. Smith, *Palestinian Parties,* 25.

46. Ibid., 26.

47. Dever, *What Did the Biblical Writers Know,* 178.

48. Smith, *Palestinian Parties,* 26.

49. Ibid., 25.

50. Kirsch, *God Against the Gods,* 31, quoting J. E. Emerton, "Yahweh and His Asherah," *Vetus Testamentum,* vol. XLIX, no. 3, July 1999, 320 (Leiden, Netherlands: E.J. Brill).

51. Dever, *Who Were the Early Israelites,* 65.

52. Smith, *Palestinian Parties*, 32.

53. Dever, *What Did the Biblical Writers Know*, 197.

54. Lang, *Wisdom and the Book of Proverbs*, 116.

55. Ibid., 124.

56. Davies, *In Search of,* 33.

57. Ibid., 12.

58. Ibid., 68.

59. Dever, *What Did the Biblical Writers Know*, 128, 269.

60. Smith, *Palestinian Parties*, 23.

61. Ibid., 31 and n. 112.

62. Lang, *Wisdom and the Book of Proverbs*, 117, and Lang, *Monotheism*, 30.

63. Lang, *Monotheism*, 30.

64. Lang, *Wisdom and the Book of Proverbs*, 119.

65. Smith, *Palestinian Parties*, 35, and Lang, *Wisdom and the Book of Proverbs*, 119.

66. Smith, *Palestinian Parties*, 41.

67. Ibid., 42–43.

68. Ibid., 44.

69. Lang, *Monotheism*, 36.

70. Davies, *In Search of,* 69–70 .

71. Lang, *Wisdom and the Book of Proverbs*, 116.

72. Smith, *Palestinian Parties*, 49–51.

73. Davies, *In Search of,* 40–41.

74. Ibid., 79.

75. Ibid., 80.

76. Lang, *Monotheism*, 41.

77. Ibid.

78. Smith, *Palestinian Parties*, 51.

79. Ibid., 54.

80. Lang, *Monotheism*, 161, n. 80.

81. Bonwick, *Egyptian Belief and Modern Thought*, 412.

82. Wheless, *Forgery in Christianity*, 22, citing Ed A. H. Sayce, editor, *Records of the Past: Being English Translations of the Ancient Monuments of Egypt and Western Asia*, vol. 9 (London: Samuel Bagster Publishing, 1875), quoted in James Freeman Clarke, *Ten Great Religions: A Comparison of All Religions,* vol. 2, 383.

83. Lang, *Monotheism,* 161, n. 81.

84. Ibid., 45.

85. Smith, *Palestinian Parties*, 82.

86. Assmann, *Moses the Egyptian*, 62, citing Bezalel Porten, *Archives From Elephantine: The Life of an Ancient Jewish Military Colony* (Los Angeles: University of California Press, 1968), and Friedmann, *Who Wrote the Bible?* 154.

87. Davies, *In Search of,* 81.

88. Ibid., 85.

89. Smith, *Palestinian Parties*, 117.

90. Ibid., 144–145.

91. Lang, *Wisdom and the Book of Proverbs,* 120.

92. Davies, *In Search of,* 116.

93. Ibid., 118.

94. Ibid., 85.

95. Friedman, *Who Wrote the Bible,* 18–20.

96. Ibid., 20.

97. Ibid., 24.

98. Ibid., 61, 73, 86.

99. Ibid., 87.

100. Ibid., 103.

101. Ibid., 146.

102. Ibid., 162, 215.

103. Ibid., 204.

104. Ibid., 152, 210–213.

105. Ibid., 217.

106. Ibid., 221–222.

107. Smith, *Palestinian Parties*, 100, 3.

108. Albright, *From the Stone Age to Christianity*, 318, 331, 346, 351.

109. Ibid., 249, 252.

110. Davies, *In Search of*, 92.

111. Ibid., 100.

112. Ibid., 101.

113. Ibid., 91.

114. Ibid., 94, 120.

115. Smith, *Palestinian Parties*, 15.

116. Ibid.

117. Dever, *What Did the Biblical Writers Know*, 100.

118. Ibid., 97–99.

119. Dever, *Who Were the Early Israelites*, 233.

120. Dever, *What Did the Biblical Writers Know*, 99.

121. Dever, *Who Were the Early Israelites*, 226.

122. Davies, *In Search of*, 133, 144.

123. Smith, *Palestinian Parties*, 3.

124. Davies, *In Search of*, 120, 149.

125. Ibid., 154, 160.

126. Lang, *Wisdom and the Book of Proverbs*, 121.

127. Smith, *Palestinian Parties*, 19.

128. Ibid.

129. Dever, *What Did the Biblical Writers Know*, 173.

130. Ibid., 186.

Chapter 6

1. Arthur Koestler, *The Ghost in the Machine* (New York: The MacMillan Co., 1967), 48.

2. Ibid., 201.

3. Beck and Cowan, *Spiral Dynamics*, 32.

4. Wilber, *Sex, Ecology, Spirituality*, 215.

5. Ken Wilber, *Integral Spirituality* (Boston: Shambhala Publications, 2006), 7.

6. Beck and Cowan, *Spiral Dynamics*, 250.

7. Wilber, *Integral Psychology*, 197–198.

8. Beck and Cowan, *Spiral Dynamics*, 50.

9. Ibid., 300.

10. Wilber, *Integral Psychology*, 197–198.

11. Beck and Cowan, *Spiral Dynamics*, 220.

12. Ibid., 50.

13. Wilber, *Sex, Ecology, Spirituality*, 25.

14. Beck and Cowan, *Spiral Dynamics*, 300.

15. Ibid., 50.

16. Ibid., 300.

17. Wilber, *Sex, Ecology, Spirituality*, 25, and *Integral Spirituality*, 68, chart.

18. Wilber, *Integral Psychology*, 197–198.

19. Beck and Cowan, *Spiral Dynamics*, 50.

20. Ibid., 301.

21. Wilber, *Integral Psychology*, 197–198.

22. Beck and Cowan, *Spiral Dynamics*, 51.

23. Ibid., 301.

24. Wilber, *Integral Spirituality*, 68, chart.

25. Beck and Cowan, *Spiral Dynamics*, 274, 276.

26. Ibid., 51, 301.

27. Wilber, *Integral Spirituality*, 68, chart.

28. Beck and Cowan, *Spiral Dynamics*, 301.

29. Wilber, *Integral Spirituality*, 68, chart.

30. Ibid., 92, 102–108, 197–198, 215.

31. Ibid., 74.

32. Ibid., 68, 178–179.

33. Ibid., 68–69.

34. Ibid., 74.

Chapter 7

1. Fowler, *Stages of Faith*, 119–121.

2. Ibid., 128.

3. Fowler, *Becoming Adult*, 54–55.

4. Fowler, *Stages of Faith*, 135–150.

5. Fowler, *Becoming Adult*, 57.

6. Fowler, *Stages of Faith*, 152–154.

7. Ibid., 161–164.

8. Fowler, *Becoming Adult*, 62.

9. Fowler, *Stages of Faith*, 177–178, 181–182.

10. Ibid., 179–181.

11. Ibid., 180.

12. Ibid., 184, 198.

13. Ibid., 186.

14. Ibid., 198.

15. Ibid., 200.

16. Ibid., 201.

17. Nicola Slee, *Women's Faith Development* (Aldershot, England: Ashgate Publishing, 2004), 165.

18. Ibid., 166.

19. Fowler, *Becoming Adult*, 2.

20. Fowler, *Stages of Faith*, 293.

21. Ibid., 294.

22. Ibid.

23. Ibid., 295.

24. Ibid.

25. Ibid., 296.

26. Ken Wilber, *A Theory of Everything* (Boston: Shambhala, 2001), 105.

27. Karen Armstrong,, *The Battle for God* (New York: Alfred A. Knopf, 2000), 91.

28. Richard Tarnas, *The Passion of the Western Mind: Understanding the Ideas that Have Shaped Our World View* (New York: Harmony Books, 1991), 239, 282.

29. Armstrong, *The Battle for God*, 179.

30. Beck and Cowan, *Spiral Dynamics*, 77–79.

31. Wilber, *Integral Spirituality*, 182.

32. Ibid., 184.

33. Ibid., 182.

34. Ibid.

35. Ibid., 192.

36. Richard N. Potter, *Authentic Spirituality: The Direct Path to Consciousness* (St. Paul: Llewellyn, 2004), xiv.

37. Wilber, *Integral Spirituality*, 191.

38. Ibid., 193.

39. David Kinnaman and Gabe Lyons, *unChristian: What a New Generation Really Thinks about Christianity and Why it Matters* (Grand Rapids, MI: Baker Books), 2007.

40. Ibid., 18.

41. Ibid., 26.

42. Ibid., 35.

43. Ibid., 27–28.

44. Ibid., 125.

45. Ibid.

46. Ibid., 126.

47. Ibid.

48. Ibid., 75.

49. Ibid.

50. Ibid., 183.

51. Wilber, *Integral Spirituality*, 200.

52. Ibid.

Chapter 8

1. Pierre Teilhard De Chardin, *The Heart of Matter* (New York: Harcourt Brace Jovanovich, 1976), 214.

2. Teasdale, *The Mystic Heart*, 230.

3. Mark I. Wallace, *Finding God in the Singing River: Christianity, Spirit, Nature* (Minneapolis: Fortress Press, 2005), 15–16.

4. Ibid.

5. Ibid.

6. Joyce & River Higginbotham, *Paganism: An Introduction to Earth-Centered Religions* (St. Paul: Llewellyn Publications, 2002), 80–87.

7. Arthur J. Bellinzoni, *The Future of Christianity* (Amherst, NY: Prometheus Books, 2006), 172.

8. Fowler, *Stages of Faith*, 152.

Bibliography

Albright, William Foxwell. *From the Stone Age to Christianity: Monotheism and the Historical Process.* Garden City, NY: Doubleday & Co., 1957.

Ambroise de Milan. *Traité sur L'Évangile de S. Luc II*, Livres VII–X. Translated by Dom Gabriel Tissot. Paris: Les Editions du Arf, 1955.

Armstrong, Karen. *The Battle for God.* New York: Alfred A. Knopf, 2000.

Assmann, Jan. *Moses the Egyptian: The Memory of Egypt in Western Monotheism.* Cambridge, MA: Harvard University Press, 1997.

Beck, Don Edward, and Christopher C. Cowan. *Spiral Dynamics: Mastering Values, Leadership, and Change.* Cambridge: Blackwell Publishers, Inc., 1996.

Bellinzoni, Arthur J. *The Future of Christianity.* Amherst, NY: Prometheus Books, 2006.

Bonwick, James. *Egyptian Belief and Modern Thought.* London: C. Kegan Paul & Co., 1878.

Borg, Marcus J. *Meeting Jesus Again for the First Time: The Historical Jesus & the Heart of Contemporary Faith.* San Francisco: HarperSanFrancisco, 1995.

Budge, E. A. Wallis. *The Egyptian Book of the Dead.* New York: Dover Publications, 1967.

———. *The Mummy.* London: Collier MacMillan Publishers, 1972.

Campbell, Joseph. *The Masks of God: Occidental Mythology.* New York: Viking Press, 1964.

Carpenter, Dennis, Selena Fox, and K. M. Scott, eds. *Pagan Spirit Gathering Village Guide 1995.* Mt. Horeb, WI: Circle Publications, 1995.

Carpenter, Edward. *Pagan and Christian Creeds.* New York: Harcourt, Brace & Co., 1920.

Clauss, Manfred. *The Roman Cult of Mithras: The God and His Mysteries.* Translated by Gordon Richard. New York: Routledge, 2000.

Cory, Isaac Preston. *Ancient Fragments of the Phoenician, Chaldaean, Egyptian, Tyrian, Carthaginian, Indian, Persian, and Other Writers.* Whitefish, MT: Kessinger Publishing, 2003.

Cumont, Franz. *The Mysteries of Mithra.* New York: Dover Books, 1903.

Dart, John. "Surveys: 'UUism' Unique Churchgoers from Elsewhere." *The Christian Century*, December 5, 2001.

Davies, Philip R. *In Search of 'Ancient Israel.'* Sheffield, England: Sheffield Academic Press, 1992, from the Journal for the Study of the Old Testament Supplement Series 148.

De Chardin, Pierre Teilhard. *The Heart of Matter.* New York: Harcourt Brace Jovanovich, 1976.

Dever, William G. *What Did the Biblical Writers Know and When Did They Know It? What Archaeology Can Tell Us about the Reality of Ancient Israel.* Grand Rapids, MI: Wm B Eerdmans Publishing Co., 2001.

———. *Who Were the Early Israelites and Where Did They Come From?* Grand Rapids, MI: Wm B. Eerdmans Publishing Co., 2003.

Doane, Thomas William. *Bible Myths and Their Parallels in Other Religions.* New York: University Books, 1971.

Doherty, Earl. *The Jesus Puzzle: Did Christianity Begin with a Mythical Christ?* Ottawa, Canada: Canadian Humanist Publications, 1999.

Dunlap, S. F. *Sod, the Son of Man.* London: Williams & Northgate, 1961.

Eisler, Riane. *The Chalice and the Blade: Our History, Our Future.* San Francisco: Harper & Row, 1979.

Euripides. *The Bacchae and Other Plays.* Translated by Philip Vellacott. London: Penguin Classics, 1954.

Fiorenza, Elisabeth Schüssler. *In Memory of Her: A Feminist Theological Reconstruction of Christian Origins.* New York: Crossroad, 1983.

Fortune, Dion. *Mystical Meditations on the Collects.* York Beach, ME: Samuel Weiser, 1990.

Fowler, James. *Becoming Adult, Becoming Christian: Adult Development and Christian Faith.* New York: Harper & Row, 1984.

———. *Stages of Faith: The Psychology of Human Development and the Quest for Meaning.* San Francisco: HarperSanFrancisco, 1995.

Frazer, James George. *Adonis, Attis, Osiris.* New York: University Books, 1961.

———. *The Golden Bough: A Study in Magic and Religion.* New York: Dover, 1922.

Friedman, Richard Elliott. *Who Wrote the Bible?* New York: Summit Books, 1987.

Godwin, Joscelyn. *Mystery Religions in the Ancient World.* San Francisco: Harper & Row, 1981.

Groothuis, Rebecca Merrill. *Good News for Women: A Biblical Picture of Gender Equality.* Grand Rapids, MI: Baker Book House, 1997.

Guignebert, Charles. *Christianity, Past and Present.* New York: The MacMillan Co., 1927.

Hanson, R. P. C. *Allegory and Event: A Study of the Sources and Significance of Origen's Interpretation of Scripture*. Richmond, VA: John Knox Press, 1959.

Harpur, Tom. *The Pagan Christ: Recovering the Lost Light*. New York: Walker & Co., 2004.

Helck, Wolfgang. *Urkunden IV: Urkunden der 18. Dynastie, vol. 22*. Berlin: Akademie Verlag, 1958.

Higginbotham, Joyce, and River Higginbotham. *Pagan Spirituality: A Guide to Personal Transformation*. St. Paul, MN: Llewellyn Publications, 2006.

———. *Paganism: An Introduction to Earth-Centered Religions*. Woodbury, MN: Llewellyn Publications, 2002.

Hoffman, R. Joseph, trans. *On the True Doctrine: A Discourse Against the Christians*, by Celsus. New York: Oxford University Press, 1987.

Inman, Thomas. *Ancient Faiths and Modern*. London: Trubner & Co., 1876.

Jameson, Mrs. *The History of Our Lord as Exemplified in Works of Art*. London: Longmans, Green & Co., 1864.

Johnson, Elizabeth A. *She Who Is: The Mystery of God in Feminist Theological Discourse*. New York: Crossroad, 1992.

Jorgensen, Danny L., and Scott E. Russell. "American NeoPaganism: The Participants' Social Identities." *Journal for the Scientific Study of Religion* 38, no. 3, (September 1999): 325–338.

Kelly, Aidan A. "An Update on Neopagan Witchcraft in America," in *Perspectives on the New Age*, ed. James R. Lewis and J. Gordon Melton, 136–151. New York: State University of New York, 1992.

King, C. W. *Gnostics and Their Remains: Ancient and Medieval*. London: David Nutt, 1887.

Kingsland, William. *The Gnosis*. London: Phanes Press, 1937.

Kinnaman, David, and Gabe Lyons. *unChristian: What a New Generation Really Thinks about Christianity . . . and Why It Matters*. Grand Rapids, MI: Baker Books, 2007.

Kirsch, Jonathan. *God Against the Gods: The History of the War Between Monotheism and Polytheism*. New York: Penguin Group, 2004.

Koestler, Arthur. *The Ghost in the Machine*. New York: The MacMillan Co., 1967.

Kuhn, Alvin Boyd. *Shadow of the Third Century: A Revaluation of Christianity*. Elizabeth, NJ: Academy Press, 1949.

———. *Who Is This King of Glory? A Critical Study of the Christos-Messiah Tradition*. Elizabeth, NJ: Academy Press, 1944.

Lane, Eugene N., ed. *Cybele, Attis & Related Cults: Essays in Memory of M. J. Vermaseren*, Leiden, Netherlands: E.J. Brill, 1996.

Lane Fox, Robin. *Pagans and Christians*. London: Penguin Books, 1986.

Lang, Bernhard. *Monotheism and the Prophetic Minority: An Essay in Biblical History and Sociology*. Sheffield, England: Almond Press, 1983.

———. *Wisdom and the Book of Proverbs: A Hebrew Goddess Redefined*. New York: Pilgrim Press, 1986.

Lightfoot, J. L., ed. *On the Syrian Goddess*, by Lucian. New York: Oxford University Press, 2003.

Lundy, J. P. *Monumental Christianity*. New York: J.W. Bouton, 1876.

Mack, Burton L. *The Lost Gospel: The Book of Q and Christian Origins*. New York: HarperSanFrancisco, 1993.

———. *Who Wrote the New Testament? The Making of the Christian Myth*. New York: HarperSanFrancisco, 1995.

Massey, Gerald. *The Historical Jesus and the Mythical Christ*. Escondido, CA: Book Tree, 2000.

McFague, Sallie. *Metaphorical Theology: Models of God in Religious Language*. Minneapolis, MN: Fortress Press, 1987.

Murphy, Arthur, tr. *The History of Cornelius Tacitus*. London: Jones & Co., 1831.

Murray, Margaret A. *Egyptian Religious Poetry*. John Murray, 1949.

Niemann, Paul J. *The Lent, Triduum, and Easter Answer Book*. San Jose, CA: Resource Publications, 1998.

Nolan, Albert. *Jesus Before Christianity*. Maryknoll, NY: Orbis Books, 1999.

Our Sunday Visitor's Catholic Almanac 2006. Huntington, IN: Our Sunday Visitor, 2005.

Pagels, Elaine. *The Gnostic Gospels*. New York: Random House, 1981.

Palmer, Martin. *The Jesus Sutras: Rediscovering the Lost Scrolls of Taoist Christianity*. New York: Ballantine Publishing Group, 2001.

Pittman, Nancy Chandler. *Christian Wicca: The Trinitarian Tradition*. Fairfield, CA: 1st Books, 2003.

Plummer, John P. *The Many Paths of the Independent Sacramental Movement*. Dallas, TX: Newt Books, 2005.

Porten, Bezalel. *Archives from Elephantine: The Life of an Ancient Jewish Military Colony*. Los Angeles: University of California Press, 1968.

Potter, Richard N. *Authentic Spirituality: The Direct Path to Consciousness*. St. Paul: Llewellyn, 2004.

Redford, Donald B. *Akhenaten: The Heretic King*. Princeton, NJ: Princeton University Press, 1984.

Renouf, Peter le Page. *Lectures on the Origin & Growth of Religion as Illustrated by the Religion of Ancient Egypt*. London: Williams & Norgate, 1880.

Slee, Nicola. *Women's Faith Development: Patterns and Processes*. Aldershot, England: Ashgate Publishing, 2004.

Smith, Morton. *Palestinian Parties and Politics That Shaped the Old Testament*. New York: Columbia University Press, 1971.

Stanton, Graham. *Gospel Truth? New Light on Jesus & the Gospels*. Valley Forge, PA: Trinity Press, 1995.

Steiner, Franklin. *The Religious Beliefs of Our Presidents*. Amherst, NY: Prometheus Books, 1995.

Tarnas, Richard. *The Passion of the Western Mind: Understanding the Ideas that Have Shaped Our World View*. New York: Harmony Books, 1991.

Taylor, Robert. *The Diegesis*. Boston: J. P. Mendum, 1873.

Teasdale, Wayne. *The Mystic Heart: Discovering a Universal Spirituality in the World's Religions*. Novato, CA: New World Library, 2001.

Time Almanac 2006. Boston: Pearson Education, 2005.

Turcan, Robert. *The Cults of the Roman Empire*. Oxford: Blackwell Publishers, 1992.

Vaganay, Léon, and Christian-Bernard Amphoux. *An Introduction to New Testament Textual Criticism*. Cambridge: Cambridge University Press, 1991.

Waite, Charles B. *History of the Christian Religion to the Year Two Hundred*. Chicago: C. V. Waite & Co., 1881.

Wallace, Mark I. *Finding God in the Singing River: Christianity, Spirit, Nature*. Minneapolis, MN: Fortress Press, 2005.

Wells, G. A. *Can We Trust the New Testament? Thoughts on the Reliability of Early Christian Testimony*. Chicago: Open Court, 2004.

Wheless, Joseph. *Forgery in Christianity*. New York: Alfred A. Knopf, 1930.

Wilber, Ken. *Integral Psychology*. Boston: Shambhala Publications, 2000.

———. *Integral Spirituality*. Boston Shambhala Publications, 2006.

———. *Sex, Ecology, Spirituality: The Spirit of Evolution*. Boston: Shambhala Publications, 2000.

———. *A Theory of Everything*. Boston: Shambhala Publications, 2001.

INDEX

To Write to the Authors

If you wish to contact the authors or would like more information about this book, please write to the authors in care of Llewellyn Worldwide and we will forward your request. Both the authors and publisher appreciate hearing from you and learning of your enjoyment of this book and how it has helped you. Llewellyn Worldwide cannot guarantee that every letter written to the authors can be answered, but all will be forwarded. Please write to:

Joyce and River Higginbotham
c/o Llewellyn Worldwide
2143 Wooddale Drive, Dept. 978-0-7387-1467-7
Woodbury, MN 55125-2989, U.S.A.
Please enclose a self-addressed stamped envelope for reply,
or $1.00 to cover costs. If outside U.S.A., enclose
international postal reply coupon.

Many of Llewellyn's authors have websites with additional information and resources. For more information, please visit our website at:

www.llewellyn.com

FREE CATALOG

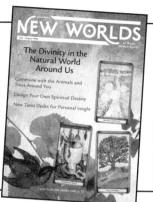

Get the latest information on our body, mind, and spirit products! To receive a **free** copy of Llewellyn's consumer catalog, *New Worlds of Mind & Spirit,* simply call 1-877-NEW-WRLD or visit our website at www.llewellyn.com and click on *New Worlds.*

LLEWELLYN ORDERING INFORMATION

Order Online:
Visit our website at www.llewellyn.com, select your books, and order them on our secure server.

Order by Phone:
- Call toll-free within the U.S. at 1-877-NEW-WRLD (1-877-639-9753). Call toll-free within Canada at 1-866-NEW-WRLD (1-866-639-9753)
- We accept VISA, MasterCard, and American Express

Order by Mail:
Send the full price of your order (MN residents add 6.5% sales tax) in U.S. funds, plus postage & handling to:

> **Llewellyn Worldwide**
> **2143 Wooddale Drive 978-0-7387-1467-7**
> **Woodbury, MN 55125-2989**

Postage & Handling:

Standard (U.S., Mexico, & Canada). If your order is:
$24.99 and under, add $3.00
$25.00 and over, FREE STANDARD SHIPPING

AK, HI, PR: $15.00 for one book plus $1.00 for each additional book.

International Orders (airmail only):
$16.00 for one book plus $3.00 for each additional book

Orders are processed within 2 business days.
Please allow for normal shipping time. Postage and handling rates subject to change.

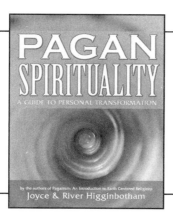

Pagan Spirituality
A Guide to Personal Transformation

Joyce & River Higginbotham

In a world filled with beginner books, deeper explanations of the Pagan faith are rarely found. Picking up where their critically acclaimed first book *Paganism* left off, bestselling authors Joyce & River Higginbotham offer intermediate-level instruction with *Pagan Spirituality*.

Respected members of their communities, the Higginbothams describe how to continue spiritual evolution though magick, communing, energy work, divination, and conscious creation in a pleasant, encouraging tone. Learn how to use journaling, thought development, visualization, and goal-setting to develop magickal techniques and further cultivate spiritual growth. This book serves to expand the reader's spiritual knowledge base by providing a balanced approach of well-established therapies, extensive personal experience, and question-and-answer sessions that directly involve the reader in their spiritual journey.

978-0-7387-0574-3, 288 pp., 7½ x 9⅛ $16.95

Paganism
An Introduction to Earth-Centered Religions

Joyce & River Higginbotham

If you want to study Paganism in more detail, this book is the place to start. Based on a course in Paganism that the authors have taught for more than a decade, it is full of exercises, meditations, and discussion questions for group or individual study.

This book presents the basic fundamentals of Paganism. It explores what Pagans are like; how the Pagan sacred year is arranged; what Pagans do in ritual; what magick is; and what Pagans believe about God, worship, human nature, and ethics.

978-0-7387-0222-3, 272 pp., 7½ x 9⅛ $15.95

Authentic Spirituality
The Direct Path to Consciousness

RICHARD N. POTTER

Our world is plagued with problems related to religions that are based on cultural and historical factors. Many people hunger for a practical and reasonable approach to spirituality that does not insult their intelligence. In other words, they are ready for an authentic spirituality of consciousness.

Lifelong mystic Richard Potter explores consciousness-based spiritual paths and demonstrates how the experience of direct mysticism can help you to open your heart and live a life of clarity, joy, peace, and love. Experiment with practices such as meditation, breathwork, sounding, and retreats.

978-0-7387-0442-5, 264 pp., 6 x 9 $15.95